Chart Your Own
Horoscope
For Beginner and Professional

Chart Your Own
Horoscope
For Beginner and Professional

Ursula Lewis

Grosset & Dunlap • **Publishers** • **New York**
A Filmways Company

Library of Congress catalog card number: 75–16862
ISBN 0-448-12114-X (paperback)
ISBN 0-448-12207-3 (hardcover)
1977 PRINTING
Printed in the United States of America

Contents

List of Tables   vii
List of Figure Captions   viii
Introduction   11

PART I Becoming Familiar with Elements of the Horoscope   13

 1 Signs, Planets, Houses — An Introduction   14
 2 Individuality Delineated by Sun Sign   21
 3 Planets Working in the Signs and Houses   26
 4 Aspects — How to Measure Them   43
 5 Aspects — How to Interpret Them   52
 6 Applying and Separating Aspects   62

PART II Other Significant Considerations in Chart Interpretation   65

 7 Angular, Succedent and Cadent Houses, Quadruplicities and Hemispheres   66
 8 Categorizing by Planetary Distribution   70
 9 Negative and Positive Positions of the Planets   74
10 The Decanates   76

PART III Important Planets in Your Everyday Life   79

11 Your Sexual Expression — Venus, Mars and the Fifth House   80
12 Your Mental Expression — Mercury and the Sun   85

PART IV Your Relationships with Others — Synastry   89

13 Using Your Chart to Find Relationships with Others   90
14 Planetary Comparison between Two People   92

PART V Important Planetary Parts   103

15 North and South Nodes of the Moon in Signs and Houses   104
16 The Arabian Parts: How to Figure Them and the Part of Fortune by Signs and Houses   109
17 The Solstice Points   113

PART VI Timing Devices   117

18 Transits and Progressions of Planets through the Houses   118
19 Pregnancy Timing and the Determination of the Sex of Children   127

PART VII Reading the Chart as a Whole   129

20 Synthesis of the Chart   130
21 Influence of Your Day of Birth   135

Appendixes   141
Appendix A: How to Set Up a Chart   142
Appendix B: Special Charts   164
Appendix C: The Calculation of Progressions   180

Bibliography   186

Index   187

List of Tables

Table 1 The Sun in the Signs and Houses   27

Table 2 The Moon in the Signs and Houses   28

Table 3 Mercury in the Signs and Houses   30

Table 4 Venus in the Signs and Houses   31

Table 5 Mars in the Signs and Houses   33

Table 6 Jupiter in the Signs and Houses   34

Table 7 Saturn in the Signs and Houses   35

Table 8 Uranus in the Signs and Houses   37

Table 9 Neptune in the Signs and Houses   38

Table 10 Pluto in the Houses   40

Table 11 Ascendants by Sign   41

Table 12 Planets in Rising Sign and Their Effect on Physique   42

Table 13 Major Aspects   43

Table 14 *Raphael's Ephemeris*, November, 1972, Showing Daily Position of the Planets, Expressed in Degrees and Based on Greenwich Time   47

Table 15 Aspects with the Sun   53

Table 16 Aspects with the Moon   54

Table 17 Aspects with Mercury   56

Table 18 Aspects with Venus   57

Table 19 Aspects with Mars   58

Table 20 Aspects with Jupiter   59

Table 21 Aspects with Saturn   60

Table 22 Aspects with Uranus   60

Table 23 Aspects with Neptune   61

Table 24 Approximate Birth Dates for Finding Decanates   77

Table 25 Interpretation of North (☊) and South (☋) Nodes of Moon by Signs and Houses   105

Table 26 The Arabian Parts   110

Table 27 Natal Aspects for Figure 34 (Ann)   134

Table 28 Position of the Solstice Points for Figure 34 (Ann)   134

Table 29 How to Figure Birth Data, House Cusps and Declinations for Sample Chart   144

Table 30 The Prime Meridians   150

Table 31 10-Second Interval Corrections   151

Table 32 Table of Houses   152

Table 33 Proportional Logarithms   156

Table 34 Position of the Solstice Points for Figure 38   162

Table 35 Practice Math Involving Mercury and the Moon   163

Table 36 Math Work for Figures 39 and 40   165

Table 37 *Raphael's Ephemeris*, November, 1972   166

Table 38 The Position of Pluto ♇ in 1972   171

Table 39 Math Work for Figures 41 and 42   173

Table 40 Math Work for Figure 43   175

Table 41 Math Work for Figure 44   178

Table 42 Major Progression for Tenth Year   183

Table 43 Minor Progression for Tenth Year   183

List of Figure Captions

Figure 1 Fire   *15*

Figure 2 Earth   *15*

Figure 3 Air   *15*

Figure 4 Water   *15*

Figure 5 The signs of the zodiac allocated to various parts of the human body   *18*

Figure 6 The flat chart or natural wheel   *19*

Figure 7 Aries, at 0°, one of the twelve signs   *45*

Figure 8 The range of Aries in this case extends from midway through the first house to midway through the second.   *50*

Figure 9 The semisquare (A), sextile (B), quintile (C), square (D), trine (E), sesquare (F), quincunx (G) and opposition (H) aspects   *67*

Figure 10 The angular houses   *67*

Figure 11 The succedent houses   *67*

Figure 12 The cadent houses   *67*

Figure 13 The cardinal cross   *68*

Figure 14 The fixed cross   *68*

Figure 15 The mutable or common cross   *68*

Figure 16 Hemisphere emphasis   *68*

Figure 17 Locomotive type   *70*

Figure 18 Bowl type   *71*

Figure 19 Splay type   *71*

Figure 20 Seesaw type   *71*

Figure 21 Bucket type   *71*

Figure 22 Bundle type   *72*

Figure 23 Splash type   *72*

Figure 24 Grand cross   *72*

Figure 25 T-square   *72*

Figure 26 Grand trine   *73*

Figure 27 Simple trine   *73*

Figure 28 Positive (P) and negative (N) ranges of the planets   *75*

Figure 29 How to figure the part of fortune   *110*

Figure 30 Solstice points: ♋ — ♊, ♌ — ♉, ♍ — ♈, ♑ — ♐, ♒ — ♏, ♓ — ♎   *114*

Figure 31 Natal planet in 12° Aries gives a solstice point of 18° Virgo and an opposite point of 18° Pisces.   *115*

Figure 32 Conception chart for woman with birth Moon 14° Aries, birth Sun 10° Cancer and solstice point 16° Virgo   *128*

Figure 33 Conception chart for woman born during a full Moon   *128*

Figure 34 Natal chart (Ann)   *133*

Figure 35 Sample birth chart with degrees and sign marked for the tenth house   *143*

Figure 36 Sample birth chart with degrees and signs marked for the tenth, eleventh, twelfth, first, second and third houses   *154*

Figure 37 Sample birth chart with degrees and signs marked for all houses   *155*

Figure 38 Completed sample birth chart   *158*

Figure 39 Sample birth chart (B, male) with degrees and signs marked   *168*

Figure 40 Completed sample birth chart (B, male)   *169*

Figure 41 Sample birth chart (C, female) with degrees and signs marked   *170*

Figure 42 Completed sample birth chart (C, female)   *172*

Figure 43 Completed sample birth chart (D, male)   *174*

Figure 44 Completed sample birth chart (E, female)   *177*

Figure 45 Birth time will determine house position of ☉.   *179*

Figure 46 Major arc progression in outer rim   *182*

Figure 47 Blank birth chart   *184*

Figure 48 Aspect form   *185*

Chart Your Own
Horoscope
For Beginner and Professional

Introduction

In recent years we have witnessed a revival of interest in astrology that has led more and more people of all ages and backgrounds to seriously study this ancient science. Some, through their concern with economic cycles, the behavior cycles of animals or the biorhythmic cycles of plants and fruit trees, have accidentally backed into astrology, as it were. Others have come to astrology more directly, recognizing that it provides a sound and proven method for predicting character traits and actions.

Every living being has a built-in clock. Human beings have their own type of clock; birds, animals and trees have theirs. More than thirty years ago Professor John H. Welsh, Harvard biologist and researcher, wrote: "So many factors have been found to affect the 'diurnal curves' [the daily rhythmic cycles] of man that the conclusions are most confusing." Since then much research has been done on human rhythmic cycles. Astrology is one tool that helps us to understand them.

No two people react exactly the same way to a given set of circumstances. Two people born at the same moment, in the same place, with identical horoscopes, will not react the same way to their life experiences. Their genetic and sociological backgrounds and their environments will be different, and these will all influence their responses. Still, research has shown that some people with identical or almost identical birth times and places do have similar if not identical experiences during their lives.

The point is that astrology is flexible and must be considered within the framework of a social structure. For instance, in our Western culture personal success is measured by different criteria than are used in a bushman's culture. And in every culture a child measures success differently than an adult.

Astrology is like an enormous jigsaw puzzle with many seemingly disassociated pieces that gradually, through sequential study, mesh into a comprehensive composite. For this reason I suggest that first you read all the chapters and study the accompanying figures and tables, which are explained in the lessons. Then work up your own chart. Finally, with your own chart in front of you, restudy the lessons from the very beginning.

I am a teacher and it has always been important to me that students learn to think for themselves. Throughout this book I emphasize that one should not and cannot interpret a person by isolated factors. The following is a quote from one of our leading astrologers, Noel Tyl: "We are one of a kind. For illustration: the least possible number of different astrological factor-combinations is 539,370,750,000,000,000,000,000,000,000,000,000, 000,000,000,000,000,000,000,000,000,000,000. This is infinitely greater than the population a million earths could ever sustain — is this not an awesome responsibility: to fulfill our individuality?" True, every character is set fundamentally at birth — the sign of the zodiac under which someone is born determines the unchanging features of his personality. But throughout life each person exercises choice to continuously reconstruct himself from the traits given at birth. This is how people differ radically from computers. It is impossible to rigidly interpret anyone's life. First, we synthesize a birth chart depicting general characteristics or isolated factors. Then we combine this chart with our knowledge of the person and his past to gain a comprehensive picture of him and his reactions to future conditions.

It is always a teacher's wish to pass on knowledge and see it utilized — astrology is meant for all. I would like to express my thanks to the many great astrologers, past and present, whose knowledge and research have brought astrology to its present plateau. It is my hope that those to follow will continue to expand the potential applications of astrology; only by first understanding ourselves can we hope to attain understanding of and compassion toward our fellowman.

This is both a textbook for the student and a reference work for the teacher and professional. I would like to thank my many faithful students who helped make this book possible.

I

Becoming Familiar with Elements of the Horoscope

1

Signs, Planets, Houses— An Introduction

Everyone is familiar, at least superficially, with the signs of the zodiac, but what astrologers call the houses will be new to many readers. For the uninitiated a brief explanation is in order.

The earth has two primary motions: its daily rotation on its axis and its annual journey around its orbit. Each motion establishes a circle, and the two circles joined together make up what is known as the flat chart or natural wheel. The circle established by the daily motion is divided into twelve equal parts, or pie-shaped wedges, called houses. The circle created by the annual orbit (the zodiac) is also divided into twelve equal parts, and these are the signs, beginning with Aries (which rules the head) and ending with Pisces (which rules the feet).

Each person's house is established by his original horizon — that is, where and when he was born determine his relationship to the universe. Since the two circles are on different planes, and since the houses have different positions in the heavens from day to day and from hour to hour on the same day, the variations in horoscopes for those born under the same sign are enormous.

A house is ruled by the planet that rules the sign on its cusp. There are ten planets, and the signs and houses each rules will be discussed in Chapter 3.

Astrology, like all the occult sciences, is based on the four elements of the universe — fire, air, earth and water. These elements in combination constitute our natural environment.

Figure 1 depicts the fire element, which is shown by the three signs Aries, Leo and Sagittarius. Fire-sign people are passionate, action-oriented and impulsive. These three signs are trine to each other. In other words, the distance from Aries to Leo is 120°, that from Leo to Sagittarius is 120° and that from Sagittarius to Aries is another 120°. The circle of the zodiac — like any circle — consists of 360°. Each of the twelve astrological signs owns 30° of the zodiac, and twelve signs times 30° equals 360°. A trine, therefore, is one-third of a circle.

Fire signs indicate courage and enthusiasm. Aries, a cardinal (or movable) sign, is the promoter and dynamo of the zodiac. Cardinal signs are always forceful, authoritative and active. Leo, a fixed sign, plays the role of a king claiming the admiration and adoration of those around him. Fixed signs are masterful and stable. Sagittarius, a mutable sign, is the idealist, the philosopher, the tutor and the missionary. All mutable signs are adaptable and flexible. The cardinal, fixed and mutable signs comprise what is called the quadruplicities. You will read more about quadruplicities in Chapter 7.

Figure 2 shows the earth element. Again, notice that the signs are 120° from each other. Earth-sign people are practical and conservative. They are Taurus, a fixed sign, which is determined, prudent and very stable; Virgo, a mutable sign, which is analytical and capable of great service to others; and Capricorn, a cardinal sign, the plodding conqueror and born diplomat.

Figure 3 shows the air element. Air-sign people need an interchange of ideas and adapt themselves to others. Gemini, a mutable sign, is independent in thought and action and is the rapid thinker. Libra, a cardinal sign, is the balancer, the uniter of lives, actions and ideas. Aquarius, a fixed sign, is the impersonal humanitarian and gatherer of wisdom. The three signs are trine to each other.

Figure 4 shows the water element. Water signs indicate emotionality and sensitivity. Cancer, a cardinal sign, is tenacious and preserving. Scorpio, a fixed sign, is the mysterious seeker, the psychic, and can be highly evolved. Pisces, a mutable sign, is sensitive, the artist and the social worker. The three signs, of course, are trine to each other.

FIGURE 1
Fire Element

FIGURE 2
Earth Element

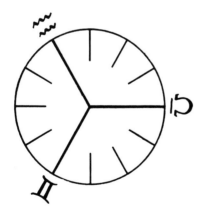

FIGURE 3
Air Element

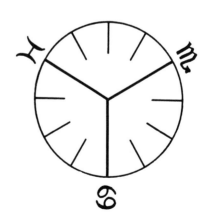

FIGURE 4
Water Element

Planets of the Zodiac

The mechanics of astrology are based on the signs and positions of ten planets that are scattered in a circular belt called the zodiac. Each of these planets rules over an area of our life. Study the key words expressing the functions of the planets and note the symbol for each.

SUN ☉
Life, vitality, ego, drive, willpower, ambition, aggression, dominance, individuality, the husband in a woman's chart, the physical body, eyes, blood circulation.

MOON ☽
Feeling, emotion, sensitivity, the soul, change, restlessness, inner personality, sentimentality, conscientiousness, subconscious mind, physiological changes (including seven-year changes), the wife in a man's chart, uterus, ovaries, breasts.

MERCURY ☿
Reasoning ability, mental activity, statistical facts, communication, analysis, skill, self-expression, musical harmony, educational capacity, nerves, lungs, shoulders, arms, hands, cell structure.

VENUS ♀
Love, art, beauty, harmony, affection, love affairs, feminine items, capacity for love, desire, vanity, selfishness, women in general, complexion, throat, venous circulation, kidneys.

MARS ♂
Energy, drive, impulse, aggression, war, sex drive, enthusiasm, independence, iron, accidents, motor nerves, surgery, temperature, red corpuscles.

JUPITER ♃
Philosophy, religion, justice, law, expansion, extravagance, wealth, optimism, appetite, vision, hips, liver, arterial blood, cell growth.

SATURN ♄
Responsibility, ambition, limitations, inhibitions, concentration, maturity, obstructions, science, chronic illnesses, skin, teeth, skeleton, rheumatism, arteries.

URANUS ♅
Invention, aviation, independence, originality, eccentricity, electricity, sudden changes, sudden accidents, revolution, inspiration, respiratory action, spasms, abnormal growths.

NEPTUNE ♆
Emotions, mystery, chaos, fantasy, dreams, freedom, music, psychism, clairvoyancy, spirituality, deception, self-deception, idealism, fraud, theft, obsession, poison, addictions, pineal gland.

PLUTO ♇
Power, destructive mass action, dictatorialness, total changes, disasters, rebirth, regeneration, atomic power, surgery, toxins, sex organs.

ARIES ♈
(fire, masculine)
Leadership, energy, courage, impetuosity, accidents, aggression, pioneering, temperament, egocentricity, nondomesticity, head, headaches, inflammations.

TAURUS ♉
(earth, feminine)
Art, creativity, domesticity, sense of values, obstinacy, sensuality, persistency, moodiness, materialism, neck, throat.

GEMINI ♊
(air, masculine)
Mentality, cleverness, progression, restlessness, sensitivity, communication, nervousness, dexterity, travel, shoulders, arms, hands, lungs.

CANCER ♋
(water, feminine)
Maternalism, domesticity, laziness, self-consciousness, tenacity, sensitivity, brooding, intuition, stomach, digestion, breasts.

LEO ♌
(fire, masculine)
Dignity, creativity, drama, domination, tactlessness, boasting, ambition, optimism, blood pressure, heart, spinal system.

VIRGO ♍
(earth, feminine)
Literature, exactingness, fault-finding, good workmanship, analysis, wit, service, patience, health, hygiene, intestines, digestion, colon.

LIBRA ♎
(air, masculine)
Harmony, art, partnerships, romance, associations, refinement, negotiation, evaluation, balance, judiciousness, kidneys, ovaries.

SCORPIO ♏
(water, feminine)
Analysis, observation, intensity, emotionality, jealousy, science, research, searching, vindictiveness, destruction, reproduction, intestines, nose.

SAGITTARIUS ♐
(fire, masculine)
Philosophy, intellectuality, curiosity, religion, lecturing, foreign affairs, journeys, legal affairs, impulsiveness, sports, self-indulgence, pride, accidents, hips, thighs.

CAPRICORN ♑
(earth, feminine)
Inhibitions, politics, administration, brooding, deliberation, concentration, egotism, contraction, thrift, caution, perseverance, colds, rheumatism, knees, skeleton.

AQUARIUS ♒
(air, masculine)
Humanitarianism, invention, electronics, civic interests, societies, social order, theories, aloofness, detachment, altruism, unconventionality, spasms, calves, ankles, blood circulation.

PISCES ♓
(water, feminine)
Emotionality, inhibitions, secretiveness, compassion, confusion, tolerance, sensitivity, sorrow, procrastination, intuition, imitations, lethargy, medicine, nursing, feet, toes, alcohol, mucous discharges, colds.

The Twelve Signs of the Zodiac

Each of the ten planets rules one or more of the twelve signs of the zodiac, and each zodiacal sign demonstrates how the energies of the ruling planet will be manifested. This is largely determined by the element the sign belongs to and whether the sign is masculine and utilizes energies directly or feminine and utilizes energies indirectly. The following list presents the key words for each of the signs. Notice the elements and the symbols for each sign.

As you will see below, each of these signs is, in turn, ruled by a specific planet or planets:

Aries is ruled by Mars, a planet of action.

Taurus is ruled by Venus, the goddess of love.

Gemini is ruled by Mercury, the messenger of the gods.

Cancer is ruled by the Moon, the feminine imaginative planet.

Leo is ruled by the Sun, the planet of vitality.

Virgo, like Gemini, is ruled by Mercury.

Libra, like Taurus, is ruled by Venus.

Scorpio is ruled by Mars (action) and Pluto, the planet of upheaval.

Sagittarius is ruled by Jupiter, the planet of expansion.

Capricorn is ruled by Saturn, the teacher and taskmaster.

Aquarius is ruled by Saturn, the planet of the ancients, and Uranus, the planet of genius and progress.

Pisces is ruled by Jupiter (expansion) and Neptune, the planet of illusion.

The three planets of historical and generational significance are: Uranus, discovered in 1830; Neptune, discovered in 1846; and Pluto, discovered in 1930. As man discovers other planets, they will be assigned to the signs with which they have correspondence.

Each of the zodiacal signs rules a part of the human body as well as a particular segment of the chart. See Figure 5, which shows the human figure. Study it for a moment. Note that:

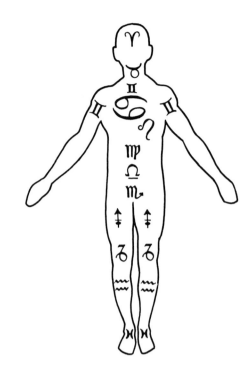

Aries ♈ rules the head.
Taurus ♉ rules the throat.
Gemini ♊ rules the lungs and both arms.
Cancer ♋ rules the breast.
Leo ♌ rules the heart.
Virgo ♍ rules the stomach.
Libra ♎ rules the intestines.
Scorpio ♏ rules the genitals.
Sagittarius ♐ rules the thighs.
Capricorn ♑ rules the knees.
Aquarius ♒ rules the calves.
Pisces ♓ rules the feet.

FIGURE 5
The signs of the zodiac allocated to various parts of the human body.

The Houses of the Zodiac

The flat chart, or natural wheel (Figure 6), is divided into twelve segments called houses, and each house corresponds naturally to one of the signs, which has rulership over it. The point where each house begins is known as a cusp.

Aries rules the cusp of the first house and the total first house.

Taurus rules the cusp of the second house and the total second house.

Gemini rules the cusp of the third house and the total third house.

Cancer rules the cusp of the fourth house and total fourth house.

Leo rules the cusp of the fifth house and the total fifth house.

Virgo rules the cusp of the sixth house and the total sixth house.

Libra rules the cusp of the seventh house and the total seventh house.

Scorpio rules the cusp of the eighth house and the total eighth house.

Sagittarius rules the cusp of the ninth house and the total ninth house.

Capricorn rules the cusp of the tenth house and the total tenth house.

Aquarius rules the cusp of the eleventh house and the total eleventh house.

Pisces rules the cusp of the twelfth house and total twelfth house.

The key words below will familiarize you with the various houses and the areas of human life they rule. As you read them, look at Figure 6 and associate the key words with the appropriate section of the circle.

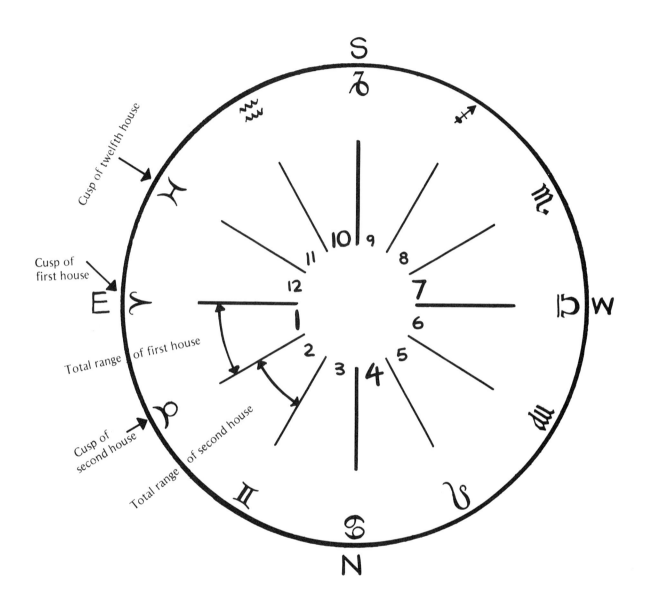

FIGURE 6
The flat chart or natural wheel.

First House (Ascendant)

Temperament, outward behavior, health pattern. This is known as the ascendant, the most important point in the chart. It reveals actions and reactions to environment and experiences.

Second House

Possessions, financial condition, gain or loss, depending on the planets' position in the chart.

Third House

Brothers, sisters, neighborhood, communication, perceptive abilities, studies, mental aptitudes.

Fourth House

One of the parents, real estate, the home, domestic affairs and conditions toward the end of life.

Fifth House

Speculations, love affairs, children, conception, sexual urges, creative expressions.

Sixth House

Employees, servants, pets, sickness, hygiene, relationship with employer and employees, dentist, chiropractor, veterinarian.

Seventh House

Marriage partners, business partners, open enemies, lawsuits, contracts, physicians, lawyers, agents.

Eighth House

Regeneration, partner's money, attitude toward life and death, money from legacies, gifts, surgery, surgeon, investigators, rehabilitation.

Ninth House

Higher education, religious and philosophical outlook, long journeys, foreign countries, publishing and publishers, law, psychic development.

Tenth House

Standing in the community, reputation, employer, social status, the other parent, employment, honor or disgrace depending on the position of planets in the chart.

Eleventh House

Friends, hopes, wishes, social alliances, income from business if self-employed, financial condition of employer if employed, unbonded relationships.

Twelfth House

Secret enemies, unexpected difficulties, sorrows, self-undoing, large animals, clandestine affairs, hospitalization, isolation.

2
Individuality Delineated by Sun Sign

You have already learned that astrology is a blending of many factors. There is no person quite like you on this earth: two persons born on the same day and in the same year, but in different localities, are not alike. They have similarities because they have the same sign and the sun was in the same position and some of the planets were in the same degree in that sign when they were born, but unless they were born at the same moment in the same place, they cannot be alike.

Your individuality is delineated by your sun sign. Basically, it shows your capacities and inner qualities and general tendencies by which you know yourself.

Aries

Aries has as its key phrase "I am." The ruler of Aries is Mars, the element is fire and the quality is cardinal. The Sun is in Aries approximately between March 20 and April 20. This is a sign of great creative action. Aries individuals charge ahead and organize, are original and refuse to be organized or ruled by others. They can be egotistical, are courageous and are quick learners. Aries love to handle a difficult situation and are good starters but do not like to finish a project: they constantly need new goals, new projects.

They are also gadget-happy. They can be tactless though they do not mean to be. Although they put on a brave front, this is merely a cover; inside they look more like a bowl of jelly. Aries are usually in good health, but since they have enormous energy, they are prone to suffer from their enthusiasms and excesses. This makes them liable to accidents, and since Aries rules the head, they are also prone to headaches and, by polarity (the opposite sign is Libra), to inflammation of the kidneys and spinal problems.

Taurus

The second sign is Taurus, and its key phrase is "I have." The ruler is Venus, the element is earth and the quality is fixed. The Sun is in Taurus approximately between April 21 and May 21. This is a stable sign, and Taurians are headstrong and possessive. Like the bull, they are slow-moving and slow-thinking, but once they learn something, they retain it forever. Taurians dislike change intensely, are usually excellent cooks and have a great gift for dealing with money. They will not be deceived by flattery, they insist on logic and they do not scatter their interests. Taurians are usually in excellent health, but since they like good food, self-indulgence often leads to weight problems and placidity. Taurus people have a strong physical magnetism for the opposite sex.

Gemini

The key phrase for Gemini is "I think." The ruler is Mercury, the element is air and the quality is mutable. The Sun is in Gemini approximately between May 22 and June 21. Gemini people are restless, nosy, news gatherers — valuable and very versatile. They are quick thinkers and too eager to know too much too fast. Therefore they often skim through life like a person skating on thin ice. They are capable of doing more than one thing at a time and like games of mental contest and wit. Often they have a marvelous stream of patter to cover up their shortcomings. Geminians need lots of rest and fresh air, and their illnesses are usually of a nervous or mental origin.

Cancer

The key phrase for Cancer is "I feel." The ruler is the Moon, the element is water and the quality is cardinal. The Sun is in Cancer approximately between June 22 and July 22. This is the sign of motherhood, tenacity, great feeling, moodiness and touchiness. Cancer people are highly emotional, very protective within the family circle and, in fact, may become fierce and warlike if they feel their offspring are being attacked. But when confronted themselves, they usually hide just like the crab under a rock. This is a highly domesticated sign, and Cancer individuals are prone to ancestor worship. They have a long memory and are collectors and hoarders of all kinds of memorabilia. They also try to get the most for their money. Since this is a water sign, Cancer individuals need to move around because they have a tendency to retain water. Because of their emotionalism, they often suffer from upset stomachs and poor digestion.

Leo

The fifth sign in the zodiac is Leo. Leo's key phrase is "I will." The ruler is the Sun, the element is fire and the quality is fixed. The Sun is in Leo approximately between July 23 and August 22. Leo, like Aries, is a powerful sign. It denotes will and determination, and at the same time kindness. Leo has a strongly developed ego and is outgoing. Like the king of the jungle, the lion, Leo has an air of confidence and can be a hunter of the opposite sex. Leo individuals are also natural showmen but do not like to win easily because they prefer to conquer. They know what they are worth and like to be appreciated, which makes them highly susceptible to flattery. They like large schemes, are good organizers, but enjoy letting others do the dirty work. Since Leo rules the heart, those born under this sign may be prone to heart disease as they get older. They also have a tendency to forget that bodies can wear out, a factor that may lead to high blood pressure.

Virgo

Virgo's key phrase is "I analyze." The ruler is Mercury, the element is earth and the quality is mutable. The Sun is in Virgo approximately between August 23 and September 22. Virgo individuals function best in service to others. They are painstaking and love detailed work but become overwhelmed by large projects. They are highly analytical and often overly critical. Those born under this sign have a high degree of intelligence and often literary gifts. They must learn to temper their critical faculties or their progress may be spoiled. Virgos carry out duties perfectly and are very fond of good workmanship. Although they are snobs at heart, they often are agreeable companions. Their behavior with the opposite sex is usually correct, tending to puritanical. Since Mercury is the ruler, Virgos usually are high-strung, which may lead to digestive difficulties.

Libra

Libra's key phrase is "I balance." It is ruled by Venus, the element is air and the quality is cardinal. The Sun is in Libra approximately between September 23 and October 22. Libras seek equilibrium above all else. They function best through union with another, are very practical, cool and detached. Libras get their way through charm. They are born strategists and can be completely impersonal; therefore, they make excellent middlemen, capable of delicate negotiations. Libras keep their feelings well under control and they like to be on the winning team. They are capable of accomplishing a great deal without appearing to work too hard. Libran women greatly love elegance and refinement and admire masculine men but will try to control them through diplomacy and charm. Libras are often good-looking and prefer and admire the rich and successful. Illnesses usually center in the kidney area.

Scorpio

The eighth sign is Scorpio; its key phrase is "I desire." Scorpio is ruled by Mars, its element is water and its quality is fixed. The Sun is in Scorpio approximately between October 23 and November 22. Scorpios are resourceful, intense, serious, and have a physical magnetism. They are often dictatorial and possess the ability to find the weak spot in another. If you become a Scorpio's enemy, he will wait to attack you at the most opportune moment. Because the sign is ruled by Mars, Scorpios are prone to be tactless, though they are usually completely surprised when it is pointed out that they have caused offense. They are very possessive and capable of experiencing great extremes of emotion. Like an animal, a Scorpio will turn against himself if he feels he has failed, and the whole force of his powerful nature may rise to great heights or sink to the lowest depths. Because of their penetrating insight, Scorpios make good psychoanalysts. Generally, they do not like to be touched because they have very sensitive skin. Since Scorpio rules the genital area, they are prone to hemorrhoids, urital strictures and disorders of the reproductive organs.

Sagittarius

Sagittarius' key phrase is "I see." It is ruled by Jupiter, the element is fire and the quality is mutable. The Sun is in Sagittarius approximately between November 23 and December 21. Sagittarians are hopeful, happy, cheerful and, like the archer, very direct. They make very loyal companions, although their heads are in the clouds. Generally, their minds are very active. But they are prone to dissipation because they lack discipline and do not like to concentrate on one thing for too long. They have enormous faith in the future, are immensely generous and seem to have no fear of poverty. They may have difficulty making distinctions between thine and mine, but only because they feel that everybody should share and share alike. Their lives are often full of contradictions and matrimonial affairs have a way of getting tangled. Because they have such a strong love of adventure, people born under this sign usually marry more than once or, sometimes, not at all. Their lives are full of change and excitement. They make great sportsmen, are fond of animals, are great travelers and quick on their feet. Ask a Sagittarian for advice and you'll get plenty — he will think of many original ways to help. Sagittarians are religious and usually have great intuitive powers. They are generally in good health although their weak spots are the hips and the liver. They are prone to arthritis, accidents and injuries because they are impulsive and move too fast.

Capricorn

The tenth sign is Capricorn. Capricorn's key phrase is "I use." It is ruled by Saturn, the element is earth and the quality is cardinal. The Sun is in Capricorn approximately between December 22 and January 20. Capricorns are capable of great diplomacy. They are very responsible people, materialistic, but often pessimistic. They are inclined to be somewhat snobbish, with an eye to the top step on the social ladder. And since they have infinite patience, they usually know how to cultivate the right people to help them get there. In their youthful years they may waste time and money, but once they reach middle age, security and a bank account become immensely important. These people never hurry, are never impulsive and are more than just generous. They must always be in charge and are great believers in a good education, which prepares them for a position of power. A Capricorn needs his belief in a higher power because once he has reached a goal and has no other place to go, he must fall back on himself. Since Saturn is the ruler of Capricorn and Saturn rules the bones, Capricorns may be susceptible to rheumatism and arthritis. Their physical constitution usually strengthens as they get older.

Aquarius

The eleventh sign is Aquarius. The key phrase is "I know." It is ruled by Saturn and Uranus, the element is air and the quality is fixed. The Sun is in Aquarius approximately between January 21 and February 19. This is the sign of humanitarian ideals and brotherhood. Aquarians seek to improve the lives of their fellowmen, and their power comes through the intellect. Like Libra, the other air sign, they are detached, impersonal and believe in justice for all. Because of their detachment, they may have difficulty in forming close personal relationships and should recognize that they were born to function impersonally. As it is a fixed sign, Aquarians are very set in their ways, but because of the Uranus rulership, they are prone to making sudden shifts in their opinions,

thoughts, ideas and plans. Because they have a great need to be free, they function better in relationships based on friendship. Aquarians somehow have the ability to make their circle of friends and associates — and action — revolve about them. When they seek power, they can become dictatorial. There is an illusive, dreamy quality in their personality, yet they also display a sense of duty and logic. Aquarius is the sign of the loner, and people born at this time will always find themselves somewhat isolated. Aquarians are honest and faithful and usually in good health. Their weak spots are the ankles, which are subject to swelling. Because of the polarity of their opposite sign — Leo, which rules the heart — their swollen ankles may signify improper heart action.

Pisces

The key phrase for Pisces is "I believe." It is ruled by Jupiter and Neptune, the element is water and the quality is mutable. The Sun is in Pisces approximately between February 20 and March 19. Pisces' symbol is two fish, each one swimming in the opposite direction. This means people born under this sign lack the ability to set and maintain a direction. They are emotional and sensitive and can easily be influenced for good or bad. Because they are highly sympathetic and great believers in the goodness of others, practicality and realism often elude them. Their deep empathetic natures often draw them to charity, and many people born under this sign have the gift of healing. They are usually highly sensual and should beware of drugs and alcohol in any form. Because Pisces is the sign of self-undoing, they are vulnerable and have no self-protective

mechanisms. They are also secretive, cannot be known intimately and rarely know themselves — though often the impulse to tell the truth will overcome them at the wrong moment. Their illnesses are usually centered in the feet. They are prone to put on weight in middle life, at which point they often become lethargic.

Note: I would like to emphasize at this point that the preceding descriptions are generalizations. You will need to study and combine many other factors in your personal chart before you gain a true picture of your own nature. It is important to analyze not only what house and sign a planet is in, but also its aspects or relationships with the other planets. All these factors must be blended. *Under no circumstances should you draw conclusions from isolated factors alone.*

3
Planets Working in the Signs and Houses

Three different people may all have horoscopes showing the Moon in Cancer so that they share emotional ups and downs, but one may have the Moon in the first house where mood changes are more prominent, another may have the Moon in the fifth house which would give him a more creative temperament, and the third may have the Moon in the tenth house which would indicate undue concern with what others think about him.

To make the material in this chapter easier to understand and handle, I shall begin with an example. Let's assume someone is born with the Sun in Virgo and in the tenth house. First read the interpretation for the Sun in Virgo, then read the interpretation for the Sun in the *tenth house* (see Table 1) and, finally, combine the information. The combined reading is as follows: the Sun in the tenth house indicates that the person has the ability to rise to the top — to attain through his own efforts a position of authority and responsibility by the application (Sun in the sign Virgo) of methodical, careful, detailed work habits. This person would make a superior boss, though he

may become lost in nonessentials and ignore larger opportunities or issues if he becomes too engrossed in details. Since the tenth house represents the reputation, this person would function best in a position where great attention to detail is required. Since the Sun represents the ego, drive, ambition, this person would be slated for greater authority than a person with the Sun in Virgo but in the *twelfth house*. The latter's drive would be directed more to a form of service, and he would not be openly authoritative but would work quietly behind the scenes, very often without getting proper credit for his performance. Since this type of situation can cause frustration, the person with the Sun in the twelfth house should become aware of his potential and realize that his restrictions are often self-imposed.

These two examples give you some idea of how an individual chart is synthesized. As you read through the following tables (1–10), note how different the charts would be for people born under the same sign but with the planets in different houses.

TABLE 1
THE SUN IN THE SIGNS AND HOUSES

SIGN	HOUSE
Aries Aggressive, enthusiastic, warlike, ambitious, ostentatious, adventurous, strong-willed, possessing good recuperative powers, tends to extreme behavior.	**First** Must learn how to use power wisely, vital, urge to rule, healthy, courageous, honorable.
Taurus Possessive, security-conscious, stubborn, pleasure-loving, enduring, determined, not easily provoked but furious when deeply angered.	**Second** Ostentatious, desires material possessions, ability to acquire money.
Gemini Versatile, changeable, restless, verbal, literary, scientific and clerical interests, affectionate, hard to understand, contradictory.	**Third** Interested in educational pursuits, able to communicate, lecture, write, teach, loves travel.
Cancer Emotional, contemplative, moody, intuitive, prone to ancestral worship, reserved, reproductive, secretive, tenacious.	**Fourth** Sentimental, strong family ties, status-conscious, good at real estate, addicted to domestic comfort, desires security.
Leo Self-confident, creative, organized, temperamental, ego-conscious, able to lead, domineering, generous, status-conscious.	**Fifth** Good at creative expression, sensual, loves pomp and splendor, strongly desires power and romance, speculative, fond of children.
Virgo Methodical, modest, good at details but can be overly critical, can become lost in nonessentials thus missing opportunities, does not show age, often shy.	**Sixth** May have weak constitution, administrative ability, responsible, can be too demanding of co-workers or employees, desires to serve
Libra Needs companionship, impersonal, sociable, artistic, sense of justice, loves peace and harmony, must learn to adjust to the needs of others, self-indulgent.	**Seventh** Must learn not to take the lead in intimate relationships, regards social status as important, may be too demanding for any form of partnership, popular, dependent.
Scorpio Strong-willed, tenacious, secretive, strongly and deeply emotional, must guard against fanaticism, critical, forceful, suspicious, empathetic, penetrating, insightful.	**Eighth** Needs regeneration of ego, interested in research, curious about the mysteries of life, likely to inherit, achieves success through marriage partner.

Sagittarius
Idealistic, cheerful, flighty, has dual nature, may swing from optimism to moodiness, loves outdoors and sports, outspoken.

Capricorn
Authoritative, ambitious, dictatorial, very self-important, industrious, quiet, serious, economical, status-conscious.

Aquarius
Humanitarian, ready to help others, good judge of character, interested in scientific and progressive methods, aloof, independent, unconventional.

Pisces
Needs to serve, strongly desires to alleviate suffering, may experience difficulties because of inhibitions and confusions, fond of occult sciences, often desires to escape through drugs or alcohol, sensual.

Ninth
Travel-minded, intellectual and scientific pursuits or interests, needs security, can be successful in law and publishing, philosophical interests.

Tenth
Ability and desire to rise to the top through own effort, notorious, slated for position of responsibility, power-driven.

Eleventh
Gets help through friends or organizations, must guard against becoming argumentative or belligerent, sociable.

Twelfth
May serve others without proper credit, severe judge of self, often negative, unconscious destructive habit patterns, destructive karmic patterns from past make it necessary now to function in a form of service, may be very withdrawn and creative.

TABLE 2

THE MOON IN THE SIGNS AND HOUSES

SIGN	HOUSE
Aries Pushy, self-assertive, jumps to conclusions, should learn to inspire others, prominence through perseverance.	**First** Changeable, inconsistent, restless, loves travel, emotionally unstable, imaginative, self-centered.
Taurus Materialistic, obstinate, romantic, should learn to broaden interests, self-reliant, practical, possessive, self-indulgent.	**Second** Susceptible to financial fluctuations, extravagant, must learn to budget, can be favorable, depending on aspects.
Gemini Has dual nature, versatile, critical, lively, moody, physically and mentally mobile, often superficial.	**Third** Travel-minded, mentally curious, nervous, experiences changes in educational interests, great need to communicate.

Cancer
Strong family ties, domestic, psychic, dislikes physical work, very emotional, brooding, needs creative outlet, overly sensitive.

Leo
Likes to give impression of grandeur, dashing, popular, capable of responsible position, must learn to curtail power drive, often status-conscious and snobbish.

Virgo
Intellectual, shrewd, analytical, logical, dedicated, reliable, tends to become buried in a maze of details.

Libra
Ambitious, gentle, romantic, affectionate, self-indulgent, needs companionship, can become too dependent.

Scorpio
Intensely emotional, manipulative, self-reliant, tactless, irritable, interested in hidden matters, psychic, critical, moody, secretive, often has convoluted emotions.

Sagittarius
Philosophical, religious, outspoken, loves outdoors, mystical, fond of animals, optimistic, idealistic, jovial, loves foreign travel, must learn to control bluntness, good sense of humor.

Capricorn
Realistic, materialistic, self-serving, ambitious, thrifty, self-important, selfish, must learn to recognize subconscious fears.

Aquarius
Detached, independent, sympathetic, ability to observe and analyze others, must learn compassion.

Pisces
Sympathetic, tremendous mood changes, talkative, feels inferior, gentle, must learn a realistic outlook on life.

Fourth
Prone to ancester worship, frequent urge to change residence or redecorate, good at real estate, good chance of an inheritance, requires roots.

Fifth
May have great interest in sports and gambling, artistic, instinctively creative, dramatic, has many love affairs, tends to have large families, loves children.

Sixth
Interested in hygiene, works well as a subordinate, must learn not to become too critical of work patterns of others, vitality is reduced.

Seventh
Desires social success, status-conscious, desires to mother mate, needs a partner, often attracts a moody partner.

Eighth
Psychic, legacy possible, can be morbid, interested in life after death, can manipulate money for others.

Ninth
Travel-minded, undergoes changes in religion and philosophies, visionary, strongly imaginative.

Tenth
Geared to public life and occupational changes, concerned with reputation, popular, desires recognition.

Eleventh
Has many friends, wide and varied interests, involved in societies and clubs, can be superficial.

Twelfth
Retiring, may live in the world of the imagination, strongly mediumistic, charitable, must have a release in helping others, subject to emotional chaos, has difficulty expressing emotions.

TABLE 3
MERCURY IN THE SIGNS AND HOUSES

SIGN	HOUSE
Aries Impulsive, quick-reacting, quick-tempered, nervous, mentally active, fighting spirit, needs to learn concentration.	**First** High-strung, witty, varied interests, quick reactions, able to communicate in words or writing, self-absorbed.
Taurus Learn best through visual demonstration, slow learner but high retention, plodding in thought and action, practical, must learn not to be obstinate.	**Second** Skillful at handling finances, may have strongly marked business and professional aptitudes.
Gemini Versatile, quick-thinking, suffers from inner confusion, high-strung, able to communicate, needs to learn not to scatter energy and emotions.	**Third** Intellectual, loves travel and study, restless, active, loves change, curious, excellent at mercurial professions.
Cancer Excellent memory, opinionated, tenacious, creative interests, loyal, dislikes change, fond of antiques and likes to collect.	**Fourth** Restless, home conditions may be subject to change causing emotional chaos, tends to save useful and useless objects.
Leo Conceited, arrogant, creative, has grand schemes, may be overly optimistic, must watch tendency to feel superior.	**Fifth** Creative, may have teaching ability, desires to speculate, able to communicate via art or drama, has clever children.
Virgo Practical, analytical, can become specialized, self-critical, must learn to expand the viewpoint.	**Sixth** Health may be affected because of mental anxieties, attentive to details, works well on a team, should give service of some kind to others to avoid self-destructive tendencies.
Libra Artistic, just, sense of form and color, tactful, needs order, may miss opportunities because of indecision.	**Seventh** Needs intellectual partnership along scientific, artistic or literary lines, attracted to younger people.
Scorpio Incisive, critical minded, needs financial security, sensual, suspicious, must learn to analyze fears and phobias.	**Eighth** Interested in the occult, scientific leanings, promise of legacy, nervous, secretive, must learn to analyze documents before signing anything.

Sagittarius
Tends to be religious and philosophical, fond of sports, outdoors and information, must learn to concentrate on a given subject.

Capricorn
Logical, takes life seriously, practical, patient, must have a goal toward which to aim, must guard against becoming too melancholy.

Aquarius
Interested in social progress, scientifically-oriented, progressive, may be unorthodox in thinking, must learn to become realistic.

Pisces
Tends to be influenced by others, lacks confidence, intuitive, has chaotic mind, must learn to overcome reticence.

Ninth
Interested in higher education and philosophy, intuitive, travel-minded, broad-minded, needs self-expression.

Tenth
Attracted to business or public life, mental ability to achieve, indications are for career in mercurial professions (literary, publishing, commerce, transport).

Eleventh
Reforming tendencies, more mental than emotional, may have unreliable friends, needs intellectual stimulation.

Twelfth
Imaginative, tends to fantasize, has habits of seclusion, should be encouraged to use latent mental abilities, worries a lot.

TABLE 4
VENUS IN THE SIGNS AND HOUSES

SIGN	HOUSE
Aries Affectionate, passionate, loves social life, creative, popular, flirtatious.	**First** Good-looking, trusting, youthful, fortunate, has sex appeal, usually makes early marriage, fond of music, art and drama, can be self-centered.
Taurus Capable of deep emotions, practical, stable, conservative, artistic interests, possession-conscious, good host or hostess, self-indulgent.	**Second** Loves and often gains money, may be extravagant, sociable, artistic, pleasure-loving.
Gemini Loves travel, restless, fickle, able to communicate through music, art or drama, can adapt to circumstances, must guard against superficiality.	**Third** Excellent at expressing ideas, interested in literature and the arts, loves travel, happy disposition, charming.
Cancer Needs to lean on others, tender, sympathetic, emotional, clinging, imaginative, mediumistic, may be prone to gain weight.	**Fourth** Interested in decorating, harmonious house is important, in later years gains security, may inherit, has good fortune in real estate dealings.

Leo
Playful, gay, loves luxury, generous, fond of opposite sex, flirtatious, needs to express self, a natural showman, dramatizes everything.

Virgo
Disappointed in love, high moral standards, may be undemonstrative, puritanical, quietly charming, reserved, critical.

Libra
Sympathetic, refined, sociable, artistic, must guard against scattering tendencies, endows good looks, idealistic, sensitive, needs affection.

Scorpio
Sensual, intensely loving nature, jealous, possessive of people and things, emotional.

Sagittarius
Intuitive, generous, idealistic, loves freedom, hypersensitive, strongly imaginative, adventurous in love affairs.

Capricorn
Conventional and stable in matters of affection, interested in business and commerce, can be too self-controlled, serious, calculating, perfectionist, often status-conscious.

Aquarius
Cool, detached, unemotional, loves independence, manipulative, has peculiar ideas about love.

Pisces
Highly emotional, mediumistic, has unfortunate love affairs, lazy, retiring, philanthropic, needs self-expression but often unable to communicate feelings.

Fifth
Loves games, pleasures, drama and sex, children may have artistic or musical ability.

Sixth
Cooperative with co-workers, usually in good health, fond of animals, sympathetic nature, often desires to serve.

Seventh
Usually marries early, discovers harmony and happiness in marriage, peace-loving, desires partnerships, artistic.

Eighth
Should learn about life's deeper meaning, likely to inherit, will have peaceful death, strong sex drive.

Ninth
Loves travel, idealistic, sympathetic, charming, cultured, mentally refined, literary and religious interests.

Tenth
Ambitious, diplomatic, rises in status, successful, benefits from superiors, popular, often has artistic leanings.

Eleventh
Able to work with groups and associations, friends and social contacts are important, profits through friendships.

Twelfth
Seeks seclusion, romantic, creative, mysterious, loves animals, peace, secret love affairs, may be subject to intrigue caused by women.

TABLE 5
MARS IN THE SIGNS AND HOUSES

SIGN	HOUSE
Aries Aggressive, argumentative, self-assured, outspoken, impulsive, independent, reckless, gadget-happy, mechanical ability, marked self-interest, impatient.	**First** Courageous, energetic, self-starting, pushy, quick-tempered, administrative ability, ambitious, tactless.
Taurus Stubborn, passionate, has practical abilities, vindictive, able to sustain an effort, smoldering temperament, organizing ability.	**Second** Strives to possess, must learn to budget, can make and lose money with equal speed.
Gemini Sharp, incisive, keen intellect and manual dexterity, quickly responds to situations, nervous, satirical.	**Third** Quick, keen mind and educational and literary interests, alert, argumentative, not always logical, hasty, nervous, high-strung.
Cancer Emotional, moody, needs security, sensitive, ambitious, sensuous, domestic, tenacious, interested in the occult.	**Fourth** Difficulties in home life, desires independence, likes to accumulate, active, combative, driving, experiences losses in real estate.
Leo Temperamental, fearless, loves excitement, tremendously self-confident, leans toward speculation, has personal magnetism.	**Fifth** Loves to gamble and speculate, may have difficulties with children, passionate, self-indulgent, capable of leadership.
Virgo Loves details, shrewd, critical, analytical, nervous, could become cantankerous in old age.	**Sixth** Hard and methodical worker, subject to fevers, wounds, cuts, burns and inflammations, should learn not to overtax strengths, may expect too much from co-workers.
Libra Perceptive, friendly, dislikes disputes, good at teamwork, survival instinct, attracted to opposite sex, needs good education.	**Seventh** Combative in relationships with others, sometimes makes early marriage, dominating, enterprising, enthusiastic, may lose spouse.
Scorpio Ambitious, highly critical, powerful emotions, perceptive, must learn self-discipline in order to be constructive.	**Eighth** Strong sex drive, difficulties in legacies, inheritance and legal involvements, mystical, may be attracted to surgery or psychology, will probably die violently.

Sagittarius
Enthusiastic, loves travel, tactless, fond of argument, daring, an independent thinker, prone to exaggerate, may go off on tangents.

Capricorn
Ambitious, obstinate, practical, self-reliant, executive and organizational ability, dutiful.

Aquarius
Strong freedom drive, reforming urge, idealistic, impatient, interested in causes.

Pisces
Makes secret enemies, self-sacrificing, lacks drive, may develop undesirable habits, lacks concentration.

Ninth
Mentally alert, loves travel, needs religious freedom, will fight for convictions, becomes more serious in later life, encounters danger in foreign travel.

Tenth
Needs to be own boss, excessively ambitious, authoritative, energetic, courageous, problems with a parent.

Eleventh
Many and varied friends but may lose them because of impulsive behavior, organization-minded, many social contacts.

Twelfth
Secretive, subject to loss of reputation, treachery and persecution, lacks energy, needs sufficient rest.

TABLE 6
JUPITER IN THE SIGNS AND HOUSES

SIGN	HOUSE
Aries Honest, leadership abilities, overly optimistic, extravagant, should learn to budget energy and finances.	**First** Optimistic, generally lucky, merciful, able to inspire others, usually has strong vitality, self-righteous.
Taurus Needs comfort, possessive, self-indulgent, loves food and drink, contemplative.	**Second** Financially successful, may be extravagant, influential, appreciates tangible assets.
Gemini Mentally alert, versatile, talkative, may be superficial, loves travel, inventive, loves literature.	**Third** Interested in literature, travel, communication and education, optimistic temperament, philosophical, good relationship with family.
Cancer Protective, sympathetic, emotional, ambitious, sociable, patriotic, loyal to family, generous but may be taken advantage of.	**Fourth** Content and secure in old age, loves pomp and splendor, vain, domestically happy, loves acquisition.

Leo
Loyal, loves speculation, popular, creative, dramatic, vital, generous, likes prestige.

Virgo
Materialistic, moral, ethical, analytical, should not bottle up emotions.

Libra
Sociable, harmonious, loves art and culture, need for excessive praise, needs companionship.

Scorpio
Intense feelings, loves a challenge, attracted to the occult, the hidden and the mysterious, tenacious drive for possession.

Sagittarius
Spiritual, religious, moral, loves travel, animals and outdoors, believes in luck, literary abilities, not necessarily a self-starter.

Capricorn
Responsible, sense of duty, able to lead, may be penny-wise and pound-foolish, egotistical.

Aquarius
Unconventional, revolutionary, scientific, idealistic, lofty.

Pisces
Intuitive, overly imaginative, artistic, charitable, fearful, sympathetic, should learn to assert self and set a definite goal.

Fifth
Loves pleasure, art, theater, luxury, drama and speculation, socially successful, has gifted children.

Sixth
Healthy but may have hypochondriacal tendencies, loyal, cooperative, should learn sensible dietary habits.

Seventh
Makes good marriage but is not necessarily happy, sociable, cooperative, attracted to professional mate.

Eighth
Excellently situated for legacies or gain through partner, interested in the occult, could handle other people's money.

Ninth
Loves study, travel and literature, philosophical, broad-minded, intuitive, religious, logical, optimistic.

Tenth
Ability to be successful, business, political, social and professional interests, influential.

Eleventh
Helpful friends and acquaintances, popular, active in social life, realizes plans.

Twelfth
Psychic, meditative, helpful to others in a quiet way, may receive help in same manner, philanthropic.

TABLE 7

SATURN IN THE SIGNS AND HOUSES

SIGN	HOUSE
Aries Ambitious, determined, may lack depth, impatient, defiant, jealous, should learn to become more realistic.	**First** Serious, persistent, self-confident, morbid at times, practical ability, learns through disappointment.

Taurus
Frugal, inhibited, functions best when under pressure, economical, stubborn, persevering.

Gemini
Logical, conscientious, shy, ability for literature, science or mathematics, may be too serious-minded.

Cancer
Tremendous desire for security, emotionally controlled, fears independence, conservative, opinionated, concerned with public welfare.

Leo
Ambitious, tends to overexert, organizing ability, hypocritical, anxious.

Virgo
Meticulous, discreet, serious, thorough, prudent, mistrustful, responsible, should watch nagging, often misunderstood.

Libra
Must always act honorably, Saturn in this sign can give extremely high esteem or standing in the community or total disgrace, scientific, emotional.

Scorpio
Obstinate, serious, occult leanings, melancholy, may be capable of extreme jealousy, shrewd type of mind, needs emotional release.

Sagittarius
Religious, philosophical, prudent, fearless, dignified, may suffer oppression through others.

Capricorn
Practical, capable, ambitious, selfish, cold, advances slowly in life, able to overcome adversity, pessimistic.

Aquarius
Freedom-loving yet serious, interested in ideologies, reserved, sociable, not resentful, observant.

Second
Responsible about finances, must learn to budget as nothing is given.

Third
Difficulty with education, travel, relatives and neighbors, but even with little education this position gives the ability to wrestle with problems of a deeper nature, may appear superficial but is not.

Fourth
Limited in domestic environment, needs to learn discipline, heritage-conscious, overanxious about old age.

Fifth
Has difficulties with children, loyal, experiences social restrictions and possibly sexual inhibitions, must use caution in any form of speculation.

Sixth
Ability to carry responsibility, works better alone, reliable, a disciplinarian, conscientious, prone to ill health and problems in employment.

Seventh
Marriage often delayed, loyal, conscientious, should learn to be affectionate, ambitious.

Eighth
Psychic, opinionated, good life expectancy, moody, responsible, serious, encounters problems with inheritance.

Ninth
Scientific, studious but may lack education which may lead to serious lack of self-worth, frustrated.

Tenth
Must have a goal, able to hold responsible position, should learn not to carry grudges, desires to instruct the masses.

Eleventh
Few but faithful friends, prefers older companions, likes to wrestle with social problems.

Pisces Philanthropic, imaginative, moody, subject to discredit, unfortunate, strong emotional nature, often source of own undoing.	**Twelfth** Morbid, able to keep a secret, secluded habits, bears sorrows in secret, reserved, lacks stamina, needs to learn self-confidence, encounters risks through treachery.

TABLE 8
URANUS IN THE SIGNS AND HOUSES

SIGN	HOUSE
Aries Freedom-loving, independent, active, original, positive, unconventional, eccentric, impulsive, rebellious.	**First** Clever, original, scientific leanings, may have difficulty getting along with others, stubborn, inventive, eccentric, changes occupation, brusque, willful, freedom-loving, erratic.
Taurus Headstrong, resourceful, smoldering, disruptive, intense, able to bulldoze through a problem or remove obstacles with force.	**Second** Experiences financial changes, ability to manipulate resources in unusual ways, finds unique manner of earning money, has financial ups and downs due to impulsiveness.
Gemini Versatile, inventive, has hunches, scientific, restless, interested in reforms, may have telepathic ability.	**Third** Too outspoken, scattering, intuitive, intellectual, loves travel, erratic, ideas come in a flash.
Cancer May be emotionally unstable, mediumistic, touchy, peculiar habits, experiences domestic difficulties, interested in home and country.	**Fourth** Changes residence, experiences upheavals in domestic life, rebellious, emotional need for security.
Leo Industrious, bold, adventurous, has leadership ability but may be eccentric in handling a situation.	**Fifth** Has unusual children, loves to gamble or speculate, unconventional ideas about sex unions, may have ability to stimulate others to self-discovery.
Virgo Scientific curiosity, teaching ability, intellectual and critical faculties, loves reform, tactless.	**Sixth** Difficulties with co-workers, works in unusual profession, high-strung, able to reorganize, prone to sudden illness.
Libra Has dual personality — sometimes extremely charming and sometimes extremely disruptive, literary abilities, scientific leanings, magnetic personality, psychic and artistic.	**Seventh** Holds peculiar freedom-loving views about marriage, drawn to eccentric type of partner, often marries too quickly.

Scorpio
Has original methods of ministering to the needs of others, emotional, independent, vengeful, energetic, determined.

Sagittarius
Scientific, intensely needs freedom, revolutionary, loves travel, intuitive, imaginative.

Capricorn
Possesses excellent leadership qualities, penetrating mind, serious, highly ambitious, authoritative.

Aquarius
Resourceful, strong mental abilities, very intuitive and imaginative, may be scientifically- or mechanically-oriented, desires to change conditions for the better.

Pisces
Highly intuitive, secretive, emotional, has unusual dreams, may be subject to scandal, experiences mood shifts.

Eighth
Unconventional ideas about life and death, curious, may be subject to sudden inheritance, psychic.

Ninth
Unconventional in ideas about philosophy and religion, travel urge, may be accident-prone, fanatical tendencies.

Tenth
Should become self-employed because unable to take orders, subject to unusual careers, independent, unconventional, original.

Eleventh
Civic-minded, many and unusual acquaintances, drawn to groups and societies, reforming urge.

Twelfth
Subject to deceit and treachery from others, eccentric, psychic, mystical, may be misunderstood by self and others, must guard against jeopardizing reputation.

TABLE 9
NEPTUNE IN THE SIGNS AND HOUSES

SIGN	HOUSE
Aries Socialistic, interested in psychic research, loves travel, dominated by feelings.	**First** Hypersensitive, must have definite objectives and aims as there may be a strong tendency to drift, nebulous.
Taurus Good sense of rhythm, musical, creative.	**Second** Has unusual type of income, must learn to budget, may spend money on needless and frivolous items.
Gemini Imaginative, prophetic, mystical, sensitive.	**Third** Intuitive, interested in the occult, may be vague in expressing feelings and emotions, loves travel, highly imaginative.

Cancer
Idealistic, spiritual, loves the sea, imaginative.

Leo
Dramatic, artistic, magnetic, kind, delusions of grandeur.

Virgo
Intellectual, mediumistic, intuitive, sensitive.

Libra
Charming, refined, idealistic, platonic, artistic, sensitive.

Scorpio
Extremely sensitive, feelings and emotions run strong, mediumistic, secretive.

Sagittarius
Visionary, loves travel and research, literary.

Capricorn
Practical ability and business insight because of psychic abilities.

Aquarius
Humane, independent, searches for inner meaning of life.

Pisces
Highly mystical and spiritual or may sink to depths of degradation.

Fourth
Needs security, has peculiar conditions in domestic environment, may be subject to theft, needs artistic type of surroundings.

Fifth
Artistic, dramatic, luxury-loving, has peculiar children, overindulgent in sensual pleasures, seductive and susceptible to seduction.

Sixth
Loves seclusion, strange health patterns, retiring, disorganized, should serve humanity in some way.

Seventh
Unusual partnerships, needs companionship, difficulty in judging motives and character of others.

Eighth
Intuitive, psychic, spiritual, partner's finances fluctuate, negative habit patterns that should be brought to the surface.

Ninth
Intuitive, travel-minded, strongly imaginative, forms own opinions about philosophies and religions, psychic abilities.

Tenth
Artistic, capable of leadership, may become famous, tends to name changes, unusual career.

Eleventh
Strange friends, may be subject to seduction, should be wary of deception, fraud and schemes.

Twelfth
Intuitive, psychic, loves seclusion, may be immoral, subject to fantasies and self-deception, may have addictive habit patterns.

Pluto

Pluto is an extremely slow-moving planet. Its period of revolution is approximately 248 years. This means that Pluto stays in each sign approximately twenty-five to thirty years, and thus influences vast groups of people born in a twenty-five- to thirty-year span. Since Pluto was only discovered in 1930, we do not have much research material on its influence. (See Table 10.)

Pluto was in Aries from approximately 1822 to 1852. It brought about social and economic revolutions.

Pluto was in Taurus from approximately 1853 to 1883. It precipitated the exploitation and utilization of the earth's resources.

Pluto was in Gemini from approximately 1883 to 1914. It induced self-expansion, intellectual development, mental and scientific achievements.

Pluto was in Cancer from approximately 1914 to 1938. It brought about technological breakthroughs.

Pluto was in Leo from approximately 1938 to 1957. It led to greater art appreciation via television.

Pluto was in Virgo from approximately 1957 to 1971. It precipitated breakthroughs in medical research.

Pluto has been in Libra from approximately 1972. Its chief influence seems to be on the necessity to balance economic factors and the recognition of the need to utilize resources in a balanced fashion. It should precipitate equality, political changes, law, order and reform.

TABLE 10
PLUTO IN THE HOUSES

First House
Experiences crises, changes, upheavals in personal life, skepticism, gives many experiences, must learn to be constructive.

Second House
Resourceful, income may come from several sources, may be subject to tremendous financial fluctuations, must learn to budget.

Third House
Searching and penetrating mind, interested in the occult, loves travel, may be cynical, subject to obscure jealousies in family, should learn to overcome hypersensitivity.

Fourth House
Subject to sudden and complete upheavals within the domestic sphere, strong hereditary ties, dictatorial tendencies, should learn cooperation with family members.

Fifth House
Dominating and jealous in romantic affairs, expects perfection from children, loves adventure, should watch gambling instinct.

Sixth House
Interested in medicine, hygiene and healing, may be self-sacrificing, must learn not to expect too great a performance from others.

Seventh House
Has power complex, competitive, at some point in life a tremendous change will occur because of the influence of another person, must learn cooperation with others.

Eighth House
Produces periodic crises, subject to sudden economic upheavals, experiences self-transformation, should guard against morbid preoccupation with death.

Ninth House Has reforming urge, adventurous, idealistic, mystical, travel-minded, should guard against becoming a religious fanatic. **Tenth House** Independent, authoritative, power complex, changes occupations, should watch ruthless dictatorial methods and attitudes as may otherwise become subject to scandal.	**Eleventh House** Interested in "isms," mass influence, visionary ideas, reforming urge, should analyze thoroughly whether aims and objectives will truly be beneficial for mankind. **Twelfth House** Subject to jealousies and emotional tension, hypersensitive, must learn to understand self in relation to the external world.

The Ascendant or Rising Sign by Element

When one of the fire signs is rising, it indicates good vitality, force and energy, strong stamina, ambition, pride, enterprise, command, a greater desire to lead than to serve, and an argumentative and temperamental nature.

When one of the air signs is rising, it means less vitality, love of art, cheerfulness, amiability, a sympathetic nature (social and communicative) and speaking abilities.

When one of the water signs is rising, the indications are for poor recuperative powers, a weak constitution, sensitivity, fear, shyness, lack of energy, emotionality and intuition.

When one of the earth signs is rising, it means general good health, a strong constitution, a cautious disposition, and a nature that is premeditative, careful, stubborn, suspicious, economical, self-protective and practical.

Table 11 gives the indications of an ascendant sign. Table 12 describes the effects on the human physique of all the planets when they are ascending.

TABLE 11
ASCENDANTS BY SIGN

Aries Frank, open, outspoken, quick-tempered but does not hold a grudge, scientific, philosophical, not easily discouraged, has willpower, aggressive, energetic. **Taurus** Self-reliant, persistent, capable of working hard to obtain goals, quiet, dogmatic, reserved, fond of beauty, art, music and literature, can be moved easily by sympathy, has a calming influence on others.	**Gemini** Investigative, experimental, dexterous, idealistic, fond of mental pursuits, restless, high-strung, indecisive, excitable, changeable, needs constant change, finds education and literature excellent emotional outlets, talkative. **Cancer** Changeable, moody, sentimental, sympathetic, talkative, good memory, fears criticism and ridicule, discreet and conventional, strong emotions, adaptable, very insecure.

Leo

Noble, good-natured, generous, has great hope, faith and fortitude, lavish, excessive energy and vitality and ardent affections, sincere, passionate, high-strung, quick to anger, grants favors readily, generally fortunate.

Virgo

Shy, modest, conservative, industrious, desires wealth but must make extra effort to save money, sensitive to surroundings and conditions of others, tends to worry, careful with details, very discriminating, should avoid drugs, conscientious.

Libra

Loves justice, neatness, order, peace, and harmony, fond of beauty in all forms, tends to be affectionate, happy, impressionable, admires modesty and refinement, finds best outlet in a profession.

Scorpio

Determined, secretive, suspicious, skeptical, sarcastic, quick-witted, quick in speech, alert, will reach high attainments through subtlety and strength of will or by force, mechanical skill, fond of investigating mysteries, penetrating gaze.

Sagittarius

Jovial, bright, hopeful, loves liberty and freedom, will allow no one to order or drive him, frank, fearless, impulsive, tactless and blunt at times, likes most things to be on a big scale (e.g., business or financial undertakings), good sense of humor, loves travel and adventure.

Capricorn

Prudent, economical, practical, quiet, serious, capable of looking after own interests, good organizer, cautious and calculating, non-demonstrative, prefers ideas to words, does well in earthy matters.

Aquarius

Determined, quiet, unobtrusive, faithful, idealistic, philosophical and humanitarian, good memory and clear reasoning power, objective, reformist, always ahead of own time, innovative inventive genius, eccentric and peculiar, interested in social issues, often possesses scientific abilities, literary ability.

Pisces

Trusting, sympathetic, idealistic, impressionable, emotional, lacks self-confidence, modest, timid, sometimes indecisive, lacks energy, has the power to make the best of circumstances, often spiritual.

TABLE 12

PLANETS IN RISING SIGN AND THEIR EFFECT ON PHYSIQUE

Mars	— Dark complexion, makes square and compact body.
Venus	— Good-looking.
Mercury	— Animated facial features.
Moon	— Fair.
Sun	— Rosy glow.
Jupiter	— More fleshy.
Saturn	— A leaden look, leathery, tends to stay slim.
Uranus	— Electric blue eyes, wiry body, light complexion, magnetic.
Neptune	— Ethereal-looking, tends to gain weight.
Pluto	— Squarish, angular, pliable features, dark complexion.

4
Aspects— How to Measure Them

In astrology the term "aspect" refers to the geometric relationships between the planets. These relationships are based on the geometric division of the 360° of the circle. Aspects are very important in chart interpretation. Whenever an aspect is formed between two or more planets, their functions are linked. For instance, if Venus and Mars are in aspect at the moment of birth, there is a definite cooperative relationship between these two planets in that person's chart.

As with signs and planets, the aspects are expressed by symbols. In Table 13, the first column lists the astrological symbols. The second column defines these symbols. The third column gives the geometric degrees involved in each particular aspect. The fourth column gives the permitted orb of the planets, exclusive of the Sun and Moon. The fifth column gives the permitted orb of the Sun and Moon — which, in most cases, are allowed wider orbs than the other planets.

Conjunction

Let's look at the first aspect, which is the conjunction.

TABLE 13

MAJOR ASPECTS

SYMBOLS	DEFINITIONS	EXACT ASPECT	EXACT PERMITTED ORB OF PLANETS	EXACT PERMITTED ORB OF	
☌	Conjunction — easy or difficult influence depending on nature of other planets involved.	8°	8°	8°	Conjunction can occur in same sign or adjoining sign but cannot exceed 8°.

	Parallel (Declination) — one planet involved may be south and the other may be north. Both planets involved in the parallel may be north or both planets involved may be south.	1°	1°	1°	All planets involved in the parallel cannot exceed 1°.
ℙ					

SYMBOLS	DEFINITIONS	EXACT ASPECT	EXACT PERMITTED ORB OF PLANETS	TOTAL RANGE ON EITHER SIDE OF EXACT PERMITTED ORB OF PLANETS	EXACT PERMITTED ORB OF — or +	TOTAL RANGE ON EITHER SIDE OF EXACT PERMITTED ORB OF
			— or +	— +		— +
∠	Semisquare	45°	4°	41°–49°	5°	40°–50°
✳	Sextile	60°	8°	52°–68°	8°	52°–68°
Q	Quintile	72°	2°	70°–74°	2°	70°–74°
□	Square	90°	8°	82°–98°	10°	80°–100°
△	Trine	120°	8°	112°–128°	10°	110°–130°
⊡	Sesquare	135°	3°	132°–138°	5°	130°–140°
⊠	Quincunx (also called inconjunct)	150°	3°	147°–153°	5°	145°–155°
☍	Opposition	180°	8°	172°–188°	10°	170°–190°

*Any of the distances between planets can be measured between any two points in the chart.

Figure 7 shows all 30° of the sign Aries. Sometimes 0° is also referred to as 30° of Pisces (the previous sign); in the figure it ranges to 0° of Taurus (the next sign). Notice that the degree numbers a sign encompasses move counterclockwise around the wheel. The arrow shows the direction in Figure 7.

The total range of any sign is 30°, whether it begins at the cusp of one house and ends at the cusp of another house, as in Aries (Figure 8), or begins at a point within one house and ends at a point within another house.

Planets that occupy the same sign are considered conjunct if they fall within the permitted orb (as shown in Table 13). Planets may also conjunct if they fall in two conjoining signs, such as Leo and Virgo, and are within the permitted orb. Conjunction symbolizes activity. When planets are in conjunction there is a concentration of the different kinds of action symbolized by the planets in question. The interpretation of a conjunction depends on the nature of the type of planet involved — in other words, whether the planets are of a malefic or benefic nature.

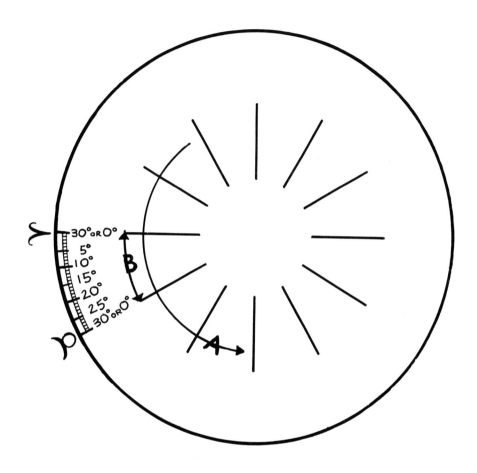

FIGURE 7
Aries, at 0°, one of the twelve signs.

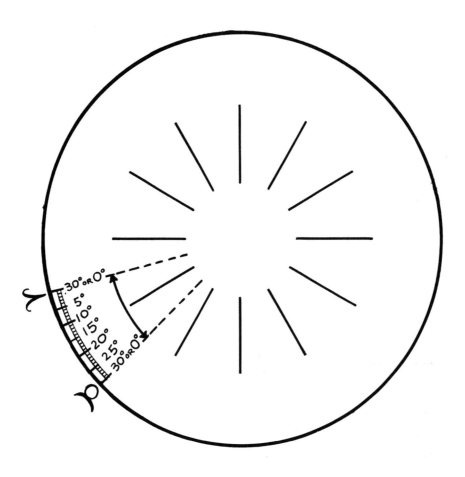

FIGURE 8
The range of Aries in this case extends from midway through the first house to midway through the second.

Parallel (Declination)

The parallel aspect occurs between two planets that have the same degree of declination (angular distance north or south of the celestial equator). In Table 14 follow the seventh day across the columns headed "Dec." (declination). Note under the heading "Neptune" that its declination for the seventh is 19°S27'. Next note under "Saturn" that its declination is 21°N22'. The difference between these two planets is slightly less than 2° so they can be considered parallel.

TABLE 14

RAPHAEL'S EPHEMERIS, NOVEMBER, 1972
SHOWING DAILY POSITION OF THE
PLANETS, EXPRESSED IN DEGREES AND
BASED ON GREENWICH TIME*

New Moon—November 6d. 1h. 22m. a.m.

22   **NOVEMBER, 1972**   [*RAPHAEL'S*

D M	Neptune Lat.	Neptune Dec.	Herschel Lat.	Herschel Dec.	Saturn Lat.	Saturn Dec.	Jupiter Lat.	Jupiter Dec.	Mars Lat.	Mars Dec.	Mars Dec.
1	1 N 35	19 S 24	0 N 36	7 S 15	1 S 40	21 N 23	0 S 5	23 S 26	0 N 46	7 S 18	7 S 33
3	1 35	19 25	0 36	7 18	1 40	21 23	0 5	23 25	0 45	7 48	8 3
5	1 35	19 26	0 36	7 21	1 40	21 22	0 5	23 24	0 44	8 18	8 33
7	1 35	19 27	0 36	7 23	1 40	21 22	0 6	23 24	0 44	8 48	9 3
9	1 35	19 28	0 36	7 26	1 40	21 21	0 6	23 23	0 43	9 18	9 32
11	1 35	19 29	0 36	7 29	1 40	21 20	0 6	23 22	0 42	9 47	10 1
13	1 35	19 29	0 36	7 31	1 40	21 20	0 6	23 21	0 41	10 16	10 30
15	1 35	19 30	0 36	7 34	1 40	21 19	0 6	23 20	0 40	10 45	10 59
17	1 34	19 31	0 36	7 36	1 40	21 18	0 6	23 18	0 39	11 13	11 28
19	1 34	19 32	0 36	7 39	1 40	21 18	0 7	23 17	0 39	11 42	11 56
21	1 34	19 33	0 36	7 41	1 40	21 17	0 7	23 16	0 38	12 10	12 23
23	1 34	19 34	0 36	7 43	1 40	21 16	0 7	23 14	0 37	12 37	12 51
25	1 34	19 34	0 36	7 46	1 40	21 15	0 7	23 13	0 36	13 4	13 18
27	1 34	19 35	0 36	7 48	1 40	21 15	0 7	23 11	0 35	13 31	13 S 45
29	1 34	19 36	0 36	7 50	1 40	21 14	0 7	23 9	0 34	13 58	—
30	1 N 34	19 S 36	0 N 36	7 S 51	1 S 40	21 N 13	0 S 8	23 S 8	0 N 33	14 S 11	

D M	D W	Sidereal Time H. M. S.	☉ Long.	☉ Dec.	☽ Long.	☽ Lat.	☽ Dec.	MIDNIGHT ☽ Long.	☽ Dec.
1	W	14 43 29	9 ♏ 9 51	14 S 33	18 ♏ 24 46	4 S 18	0 N 37	24 ♍ 37 21	2 S 3
2	Th	14 47 26	10 9 57	14 52	0 ♎ 47 20	4 46	4 S 41	6 ♎ 54 59	7 15
3	F	14 51 22	11 10 4	15 11	13 0 31	5 0	9 44	19 4 11	12 7
4	S	14 55 19	12 10 13	15 30	25 6 7	5 0	14 22	1 ♏ 6 31	16 28
5	☉	14 59 15	13 10 24	15 48	7 ♏ 5 31	4 47	18 24	13 3 17	20 9
6	M	15 3 12	14 10 37	16 6	18 59 57	4 22	21 40	24 55 42	22 58
7	Tu	15 7 8	15 10 52	16 24	0 ♐ 50 44	3 45	24 0	6 ♐ 45 15	24 47
8	W	15 11 5	16 11 8	16 41	12 39 30	2 59	25 16	18 33 48	25 29
9	Th	15 15 1	17 11 27	16 58	24 28 29	2 4	25 24	0 ♑ 23 56	25 1
10	F	15 18 58	18 11 46	17 15	6 ♑ 20 34	1 4	24 22	12 18 52	23 25
11	S	15 22 55	19 12 8	17 32	18 19 22	0 S 1	22 12	24 22 35	20 43
12	☉	15 26 51	20 12 30	17 48	0 ♒ 29 9	1 N 4	19 0	6 ♒ 39 38	17 3
13	M	15 30 48	21 12 54	18 4	12 54 41	2 7	14 54	19 14 55	12 33
14	Tu	15 34 44	22 13 20	18 20	25 40 55	3 6	10 2	2 ♓ 13 13	7 22
15	W	15 38 41	23 13 46	18 35	8 ♓ 52 20	3 57	4 S 35	15 38 38	1 S 41
16	Th	15 42 37	24 14 14	18 50	22 32 21	4 36	1 N 16	29 33 37	4 N 16
17	F	15 46 34	25 14 44	19 5	6 ♈ 42 19	5 1	7 16	13 ♈ 58 9	10 12
18	S	15 50 30	26 15 14	19 19	21 20 36	5 6	13 3	28 48 52	15 45
19	☉	15 54 27	27 15 46	19 33	6 ♉ 22 1	4 51	18 13	13 ♉ 58 50	20 26
20	M	15 58 24	28 16 20	19 47	21 38 1	4 16	22 17	29 18 9	23 45
21	Tu	16 2 20	29 ♏ 16 55	20 0	6 ♊ 57 48	3 21	24 47	14 ♊ 35 34	25 21
22	W	16 6 17	0 ♐ 17 31	20 13	22 10 9	2 13	25 26	29 40 26	25 2
23	Th	16 10 13	1 18 10	20 25	7 ♋ 5 26	0 N 57	24 12	14 ♋ 24 27	22 57
24	F	16 14 10	2 18 49	20 38	21 36 56	0 S 21	21 21	28 42 35	19 27
25	S	16 18 6	3 19 30	20 49	5 ♌ 41 16	1 36	17 18	12 ♌ 33 14	14 57
26	☉	16 22 3	4 20 13	21 1	19 18 6	2 43	12 27	25 56 43	9 51
27	M	16 26 0	5 20 57	21 12	2 ♍ 29 17	3 39	7 11	8 ♍ 56 15	4 N 28
28	Tu	16 29 56	6 21 43	21 22	15 18 6	4 22	1 N 45	21 35 20	0 S 56
29	W	16 33 53	7 22 31	21 33	27 48 27	4 52	3 S 36	3 ♎ 57 58	6 11
30	Th	16 37 49	8 ♐ 23 20	21 S 42	10 ♎ 4 20	5 S 7	8 S 42	16 ♎ 8 1	11 S 7

First Quarter—November 14d. 5h. 1m. a.m.

E P H E M E R I S] **NOVEMBER, 1972** 23

D M	Venus Lat.	Venus Dec.		Mercury Lat.	Mercury Dec.		☽ Node	Mutual Aspects
1	1N 33	0N 39	0N 12	2 S 41	23 S 12	23 S 28	20 ♑ 27	1. ⊙⊥♇. ♂P♅.
3	1 36	0 S 15	0 S 42	2 46	23 43	23 56	20 21	2. ☿✳♀, P♃, ✳♇. ♂♂♇.
5	1 39	1 9	1 37	2 47	24 8	24 18	20 14	3. ☿♂♇. ♀⊥♇.
7	1 42	2 4	2 31	2 47	24 26	24 33	20 8	4. ⊙⊥♃,∠♅. ♀□♃.
9	1 44	2 59	3 26	2 44	24 38	24 41	20 2	5. ⊙±♄. 6. ♂□♃.
11	1 46	3 54	4 21	2 36	24 42	24 41	19 55	7. ⊙⊥♀. 10. ⊙∠♇.
13	1 48	4 48	5 16	2 24	24 38	24 32	19 49	11. ⊙♒♄. 12. ♂♃.
15	1 49	5 43	6 10	2 7	24 24	24 13	19 43	13. ♂⊥♅. 14. ⊙∠♃.
17	1 50	6 37	7 4	1 45	24 0	23 43	19 36	15. Stat. ♀△♄.
19	1 51	7 31	7 58	1 16	23 24	23 1	19 30	16. ♀∠♅. 17. ♀♂♅.
21	1 51	8 24	8 51	0 41	22 36	22 7	19 24	19. ⊙⊥♅,P♅. ♀P♃. ♀P♅.
23	1 51	9 17	9 43	0 S 2	21 36	21 3	19 17	20. ☿♂♀.
25	1 50	10 9	10 35	0N 39	20 29	19 54	19 11	21. ☿⊥♂. ♂□♄,⅄♇.
27	1 50	11 1	11 S 26	1 18	19 20	19 4	19 4	22. ☿♀♃. ♀□♃.
29	1 48	11 51	—	1 51	18 18	18 S 48	18 58	23. ☿⊥♀. ♂♅♅.
30	1N 48	12 S 16		2N 5	17 S 51		18 ♑ 55	24. ☿P♅. ✳♂,Ph,∠♅. 25. ⊙P♀,⊥♃. ♂♂♅. 26. ⊙♂☿,✳♇. ♀✳♀,⊥♃. 27. ⊙Ph,♂♀. ♀P♅. ♀□ [♄,⅄♇. [✳♇. ♂P♇. 28. ⊙⊥♅. ♀⅄♀.

D M	♆ Long.	♅ Long.	♄ Long.	♃ Long.	♂ Long.	♀ Long.	☿ Long.	Lunar Aspects ⊙ ♇ ♆ ♅ ♄ ♃ ♂ ♀ ☿
1	4 ♐ 3	19 ♎ 59	19 ♊ 48	5 ♑ 3	20 ♎ 30	1 ♎ 55	2 ♐ 1	⅄ □ ⅄
2	4 5	20 3	19 ℞ 45	5 13	21 9	3 7	3 9	✳ ♂ ✳ □ ♂ ✳
3	4 7	20 6	19 42	5 24	21 49	4 20	4 16	⅄ ∠ ♂ △ ♂ ∠
4	4 9	20 10	19 38	5 34	22 28	5 32	5 20	⅄ ⅄ ∠ □ ✳ ⅄ ⅄
5	4 11	20 13	19 35	5 45	23 8	6 44	6 22	
6	4 13	20 17	19 31	5 56	23 47	7 57	7 20	♂ ∠ ⅄ ∠ ⅄ ∠
7	4 15	20 20	19 28	6 7	24 26	9 10	8 15	✳ ♂ ∠ ⅄
8	4 18	20 24	19 24	6 18	25 6	10 22	9 6	⅄ ✳ ∠ ✳ ♂
9	4 20	20 28	19 20	6 30	25 45	11 35	9 52	✳ ♂ ♂ ∠ ✳
10	4 22	20 31	19 17	6 41	26 25	12 48	10 34	∠ □ ⅄ ♂ ⅄
11	4 24	20 34	19 13	6 52	27 4	14 1	11 10	✳ ∠ □ □
12	4 26	20 38	19 9	7 4	27 44	15 14	11 40	△ ✳ □ □ ∠
13	4 28	20 41	19 5	7 15	28 24	16 27	12 3	□ △ ⅄ △ ✳
14	4 31	20 45	19 1	7 27	29 3	17 40	12 19	□ △ ∠ △
15	4 33	20 48	18 56	7 39	29 ♎ 43	18 54	12 27	□ □ ✳ □ □
16	4 35	20 51	18 52	7 51	0 ♏ 23	20 7	12 ℞ 25	△ □ □ △
17	4 37	20 55	18 48	8 3	1 2	21 20	12 14	□ ♂ △ □ ♂ □
18	4 40	20 58	18 44	8 15	1 42	22 34	11 53	□ ♂ ✳ ♂ □
19	4 42	21 1	18 39	8 27	2 22	23 47	11 22	∠ △ ♂
20	4 44	21 4	18 35	8 39	3 2	25 1	10 39	♂ □ ⅄ ∠
21	4 46	21 8	18 30	8 51	3 41	26 14	9 47	△ ♂ □ ♂
22	4 49	21 11	18 26	9 3	4 21	27 28	8 45	△ ♂ △ ♂
23	4 51	21 14	18 21	9 15	5 1	28 42	7 35	□ ♂
24	4 53	21 17	18 17	9 28	5 41	29 ♎ 56	6 18	□ □ □ ⅄ □
25	4 55	21 20	18 12	9 40	6 21	0 ♏ 10	4 58	△ ✳ △ □ □ △
26	4 58	21 23	18 7	9 53	7 2	23	3 35	∠ ✳ ✳ □
27	5 0	21 26	18 3	10 3	7 41	3 37	2 14	□ ⅄ ✳ ✳ □
28	5 2	21 29	17 58	10 18	8 21	4 51	0 ♐ 57	⅄ □ △
29	5 4	21 32	17 53	10 31	9 1	6 5	29 ♏ 46	∠ ⅄ ✳
30	5 ♐ 7	21 ♎ 35	17 ♊ 48	10 ♑ 44	9 ♏ 41	7 ♏ 20	28 ♏ 44	✳ ♂ ✳ □ ⅄ ⅄ ∠

In order to determine the exact difference between the two planets, we subtract 19°S27' (Neptune) from 21°N22' (Saturn). Now, you cannot subtract 27' from 22', but since each degree consists of 60 minutes, the computation looks like this: Saturn 20°82' minus Neptune 19°27' equals 1°55' (difference).

In Table 14 look at the declination column of the Moon. Reading from the top to the bottom of

the column, you will notice that the declination increases or decreases — in other words, changes direction, shifting back and forth between the north and south declinations. This kind of shift occurs with all planets, but the Moon undergoes the fastest changes in this respect.

A parallel is a powerful aspect. If a chart shows one planet south and the other north by declination, this is an opposition or separative type of

48 **Becoming Familiar with Elements of the Horoscope**

pattern and indicates loss of either a person or a condition. If the planets in question are both north or both south, this represents a holding pattern. Parallels are always read in conjunction with other planetary aspects and are used to refine interpretations.

The Other Aspects

Now let's go over the remaining aspects shown in Table 13. In order to do this we will have to refer to Figure 9. The *semisquare* is indicated by A. It consists of one-eighth (45°) of a circle (360°). The permitted total orb on either side of the exact semisquare aspect of 45° is 4°, which means that the total range is from 4° *less* the exact aspect of 45° — in other words, from 41° to 45° to 4° more than the exact aspect of 45°, or from 45° to 49°. Thus the *total* range of the *exact* permitted *aspect* is from 41° to 49°. Since the permitted orb of the Sun and Moon is greater, an extra-degree leeway is given on either side of the exact permitted aspect. The orb for the aspect extends in this case *from 40° to 45°* (45° is the exact aspect of the semisquare), and *from 45° to 50°*. Note on Table 13 that the total permitted orb is 5° for the Sun and Moon, and the range is from 5° less or 5° more than the exact aspect.

If we assume Saturn is at 20° of a sign — say, Aries — and another planet — say, Mars — is at 5° of Gemini, the exact difference between the two planets would be 45°. This is considered an exact semisquare aspect.

If we assume that one planet is at 20° of Aries and the other is at 1° of Gemini, the exact distance between the two planets is 41° — which is within the accepted orb between the two planets.

Now let's consider the aspects with the permitted orb for the Sun and Moon. From 5° of Aries to 20° of Taurus, for example, shows an exact 45° aspect. From 0° of Aries to 20° of Taurus shows a distance of 50°. These examples are within the permitted orb for the Sun and Moon.

Any time either the Sun or the Moon is involved with another planet, an extra range is given, as you will notice on Table 13. If the Sun and the Moon together form an aspect, *do not* double the permitted orb. It stays the same.

The semisquare aspect is considered a physical aspect. It indicates friction and creates occasional difficulties. The lesson the native* has to learn is found in the nature of the two planets involved in the aspect. Interpretation should involve studying the kinds of people who are ruled by the houses that these two planets occupy in the natal (birth) chart. Study also the houses ruled by the two planets involved in the aspect.

The next aspect to be considered is the *sextile*. The sextile consists of one-sixth (60°) of a circle (360°). In general, this aspect (B in Figure 9) occurs between planets that fall within a 60° angle. Table 13 shows that the permitted orb on either side of an exact aspect for both the planets and the Sun and the Moon is 8°. The sextile is considered a mental aspect and also indicates an ability to achieve if the necessary effort is made by the native. The opportunities it brings are designated by the natal house position of the planets involved. Be sure that in every case you also analyze the other houses that are ruled by the two planets involved in the aspect. The people and conditions these houses rule will give you clues as to how the sextile can best be utilized. In essence, the sextile shows the native that if he makes an effort, he can achieve. The time when this natal aspect becomes activated will be shown by the progressions and transits.† This holds true for all the aspects found in a chart that shows the strength, weakness, opportunity and hindrance areas encountered in a lifetime.

Next let's discuss the *quintile*. Look at C in Figure 9. The exact aspect is 72° (the orb and range are shown in Table 13). Quintiles are not often found, but when this aspect exists between two

---

* Term astrologers use for the person whose chart is being analyzed. The birth chart is sometimes called the *natal chart*, and a horoscope is sometimes called a *nativity*.

† Progressions and transits are used to time events and will be discussed in Chapter 18.

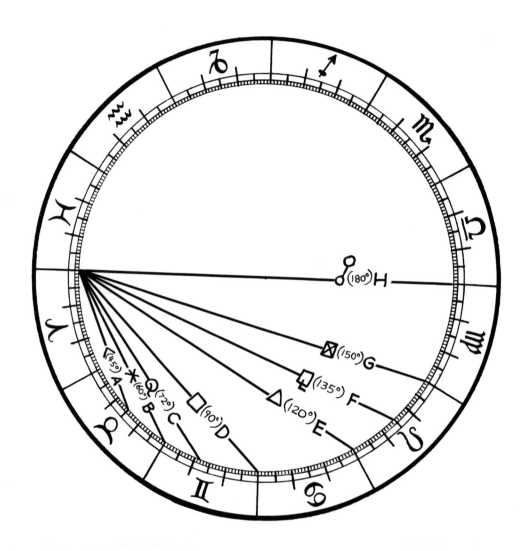

FIGURE 9
The semisquare (A), sextile (B), quintile (C), square (D),
trine (E), sesquare (F), quincunx (G) and opposition (H)
aspects.

planets in a chart, it indicates some built-in talent that can be used successfully in life. The nature of the two planets and the houses they are in and rule have to be taken into consideration.

The next aspect is the *square*. (Continue to refer to Table 13 as we discuss the remaining aspects.) For example, if at birth the Moon was at 20° Leo and Venus at 20° Taurus, this would be considered an exact Moon–Venus square. A square represents a conflict or struggle and indicates there will be karmic lessons and experiences in this life because of previous misuse of free will. If a chart does not show a square aspect, no progress can be made. This aspect shows where the native must apply himself for constructive achievement. It also indicates the area where new experiences will have to be sought and is therefore considered a learning aspect. Squares in a chart are not malefic, as is so often taught. Rather they give the native the crucial opportunity to gain strength in handling everyday problems. Without squares, achievement is literally impossible.

The *trine* aspect (E in Figure 9) is found where two planets fall within a 120° angle of each other. This is a birthright aspect and indicates consequences of actions in former lives. The trine shows gain, ease of expression and luck. This aspect represents an enormous protective pattern in the chart. However, it should only be classified as helping the native to advance if squares are present at the same time to make him work and earn that advancement. Without coexisting squares, trines do not build backbone because the effort and active energy induced by the square is lacking. In other words, while trines are beneficial by nature, without the help of squares in the chart, they produce only laziness, daydreaming and the inability to take advantage of the opportunities they bring.

The range of the *sesquare* aspect is shown by F in Figure 9. Like the semisquare, the sesquare is a physical aspect and thus is dynamic. It shows health problems, identified by the two planets involved in the aspect, and — like the semisquare and the square — indicates difficulties and irritability with the people ruled by the houses that the two planets forming the aspect are found in. Let me again remind you always to look at the houses that are ruled by the two planets in aspect when making up a chart.

The range of the *quincunx* aspect (often referred to as minor aspect) is shown in G in Figure 9. The quincunx is a regenerating, reorganizing and transforming type of aspect. It indicates an ability to do research work and shows a karmic necessity to pay greater attention to personal health and to perform a service identified by the two planets involved and the houses they occupy. Again, as in every aspect, for further clues look at the houses the two planets involved rule. For instance, Saturn may be found in Gemini, in the twelfth house, but the sign of Aquarius, which Saturn rules, is found on the cusp of the ninth house. This means that the ninth house must also be taken into consideration when analyzing the aspects.

The *opposition* (H in Figure 9) is one of the easiest aspects to spot immediately. It occurs between two planets approximately 180° apart (opposite each other on the circle) that fall in opposite signs within a planetary orb of 8°–10°. The latter orb, of course, is only allowed to the Sun and Moon (see Table 13). An example of this aspect is the Moon falling at 20° Virgo and Mercury falling at 15° Pisces. In this case, the planetary orb is permissible. Opposition shows where cooperation may be difficult. It indicates the tension between two simultaneous planetary drives in different directions and often results in a separative effect. To understand what specific life areas are being affected by this aspect, you must study the planets involved and the houses they fall in. For instance, a Pluto–Venus opposition from the fifth to the eleventh house would indicate great upheavals and loss in the area of love and romance. The opposition is a strong lesson aspect, where self-discipline and self-awareness must be learned. This aspect will also teach the native to become aware of his outside environment, as well as to respect and accept the habit patterns of other people. Unless the native rises to this aspect, it can be a serious limiting force and a significant impediment to his personal happiness.

5
Aspects— How to Interpret Them

When reading a chart, you should first analyze the Sun sign that a person belongs to, then the element that characterizes his rising sign at birth (fire, earth, air or water), then the actual rising sign, then the planets present in the signs and houses and, finally, the aspects between these planets. Sounds formidable? Well, only in the beginning. With practice, it all falls into place. Read this chapter through several times, but don't force yourself to memorize it.

As you look at Tables 15–23, you will notice that the first column shows the planets in aspect with each other, the second column gives the ☌ (conjunction) interpretation, the third column gives the ✳ (sextile) and △ (trine) interpretations and the fourth column gives the ∠ (semisquare), □ (square), ⛝ ses-square and ☍ (opposition) interpretations.

Note the order of the tables in this chapter. Table 15 shows the Sun in aspect with the Moon and the other eight planets. Then the Sun is eliminated and Table 16 shows the Moon in aspect with Mercury and the remaining seven planets. Then the Moon is eliminated and Table 17 shows Mercury in aspect with Venus and the

remaining six planets. And so on. The same order of planets is maintained throughout the tables. In figuring aspects in your own chart retain this order so that you do not lose an aspect between planets.

Now, for an example. Let's take a person who has Mars (♂) in Aries (♈) in the fifth house trine (△) to Pluto (♇) in Leo (♌) in the ninth house. At the same time, Mars is also sextile (✳) to Uranus (♅) in Gemini (♊) in the eighth house. Also, Mars is in opposition (☍) to Neptune (♆) in Virgo (♍) in the eleventh house.

First blend Mars in Aries and Mars in the fifth house. Then blend Pluto in Leo in the ninth house, then Uranus in Gemini in the eighth house, then Neptune in Virgo in the eleventh house.

Assuming you have familiarized yourself with the planets by signs and houses, you should now learn the meaning of the aspects to see how the potential of the planet is utilized within the framework of the whole chart. Remember, the sextile is considered a mental aspect and it shows the ability to achieve if the native makes the necessary effort. In other words, the interpretation of Mars sextile Uranus would be handled on a conscious level. Briefly, the interpretation of Mars sextile Uranus reads: "Scientific, inventive, original, practical, self-reliant, fearless." So if the native makes the effort, he can handle his problems in a self-reliant, original manner. This person also has an aptitude for science and invention. Since Mars in Aries is by nature a self-assured signature, this aspect reinforces the natural tendency to self-reliance. Uranus in the eighth house shows a psychic tendency, which, because of the sextile, should be developed further.

A trine (in this case we have Mars trine Pluto) shows a certain amount of luck, ease of expression and an inborn ability to achieve advancement. However, a conscious effort must be made (Mars sextile Uranus) to utilize great abilities indicated by this aspect.

The opposition of Mars/Neptune shows occasional overimagination and mischanneling of energy, especially where others are concerned. Remember, the eleventh house deals with associates such as friends, and the fifth house — where Mars is positioned — deals with romance, so it is quite possible that cooperation with others may at times be difficult. The person must learn self-discipline and self-awareness, especially in matters of love and affection. That these can be learned is shown by Mars sextile Uranus.

In the beginning it will probably be easier to write out each separate interpretation; for instance, the meaning of Mars, the meaning of the sign Aries, the meaning of Mars in Aries; then the meaning of Mars in the fifth house, the meaning of Mars sextile Uranus, the meaning of Mars trine Pluto, etc. Then calmly sit down and analyze all these factors to form a comprehensive whole.

Again, however, I would like to emphasize that it is an error to rely on isolated factors alone. These are only parts of a whole, and the entire person can only be known when you build up a composite picture. Each of us is unique.

Note: It is important to analyze not only the aspects between planets but also the houses and signs that these planets occupy and rule. *Remember, under no circumstances use isolated factors.* A planet may be disharmoniously situated with another planet and, at the same time, harmoniously situated with a third planet, which, while it weakens the harmonious tendencies to a degree, also weakens the disharmonious tendencies. Make as many charts as possible to gain practice in the art of interpretation.

TABLE 15

ASPECTS WITH THE SUN

	☌	✳ △	∠ ⊾ □ ☍
☉ **with** ☽	Desires harmony, tends to overexert physically, has periodic states of depression, is subjective.	Enjoys physical well-being, harmony at home, success, ambition, good luck.	Experiences frustrations, disharmony with others, emotional conflicts and crises.
☉ **with** ☿	Artistic, loves luxury, good memory, mathematical abilities, interested in literature.	Sun and Mercury are never more than 28° apart; therefore the other aspects cannot occur.	
☉ **with** ♀	Cultured, loves luxury, gentleness, social, talent for music and art, affectionate.	Sun and Venus are never more than 48° apart; therefore only the semisextile aspect is possible.	

	⊙	⊙	⊙
			Irresponsible, lazy, complacent.
⊙ with ♂	Impulsive, strong physique, energetic.	Abundant energy, leadership capacities, tact.	Argumentative, quarrelsome, reckless, impulsive.
⊙ with ♃	Lucky in life, protected, good health, cooperates with others, honorable, sympathetic, optimistic.	Socially popular, prominent, executive ability, philosophical, positive, life-loving.	Extravagant, swaggering, overindulgent, unrealistic, tends to overeat.
⊙ with ♄	Emotionally supressed, pessimistic, learns through hard knocks, thrifty, misses opportunities, tenacious.	Serious, capable, patient, accepts conditions, ability for organization, prospers.	Selfish, oppressed, self-pitying, pessimistic, damaged ego.
⊙ with ♅	Enjoys public success, magnetic, independent, rebellious, eccentric, needs to control emotions.	Organizing ability, makes sudden gains, inventive, genius.	Has stormy relationships with others, self-willed, unconventional, tactless, erratic.
⊙ with ♆	Charming, artistic, empathetic, mystical, intuitive, musical, ability to influence public.	Prominent, strongly imaginative, psychic, intuitive, visionary.	Experiences chaotic conditions, impractical, sensuous, subject to treachery, tends to escapism, lives in a dream-world.
⊙ with ♇	Crisis-prone, boastful, presumptuous, temperamental, power-driven.	Mediumistic, reforming, able to regenerate self, progressive.	Capable of ruthless behavior, dictatorial, needs to learn faith, crisis-prone, subject to upheavals, power-driven, manipulative.

TABLE 16
ASPECTS WITH THE MOON

	☌	✶ △	∠ ⊾ □ ☍
☽ with ☿	Above-average intelligence, good memory, loves change to such an extent it may disrupt life, restless, high-strung.	Charming, socially successful, intelligent, alert, commonsensical.	High-strung, unable to concentrate, indecisive, resentful, indiscreet, worried, restless.

☽ with ♀	Charismatic, artistic, happy in marriage, loves luxury, refined.	Popular, artistic interests, enjoys domestic serenity, sensuous, happy, affectionate, self-expressive in a refined way.	Self-indulgent, moody, gossiping, envious, has misunderstandings with others and domestic difficulties, overly sensitive, strong need for love.
☽ with ♂	Restless, intense, overreacts, irritable.	Ambitious, able to make money, has drive, makes gains, seeks security, good constitution, enterprising.	Irritable, argumentative, has financial difficulties, temperamental, moody, rash.
☽ with ♃	Optimistic, will rise in life, kind and in good health but should guard against weight gain.	Lucky, successful, may inherit, optimistic, helped by others.	Extravagant, emotionally rash, unreliable associations, should not trust luck, should not get involved in schemes, tends to overeat.
☽ with ♄	Timid, feels inferior, moody, misses opportunities, overcautious, serious.	Thrifty, practical, trustworthy, capable of handling responsible positions.	Morbid, shy, subject to limitations and hardships, has difficulties in home environment, jealous, critical, finds it difficult to show feelings.
☽ with ♅	Independent, eccentric, popular, charismatic, inventive abilities, extravagant.	Ambitious, imaginative, psychic, romantic, has many friends, sparkles and is full of energy.	Cantankerous, high-strung, bohemian, careless, rebellious, theatrical, mercurial, erratic, unstable.
☽ with ♆	Overly sensitive, daydreaming, impractical, retiring, mystical, escapist tendencies.	Psychic, artistic, imaginative, personally popular, loves to travel.	Daydreams, lives in realm of unrealities, impractical, associates may prove unreliable, subject to self-delusions, tends to escape, can be deceived by women.
☽ with ♇	Moody, sensitive, sensuous, irritable, revengeful, may have psychometric abilities, adventurous.	Able to achieve, prophetic, visionary, adventurous.	Experiences upsetting conditions, fanatical tendencies, obstinate, destructive, violent temper, manipulative, irresponsible.

TABLE 17

ASPECTS WITH MERCURY

	☌	✶ △	∠ ⊾ □ ☍
☿ **with** ♀	Excellent at self-expression, charming in speech and manner, artistic, should cultivate responsibility, loves pleasure and the arts.	Mercury and Venus can never be more than 76° apart. (Interpretation same as for the conjunction.)	Only the semisquare can occur. Sometimes shirks responsibility, spends on trivial items.
☿ **with** ♂	Marked mental energy and analytical ability, quick physical and mental reactions, fast speaker, impulsive.	Same as the conjunction, but indicates coordinated and smooth-flowing mental and physical expression.	Hypercritical, irritable, bad-tempered, sarcastic, argumentative, selfish, must learn to reason before drawing conclusions.
☿ **with** ♃	Optimistic, intellectual, tolerant, might show signs of superiority, oratorical and scientific ability, philosophically inclined.	Same as the conjunction but more thorough in intellectual pursuits.	Poor judgment, subject to fraud, untruthful, fuzzy thinker, impatient, indiscreet, vacillatory, tends to exaggerate.
☿ **with** ♄	Serious, inhibited, over-conservative, great powers of concentration, skeptical.	Orderly mind, methodical, able to organize, cautious, responsible.	One-track mind, rigid, inhibited, obstinate, brusque in speech and writing, critical.
☿ **with** ♅	Inventive, experiences thoughts as coming in a flash, lightening perception, original, restless, hasty.	Inventive, scientific, excellent in debate, dramatic, clever, sense of rhythm and timing, progressive attitude.	Unconventional, eccentric, nervous, scatters energies, opinionated.
☿ **with** ♆	Sensitive, strongly imaginative, subject to self-deception, needs to take time out to relax, experiences inner confusion.	Visionary, mediumistic, psychic, poetic, refined, sympathetic, compassionate, artistic.	Vivid imagination, touchy, impaired reasoning ability, nervous, deceptive, gullible, unreliable, impaired judgment, chaotic, obsessive.
☿ **with** ♇	Nagging, overzealous, irritable, restless.	Diplomatic, could make a good critic, spellbinding, excellent powers of observation, penetrating perceptions.	Destructive, irritable, sarcastic, cynical, draws mental conclusions too quickly, explosive, violent.

TABLE 18
ASPECTS WITH VENUS

	♂	✳ △	∠ ⊿ □ ☌
♀ **with** ♂	Strongly sexual, charismatic, loves excitement and sports, self-confident, optimistic.	Affectionate, sensuous, artistic, sense of color, rhythm and timing, creative.	Highly sexed, lacks tact, careless in money matters, self-indulgent, difficulties in the social world and in self-expression.
♀ **with** ♃	Strong artistic abilities, numerous love affairs, works better with a partner than alone, charming.	Artistic, popular, charming, good relationships with others, financial security, sentimental.	Self-conceit, intensely driven to seek partner, clingy, abuses charm, overly demonstrative, self-indulgent habits.
♀ **with** ♄	Delayed marriage or marries an older person, jealous, undemonstrative, emotional difficulties.	Stable marriage, loyal, business ability, faithful, responsible, practical.	Experiences emotional difficulties, jealousy, sorrow, inhibitions and estrangements, often does not marry.
♀ **with** ♅	Unusual and original ideas about art and love, dramatic, self-willed, romantic, financial advantages, charismatic, independent.	Popular, artistic, financial opportunities, loves speculation, experiences beneficial changes, charismatic, desires freedom and romantic excitement.	Forms unconventional partnerships and peculiar love relationships, emotional difficulties, loses through speculation, intense reaction to others, emotionally erratic, freedom-loving.
♀ **with** ♆	Sensitive, imaginative, artistic, self-delusioned, unrealistic viewpoint toward life.	All artistic expressions are enhanced, psychic, popular, sentimental.	Should watch reputation, self-indulgent, financial losses because of impracticality, deceived through others, especially women.
♀ **with** ♇	Has many love affairs, easily hurt, hypersensitive, fanatical tendencies, possessive.	Mediumistic, creative, ingenious, excellent color sense, gifted, able to succeed, perceptive.	Immoral, difficulty with others especially in close relationships, easily hurt, coarse, crude, self-serving, experiences romantic upheavals.

TABLE 19

ASPECTS WITH MARS

	☌	✶ △	∠ ⊾ □ ☍
♂ with ♃	Tremendously energetic, daring, courageous, adventurous, leadership ability, can make money quickly but spends it with equal speed, reckless, may be unscrupulous.	Fun-loving, adventurous, energetic, will get help in time of need, loves display, enjoys financial protection.	Has gambling instinct, reckless, extravagant, swaggering, opinionated, rebellious, tends to exaggerate.
♂ with ♄	Suspicious, tends to be malicious, mistrustful, temperamental.	Fantastic endurance, conventional, good at details, thorough, leadership qualities, materialistic.	Impatient, experiences physical and emotional strains, sadistic, bad-tempered, suspicious, tends to be ruthless.
♂ with ♅	High-strung, nervous, stubborn, irritable, needs freedom of thought and action, develops original working methods, energetic.	Scientific, inventive, original, practical, self-reliant, fearless.	Irrational, temperamental, high-strung, brutal, frank, obstinate, tactless.
♂ with ♆	Conceited, self-indulgent, self-centered, may have tendency to persecution complex, addictive tendencies.	Popular, enthusiastic, executive ability, inspirational, visionary, charismatic.	Fearful, overly imaginative, unrealistic, elusive, mischannels energy, inferiority complex, self-destructive, subject to addiction.
♂ with ♇	Explosive, temperamental, self-torturing, stubborn, destructive tendencies.	Capable of great achievements, ambitious, self-confident, great physical and mental energy.	Cruel, unscrupulous, fool-hardy, vindictive, brutal, argumentative, violent temper.

TABLE 20
ASPECTS WITH JUPITER

	☌	✶ △	∠ ⊡ □ ☍
♃ **with** ♄	Honest, penny-wise and pound-foolish, good at sound investments, subject to alternating periods of optimism and depression.	Practical abilities, common sense, prosperous, honest, patient, confident, diplomatic.	Matures early because of tests in life, materialistic, difficult rise in life, must work hard for everything.
♃ **with** ♅	Tends to be philanthropic, philosophic and religious, independent, freedom-loving, optimistic, original, inventive, loves to travel.	Leadership qualities, gets help from superiors, inspirational, intuitive, philosophical, desires to develop self.	Headstrong, rebellious, opinionated, exaggerates, tactless, experiences losses because of premature actions.
♃ **with** ♆	Sympathetic, mystical, religious, artistic, poetic, emotional, has a touch with money but may spend excessively.	Humanitarian, imaginative, idealistic, generous, psychic, visionary, poetic.	Subject to peculiar beliefs, emotional disturbances and financial irresponsibility, hypersensitive, not good at speculation, misunderstood by others and self.
♃ **with** ♇	Tends to exaggerate, extremely ambitious, has willpower, courage and enthusiasm.	Honorable, organizational and leadership abilities, tremendously capable of influencing others.	Arrogant, fanatical, conflicts with authority, extravagant, tends to squander, destructive.

TABLE 21
ASPECTS WITH SATURN

	☌	⚹ △	∠ ⬦ □ ☍
♄ with ♅	Wastes energy, difficulty in concentrating, seeks practical objectives, eccentric, inhibited, emotional.	Ambitious, responsible, honorable, concentrative ability, inventive, perceptive, thorough, serious.	Vague, philosophical ideas, restless, argumentative, frustrated, lacks concentration, illogical, eccentric, impulsive, aggressive.
♄ with ♆	Inferiority complex, self-deluded, must guard reputation, financial difficulties, misdirects energy, subject to treachery.	Keenly intuitive, skilled at business, practical, organizing ability, self-reliant, sympathetic, able to make dreams come true.	Inferiority complex, subject to criticism, inhibited, tends to be hypochondriacal, self-deluded, moody.
♄ with ♇	Foolish, suspicious, impatient, suicidal tendencies, has power urge but this may be misdirected, self-destructive, envious.	Able to endure, self-disciplined, thorough, tenacious, leadership quality, courageous, loves research.	Unsympathetic, egotistical, violent, suicidal tendencies, subject to depression, harsh disciplinarian.

TABLE 22
ASPECTS WITH URANUS

	☌	⚹ △	∠ ⬦ □ ☍
♅ with ♆	Restless, must guard against scandals, confused, chaotic, self-deluded.	Executive ability, loves travel, intuitive, psychic, inventive, idealistic.	Self-deluded, confused, nervous, oversensitive, confused ideas, impaired psychic faculties.
♅ with ♇	Subject to sudden upheavals and changes, foolhardy, inventive, violent, excitable, fanatic.	Makes record-breaking achievement, stamina, ability to re-create.	Subject to upsets, great changes, upheaval and violence, fanatical, destructive tendencies.

TABLE 23
ASPECTS WITH NEPTUNE

♆ with ♇	☌	⚹ △	∠ ⫾ □ ☍
	Unusual and peculiar ideas and objectives and strange longings, adventurous, confused, chaotic, destructive tendencies.	Ability to orientate self to needs of others, mystical, spiritual, intuitive knowledge of higher forces and depth perception, strives for inner knowledge.	Crisis-prone, experiences turning points of unusual nature in life, prone to deception, subject to strange changes, able to decipher motives of others, to deceive others and to hide own faults, misdirected abilities.

6
Applying and Separating Aspects

Determining whether an aspect is applying or separating makes greater refinement in chart reading possible. Aspects are referred to as either *major* or *minor*. Don't let the term *minor* mislead you — major and minor aspects are of equal importance in astrology. Historically, minor aspects were considered to be secondary qualities, but today — in the light of new research and technological advancement — most astrologers, while retaining the old terminology, recognize the import and value of the so-called minor aspects.

Analyzing Applying and Separating Aspects

In an applying aspect the faster-moving planet is moving toward the slower-moving planet.

Example:

$$♀12♈ \text{ with } ☽9♊$$
$$\text{or}$$
$$☽8♒ \text{ with } ♀12♈$$

In either case the ☽ is *applying to* ✳ of ♀ as ☽ is faster than ♀.

In a separating aspect the faster-moving planet is separating from the slower planet.

Example:

$$♀12♈ \text{ with } ☽14♊$$
$$\text{or}$$
$$☽16♒ \text{ with } ♀12♈$$

In either case the ☽ is *separating from* ✳ of ♀ as ☽ is faster than ♀.

Note: The parallel aspect and influence have been discussed previously. The influence of two planets involved in an applying or separating aspect, and *also* parallel, would be a major factor in the native's development pattern. In every case it is important to analyze the nature of the two planets involved in the aspect and the houses that these planets occupy.

30° ⌄
(Semisextile)
2° Orb for Planets (5° if ☉ / ☽ Are Involved)
This is a minor aspect and its influence often goes unnoticed by the native.

The applying aspect has a twelfth-house influence: Subconscious experiences from other lives will gradually be utilized for further development in this life.

The separating aspect has a second-house influence: Practical development and gain are possible providing the native makes the effort.

36° ⊥
(Semiquintile)
1° Orb for Planets (2° if ☉ / ☽ Are Involved)
This is a minor aspect and deals with subtle inner mental forces.

The applying aspect has an eleventh-house influence: Group activities and occult and scientific interests can be utilized by the native for further development.

The separating aspect has a second-house influence: Mental abilities are geared to the practical utilization of resources.

45° ∠
(Semisquare)
4° Orb for Planets (5° if ☉ / ☽ Are Involved)
This is major aspect and indicates periodic setbacks and irritations throughout the native's life.

The applying aspect has an eleventh-house influence: The realization of desires is often thwarted by friends, groups or social contacts.

The separating aspect has a second-house influence: The steady development of practical resources is periodically interrupted.

60° ✳
(Sextile)
8° Orb for Planets (8° if ☉ / ☽ Are Involved)
This is a major aspect and concerns opportunity.

The applying aspect has an eleventh-house influence: Cooperation by and through friends and groups for the gratification of personal desires and development can be had if the native makes the necessary effort to gain it.

The separating aspect has a third-house influence: Opportunity is present, to be taken advantage of by using mental faculties. Intellectual development should be pursued for the utilization of the native's full potential.

72° Q
(Quintile)
2° Orb for Planets (2° if ☉ / ☽ Are Involved)
This is a minor, but nonetheless important, aspect as it indicates originality (particularly in mathematics) and the ability to solve complicated mental problems and to apply the results practically and concretely. This is sometimes referred to as the "genius aspect."

The applying aspect has a tenth-house influence: Long-range plans are worked out to serve professional ambitions and career. The unfoldment or utilization of the specific talent and genius often does not take place until age thirty-six.

The separating aspect has a third-house influence: Special talents and genius are utilized strictly in the mental realm. This gives the native the penetrating insight to perceive conditions clearly.

90° ☐
(Square)
8° Orb for Planets (10° if ☉ / ☽ Are Involved)
This is a major aspect and shows where constant adjustments, energy and effort have to be expanded to get results.

The applying aspect has a tenth-house influence: Many hardships and problems will have to be faced and handled in order to build character since the native abused his free will in previous incarnations. New experiences will contribute to future development and perfection.

The separating aspect has a fourth-house influence: Ingrained habit patterns and errors from previous lives must be corrected through untiring effort if personal development is to be made. Constant self-improvement must be practiced. The native must expend energy to develop new abilities.

108° V
(Tredecile)
3° Orb for Planets (3° if ☉ / ☽ Are Involved)
This is considered a minor aspect and deals with mental development and unfoldment.

The applying aspect has a ninth-house influence:

This indicates mental growth in the realms of philosophy, religion and higher education.

The separating aspect has a fourth-house influence: Mental development is utilized in practical everyday affairs.

120° △
(Trine)
8° Orb for Planets (10° if ☉ / ☽ Are Involved)

This is a major aspect and shows creativity, spiritual awareness and general good fortune, earned as reward due to past good karma.

The applying aspect has a ninth-house influence: Spiritual awareness gained in previous lives should be used as the building block for further enlightenment.

The separating aspect has a fifth-house influence: The ability for self-expression is present. Creative abilities are also evident and should be utilized in some manner.

135° ⌑
(Sesquare)
3° Orb for Planets (5° if ☉ / ☽ Are Involved)

This is considered a major aspect and gives periodic negative tendencies — dominance, aggression and impulsiveness — that are activated by others in the environment.

The applying aspect has an eighth-house influence: Changes and upheaval periodically upset the native's equilibrium, making it necessary for him to rearrange his plans.

The separating aspect has a fifth-house influence: The native has difficulty with self-expression or experiences inhibitions. Children may present problems.

144° ±
(Biquintile)
2° Orb for Planets (3° if ☉ / ☽ Are Involved)

This is considered a minor aspect and deals with mental abilities in the area of the occult, creativity, ESP and clairvoyance and associated subtle forces.

The applying aspect has an eighth-house influence: Occult interests and abilities rooted in past incarnations can be activated for further development.

The separating aspect has a fifth-house influence: Gives native ability to express himself in any creative area.

150° ⊠
(Quincunx)
3° Orb for Planets (5° if ☉ / ☽ Are Involved)

This is considered a minor aspect, but nonetheless a very important one. It deals with transformation, changes in mental outlook and health patterns, death and regeneration.

The applying aspect has an eighth-house influence: The native must reorganize financial interests held in any form of partnership. Personal changes and transformation become of prime importance when activated by progression or at time of transit.

The separating aspect has a sixth-house influence.

180° ☍
(Opposition)
8° Orb for Planets (10° if ☉ / ☽ Are Involved)

This is a major aspect and has a first- and seventh-house influence. It indicates awareness, reaching out of the self to make contact with others, becoming cognizant of potential for relationship with others. It teaches recognition of individuality of self and others. Friends, marriage and business partners and the public at large all will act as catalysts. Self-discipline and harmony must be learned if the native is to achieve his growth potential.

II

Other Significant Considerations in Chart Interpretation

7

Angular, Succedent and Cadent Houses, Quadruplicities and Hemispheres

Houses

The first, fourth, seventh and tenth houses are called *angular* houses. (See Figure 10.) In a chart, any planets found in these angular houses are strong, exercise great power and are very dynamic or activating, i.e., they set processes in motion and represent the primary areas of experience. Angular-positioned planets indicate tremendous ability for self-expression and great freedom of function. The first house is the east (sunrise); the tenth house is the south (noon); the seventh house is the west (sunset); and the fourth house is the north (midnight).

Figure 11 shows the *succedent* houses. These are succedent because they directly follow the angular houses and are reactive to the action expressed in the angular houses. The succedent houses are the second, fifth, eighth and eleventh. Planets found in these houses give stability and fixed purpose.

Figure 12 shows the *cadent* houses. Cadent houses come before angular houses and are therefore the third, sixth, ninth and twelfth houses. These represent versatility, changeability and intuition. Planets found in them do not provide much opportunity for action except when they are moving by progression, but they harmonize the processes begun by the angular houses and stabilized by the succedent houses.

If you memorize the four angular houses — one, four, seven and ten — you will have no trouble remembering which are the succedent houses (the four that follow the angular houses) and which the cadent (the four that precede the angular houses).

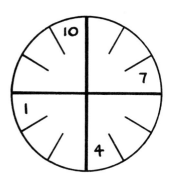

FIGURE 10
The angular houses.

FIGURE 11
The succedent houses.

FIGURE 12
The cadent houses.

Quadruplicities

Figures 13, 14 and 15 show the qualities. All the zodiacal signs correspond to one of three qualities — cardinal, fixed or mutable — which are referred to as the *quadratures*. Each quadrature contains all four elements (fire, earth, air and water). The cardinal cross (Figure 13) is composed of Aries (a fire sign) in opposition to Libra (an air sign), and Cancer (a water sign) in opposition to Capricorn (an earth sign). Cardinal signs are forceful, authoritative, active and have the most power when positioned in angular houses.

The fixed cross (Figure 14) is composed of Taurus (an earth sign) in opposition to Scorpio (a water sign), and Leo (a fire sign) in opposition to Aquarius (an air sign). Fixed signs are masterful, stable, rigid and have great fixity of purpose. Should these signs occur in your own chart in an angular position, it would indicate you are determined, organized and habit-bound.

The mutable or common cross (Figure 15) is composed of Gemini (an air sign) in opposition to Sagittarius (a fire sign), and Virgo (an earth sign) in opposition to Pisces (a water sign). Mutable signs are adaptable and flexible. When mutable signs are found in angular positions, the native then has greater capacity for action; when found on cusps of succedent houses, these signs become more stable.

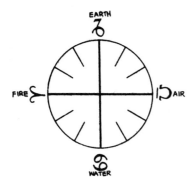

FIGURE 13
The cardinal cross.

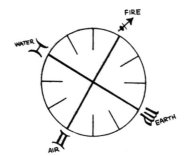

FIGURE 15
The mutable or common cross.

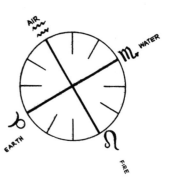

FIGURE 14
The fixed cross.

Hemispheres

The hemispheres in the chart that most of the planets occupy also have significance. Basically, they show the spheres of activity where the native's energies will tend to focalize and whether these will be working in an internal, external, personal or impersonal way. The immediate notation of this is an important initial step in horoscope interpretation.

Figure 16 shows the location of hemisphere emphasis. If most of the planets in a chart are found on the eastern side of the chart (referred to as the oriental side) — which extends from the cusp of the tenth house to the beginning of the cusp of the fourth house — this means a self-reliant nature. The native is a self-starter and often takes on more than he can manage. The road his life takes, therefore, is his personal choice.

If most planets on the western (occidental) side of the chart — which extends from the beginning of the cusp of the fourth house to the beginning of the cusp of the tenth house — he functions on an impersonal plane. The native's life, therefore, is somewhat dependent on other people. This

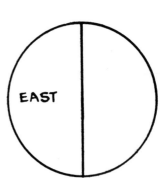

FIGURE 16
Hemisphere emphasis.

person will very often find himself imposed on by others in his needs and personal emergencies.

If most planets are situated on the south (diurnal) side of the chart — extending from the cusp of the seventh house to the cusp of the first house — it indicates a large scope of interests. The native is generally independent, proud and somewhat lucky. He usually desires leadership and has many interests, geared toward gaining recognition.

If most planets are on the north (nocturnal) side of the chart — which extends from the cusp of the first house and ends at the cusp of the seventh house — they function strictly on the inner plane. This indicates narrow interests and also makes the native introverted and domestic. This person is prone to be somewhat moody and gloomy because the north side of the chart represents the night.

It is, of course, quite possible for a chart to show a combination. For instance, the same number of planets may appear on the east side as appear on the south side. This, incidentally, is one of the best combinations: not only does it make the native a self-starter but it also makes him a happy and gregarious person.

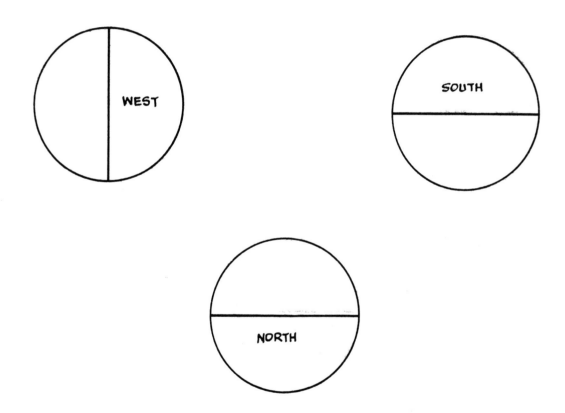

8
Categorizing by Planetary Distribution

The next thing to look for in chart interpretation is the way the planets are distributed within the circle. This gives the next clue or insight into a person. You will find that most people's planetary distribution fits into one of seven classifications — locomotive, bowl, splay, seesaw, bucket, bundle and splash. There are, of course, deviations from the norm, which make some charts difficult to classify, but with practice, and by working with the charts of people who are familiar to you, you will quickly become adept at interpreting charts.

Planetary Classifications

The Locomotive Type
About two-thirds of the chart (Figure 17) contains planets and one-third is empty. People whose charts are classified as locomotive require continual opportunity, need appreciation, are unreasonably ambitious and desire success and power. Self-confidence is rooted in their personal experience. They have an exceptional fund of energy at their disposal.

The leading planet — the first clockwise-oriented planet — and the house this planet is in are often important. If locomotive types are thwarted or frustrated, they may become rebellious.

FIGURE 17
Locomotive type.

70

The Bowl Type

More than one-third, but less than one-half, of the circle is empty. (See Figure 18.)

This arrangement indicates self-sufficiency and an uncompromising effort to compel recognition and acceptance from others. The bowl type shows conscious and exaggerated self-importance, tireless self-improvement and honesty. He tends to absorb experience. The leading planet will be revealing. Venus and Jupiter leading and well aspected will be helpful, while Mars, Saturn, Uranus and Pluto, if negatively aspected, could be detrimental. Extra force is shown if the planets fall above, below, east or west of the horizon.

The Splay Type

This is generally a threefold arrangement, though it is not always easy to define as such. (See Figure 19.)

This pattern gives the native the potential for marked genius and an extraordinary chance to put his seal on human destiny. He may be very decent or he may be in some way perverted. Certainly he dislikes being regimented or pigeonholed and will desperately try to escape being trapped within the boundaries of discipline or routine. His temperament will "poke" out into experience according to his own tastes.

The Seesaw Type

The ideal is an hourglass arrangement with two groups facing each other. (See Figure 20.)

The seesaw type has the unusal ability to communicate or share his intelligence. Genius is possible and would be shown by the planet that deviates from the hourglass arrangement. At worst, these people consider unorthodox ideas and see life through a different colored glass than the rest of us.

The Bucket Type

A singleton, or one planet, across from all the others. (See Figure 21.)

With a T-cross there is a capacity for enduring accomplishments. Achievement is important for the native's psychological well-being. The instinct for self-preservation may be lacking, so this pattern type often undergoes self-defeating experiences. He may be confused and if he dissipates his resources, may resort to ruthless tactics to achieve his ends and ambitions.

FIGURE 18
Bowl type.

FIGURE 19
Splay type.

FIGURE 20
Seesaw type.

FIGURE 21
Bucket type.

The Bundle Type

This is a rare grouping. All the planets are contained in one-third of the circle or less. (See Figure 22.)

This arrangement indicates a complacent and provincial person incapable of well-rounded development. But he has need for self-fulfillment, so he often tends to be a specialist. His thinking is rather confined, but he is capable of mastering a given subject in depth.

The Splash Type

This arrangement is easily recognized because the planets occupy as many signs as possible. It is the pattern with a wheel-like distribution. (See Figure 23.) The difference between this and the splay type is that the latter needs at least one stellium (a grouping of four or more planets in one sign or house).

Universality, exceptional achievement or waste are shown by this pattern. The native needs a well-rounded education because scattering tendencies are present.

FIGURE 22
Bundle type.

FIGURE 23
Splash type.

Planetary Configurations

The Grand Cross

Now look at Figure 24, which shows the grand cross configuration within a chart. One planet is in Sagittarius and another is in opposition in Gemini, and at the same time there is a planet in Virgo and another one in opposition to it in the sign of Pisces. In other words, we have two sets of planets in opposition placed so that they are at 90° intervals around the chart, plus or minus the permitted orb.

People who are born with a grand cross have to meet continual tests and crises in their lives. The grand cross configuration occurs where two sets of planets are in opposition and on either side square to two or more planets.

The T-Square

This configuration shows accomplishment and achievement. (See Figure 25.) Two planets are in opposition to each other, and one planet is in square aspect to the two opposing planets. For

FIGURE 24
Grand cross.

FIGURE 25
T-square.

instance, we have one planet in Aries, another in opposition in Libra and a third in Capricorn. The configuration looks like a "T." The planet that has the short leg of the "T" is the one that makes a square to the other two and carries the weight or responsibility for making accomplishment possible.

The Grand Trine
This configuration indicates ease and effortless good fortune. Therefore it very often signifies nonachievement. In a grand trine three planets are found 120° apart from each other (plus allowance for permitted orb). An example of this would be planets in Aries, Leo and Sagittarius. (See Figure 26.)

The Simple Trine
A simple trine occurs when two planets are 120° apart from each other (plus allowance for permitted orb). This is a harmonious combination; both planets and the signs and houses they occupy must be evaluated. An example of a simple trine is one planet in Virgo and the other planet in Capricorn (see Figure 27). A trine gives natural ease of expression. A trine can occur between two signs of the same element, such as earth (Virgo and Capricorn in our example), or, depending on the degree the two planets occupy, between two signs of different elements. (28° Virgo or 2° Aquarius gives an earth-and-air combination.)

FIGURE 26
Grand trine.

FIGURE 27
Simple trine.

9
Negative and Positive Positions of the Planets

The positive and negative ranges of the planets are shown in Figure 28. For example, if a planet is in 12° Leo, it is in the negative range. If another planet is in 14° Virgo, that planet would be in a positive range.

Most planets in a positive position indicate greater optimism, more self-expression and a realistic, direct approach to life. On the other hand, most planets in negative positions give greater introspection, receptivity and — depending on other factors in the chart — too much self-repression.

When making up a chart, determine how many of the ten planets are in a positive position and how many are in a negative position. If five planets are positive and five negative, the indication is for an emotionally balanced person.

At the risk of being repetitious, let me remind you again never to interpret a person by isolated factors in his or her chart. At *all times* the whole chart has to be taken into consideration. This, of course, takes time and practice.

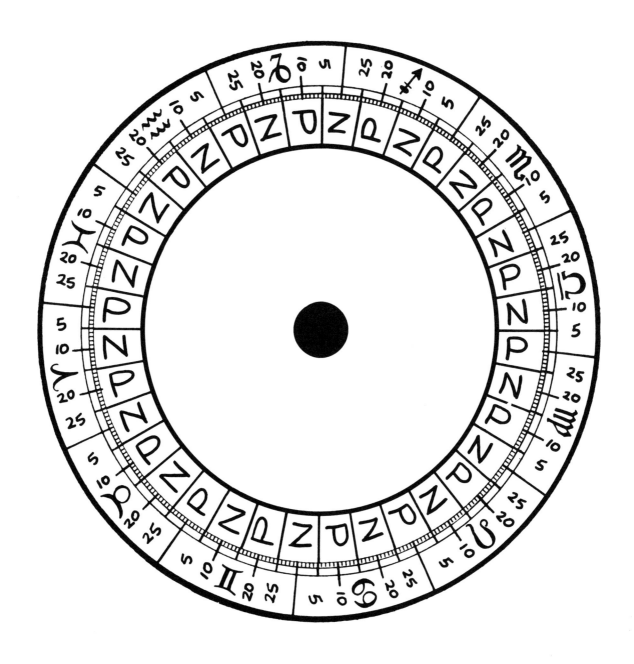

FIGURE 28
Positive (P) and negative (N) ranges of the planets.

10
The Decanates

Each sign, since it consists of 30°, can be divided into three decanates of 10° each. In other words, every sign from 0° to 9°59' belongs to the first decanate, and any natal planet situated in the first decanate partakes of or is influenced by that sign and the planet that rules it. Any planet situated in the second decanate, which ranges from 10° of a sign to 19°59', is *sub*influenced by the next sign counting in a counterclockwise direction of the *same element*. Any natal planet in the third decanate, which ranges from 20° of a sign to 29°59', is *sub*influenced by the third sign counting in a counterclockwise direction of the same element.

Assuming that a natal planet is positioned in the first decanate of Libra, this planet would take on the attributes of the sign Libra and the planet Venus, which rules Libra. Any natal planet situated in the second decanate of Libra would also take on the attributes of Libra and Venus, but in addition would be subinfluenced by the next counterclockwise air sign, Aquarius, which is ruled by Uranus and Saturn. A natal planet in the third decanate of Libra, again, would take on the attributes of Libra and Venus, but in addition would be subinfluenced by the third counterclockwise air sign, Gemini, which is ruled by Mercury.

Since this is a difficult concept to grasp, one more example: A planet in the first decanate of Aquarius takes on the attributes of the sign Aquarius and of the planets Uranus and Saturn, which rule the sign. A planet in the second decanate of Aquarius, in addition to taking on the influence of the sign and its ruling planet, also takes on a subinfluence coming from the next air sign, which is Gemini. A planet in the third decanate of Aquarius takes on the influence of Aquarius, *plus* the subinfluence coming from the third air sign, Libra.

Table 24 shows the decanate for all the signs with approximate dates when the sun is in various decantes. In Chapter 20, where a complete synthesis of a natal chart is given, you will see how these refinements help in evaluating a chart.

TABLE 24

APPROXIMATE BIRTH DATES FOR
FINDING DECANATES

Date	Sign	Decanate	Ruling Planets and Sub-influences
March 21 – March 30	Aries	1	♈
March 31 – April 10	Aries	2	♈ plus ♌
April 11 – April 20	Aries	3	♈ plus ♐
April 21 – April 30	Taurus	1	♉
May 1 – May 10	Taurus	2	♉ plus ♍
May 11 – May 20	Taurus	3	♉ plus ♑
May 21 – May 31	Gemini	1	♊
June 1 – June 10	Gemini	2	♊ plus ♎
June 11 – June 20	Gemini	3	♊ plus ♒
June 21 – July 1	Cancer	1	♋
July 2 – July 11	Cancer	2	♋ plus ♏
July 12 – July 21	Cancer	3	♋ plus ♓
July 22 – August 1	Leo	1	♌
August 2 – August 11	Leo	2	♌ plus ♐
August 12 – August 22	Leo	3	♌ plus ♈
August 23 – September 1	Virgo	1	♍
September 2 – September 11	Virgo	2	♍ plus ♑
September 12 – September 22	Virgo	3	♍ plus ♉
September 23 – October 2	Libra	1	♎
October 3 – October 12	Libra	2	♎ plus ♒
October 13 – October 22	Libra	3	♎ plus ♊
October 23 – November 1	Scorpio	1	♏
November 2 – November 12	Scorpio	2	♏ plus ♓
November 13 – November 22	Scorpio	3	♏ plus ♋
November 23 – December 2	Sagittarius	1	♐
December 3 – December 12	Sagittarius	2	♐ plus ♈
December 13 – December 21	Sagittarius	3	♐ plus ♌
December 22 – December 30	Capricorn	1	♑
December 31 – January 9	Capricorn	2	♑ plus ♉
January 10 – January 19	Capricorn	3	♑ plus ♍

January 20 – January 29	Aquarius	1	♒
January 30 – February 8	Aquarius	2	♒ plus ♊
February 9 – February 18	Aquarius	3	♒ plus ♎
February 19 – February 28	Pisces	1	♓
March 1 – March 10	Pisces	2	♓ plus ♋
March 11 – March 20	Pisces	3	♓ plus ♏

III

Important Planets in Your Everyday Life

11
Your Sexual Expression— Venus, Mars and the Fifth House

Venus and Mars are the planets of romance and sex. From an astrological point of view, Venus represents pleasure through the emotions and Mars represents the sexual drive.

In order to achieve sexual harmony, it is important to understand the *emotional* as well as the *physical* needs and drives of a partner. In this chapter we will discuss Mars first in a man's chart and then in a woman's chart, and Venus in a man's chart and in a woman's. I suggest that you read the information on Venus several times in the various signs and the information on Mars in the various signs.

Since the fifth house rules love affairs and sexual urges, it, too, must be analyzed in a natal chart. The sign that rules the cusp of the fifth house is highly significant for an evaluation of the native's sexual needs.

Let us take some examples. The first will be a man who has Venus (♀) in Virgo (♍), Mars (♂) in Virgo (♍) and the sign of Pisces (♓) on the cusp of the fifth house. He would be attracted to a woman who is realistic (Venus in Virgo) and dedicated to him without being overtly demonstrative. Pisces on the cusp of the fifth house shows that he needs a partner who is romantic, but since his Mars and Venus are in Virgo, at first he may appear cold to her. This is because he has a tremendous fear of being rebuffed, so he needs a woman who offers encouragement. She must have a lot of understanding, patience and warmth, but at the same time, she should never make him feel he is being smothered. Obviously, this is a complex pattern.

Take another example — a woman who has Venus (♀) in Cancer (♋), Mars (♂) in Aries (♈) and Pisces (♓) on the cusp of the fifth house. Her Venus in Cancer indicates that she needs a man she can mother, and she is looking for the same in return from him, as well as someone who understands her moods. Her Mars in Aries demands that her partner be forceful and self-confident.

But even if he isn't, she would like him to appear that way. Pisces on the cusp of her fifth house — as in the previous example — shows strong romantic leanings, but in her case this is emphasized more strongly because her Venus is positioned in Cancer. Since she is more demonstrative than the man in the first example, she is capable of overt romantic expressions. If these two people were to marry, the woman would have to learn to pull back somewhat, and the man in turn would have to recognize her need for romantic gestures. Through a mutual understanding of their needs, drives, actions and reactions, both could develop an excellent relationship.

Mars in a Man's Chart
(His Needs and Reactions)

♂ in ♈

This makes a man enthusiastic, aggressive and passionate. He does not like to win a woman easily and enjoys the chase as much as the prize.

♂ in ♉

This man is sensual and fond of all the earthly pleasures. The road to his love is through his stomach.

♂ in ♊

He is a bit flirtatious. Still, he needs an intellectual woman because he has a somewhat cerebral attitude toward his relationships.

♂ in ♋

This describes a man who is sensitive — in fact, moody — at times too thin-skinned. He has a strong protective attitude toward his loved ones and needs a woman who will, in turn, mother him.

♂ in ♌

This man is warm-hearted and warm-blooded and has a strong need to be admired. "Scratch his fur and watch him purr" is the key to his responses.

♂ in ♍

This type of man appears cold, distant and analytical, but only because he fears rebuff. He needs a woman who will give him plenty of warmth and encouragement.

♂ in ♎

He needs a companion but is repelled by coarseness or improper behavior. He is fond of pleasant and aesthetic pastimes.

♂ in ♏

This is an intensely passionate man. At first he may strike a woman as aloof but, once committed, watch out!

♂ in ♐

This man is somewhat self-indulgent and freedom-loving, though he is also tender and affectionate. The kind of woman he needs is one who can offer a change of pace to keep him interested.

♂ in ♑

He needs a woman of great tenderness and gentleness. He is extremely sensitive and easily offended.

♂ in ♒

This man is so freedom-loving that he will reject any relationship, whether romantic or friendly, in which he is not trusted. He loves the unusual and is drawn to a woman who is willing to be experimental.

♂ in ♓

This highly romantic man needs a similar type of woman. He is affectionate, warm, compassionate, understanding and gentle. Perfume, soft lights and the slightly mysterious whet his appetite.

Mars in a Woman's Chart (The Kind of Man She Will Be Attracted to)

♂ in ♈
This woman is attracted to a man who behaves in a dominant, forceful and self-confident manner.

♂ in ♉
She is attracted to the man who has a well-defined goal, who shows promise of financial security or who is already well established.

♂ in ♊
She wants a man who is stimulating intellectually and who has a continued interest in bettering himself.

♂ in ♋
The kind of man who will provide for her, treat her gently and protect her appeals to this woman.

♂ in ♌
She likes a man who is sure of himself, outgoing and stylish in his appearance.

♂ in ♍
She is attracted to the intelligent, practical and conventional man. But — he must be able to make her feel important.

♂ in ♎
This woman likes a man who is romantic, well groomed, calm and organized.

♂ in ♏
She is attracted to the man who is passionate at all hours of the day. The professional type may be especially appealing to her. He must give off an aura of superiority.

♂ in ♐
She loves a man who is outgoing, exciting and idealistic. He must have an interest in sports, animals or outdoor activities.

♂ in ♑
She is attracted to a man who sets very high goals for himself because she admires achievement and practical, realistic attitudes. He must be able to behave correctly in public.

♂ in ♒
She is drawn to the man who will not possess her. She likes him to be somewhat unconventional and come up with unexpected and original ideas and gestures. It would also help if he were a bit of a genius.

♂ in ♓
She is attracted to a man who is gentle, kind, romantic and at the same time shows great strength of character. She needs to be dominated in a gentle manner.

Venus in a Man's Chart (The Kind of Woman He Will Be Attracted to)

♀ in ♈
He is attracted to the woman who is outgoing, independent, scintillating and has a sense of adventure.

♀ in ♉
He likes a woman who is a good cook, loyal, domestic and loving.

♀ in ♊
This man finds the woman who is intelligent, entertaining, witty and a good sport very appealing.

♀ in ♋
He wants a mature woman who will mother him, cook for him and take care of all his comforts.

♀ in ♌

This man is attracted to the woman who is dramatic, who stands out in a crowd and who is demonstrative in her affection toward him.

♀ in ♍

He likes a woman who is realistic and dedicated to his needs without being overtly demonstrative toward him.

♀ in ♎

He is attracted to the woman who is gentle, romantic and well groomed. The soft, feminine type of woman is especially appealing to him.

♀ in ♏

The woman who is intensely passionate and is able to surround herself with an aura of the mystical appeals to this man.

♀ in ♐

He likes a woman who has a direct approach to life. The lean type of woman who has an interest in the outdoors and sports appeals to him. The demanding, clinging-vine type does not.

♀ in ♑

This man is attracted to the woman who has self-esteem, who has achieved a high social position or who acts at least competent within her own sphere of activity. In public she must appear serene, but in private she must be able to display passion and sensuality.

♀ in ♒

He is attracted to the unusual and independent woman. He doesn't even mind if she is somewhat eccentric. She should value her freedom, yet he wants her to be loyal only to him.

♀ in ♓

The woman who is sensitive, artistic and extremely feminine appeals to this man. He has a great need to protect the woman of his affection.

Venus in a Woman's Chart
(Her Needs and Reactions)

♀ in ♈

She needs a man who will be dominant and earthy. The slightest show of insecurity on his part will turn her off.

♀ in ♉

This woman is sensuous and incurably romantic and wants a man who will appreciate this. He must also provide financial security.

♀ in ♊

This woman needs a man who is her intellectual superior. A man who is unimaginative is not for her.

♀ in ♋

She likes to be mothered, but she also likes to be able to mother a man. She has moods and needs someone who can read them.

♀ in ♌

This is a dramatic woman. Her ideal man is responsive and ardent and very often someone who will enhance her social stature.

♀ in ♍

She needs to serve and take care of a man. But she cannot always show her emotions, and he must understand this.

♀ in ♎

Her need is for a very romantic man who is suave and well groomed, one who says the right words and does the right thing at the right time.

♀ in ♏

She has complex emotions and needs a strong man who will understand them. She is possessive, yet does not like to feel possessed.

♀ in ♐

Variety and change of pace are vitally important to keep this woman interested. She needs plenty of compliments.

♀ in ♑

This is a reserved woman, often incapable of demonstrative behavior, but once a man accepts her reserve and earns her respect, she will be extremely loyal to him.

♀ in ♒

This is the kind of woman who appreciates originality in thought and action. The conservative, straight-laced type of man is not for her.

♀ in ♓

This woman is capable of unreserved love but only for a man who showers her with affection, is highly romantic and able to make decisions for her.

The Sign Ruling the Cusp of the Fifth House

♈

This position gives love at first sight. These people need a partner who will create a challenge. They also need to play the role of initiator in sexual activity.

♉

These people need a partner who will be loyal, kind and gentle. They desire to be touched and fondled. They can be too naive and trusting.

♊

These people may make a game out of sex. They need a partner who is mentally stimulating.

♋

These people need a partner who is intuitive and understanding. They like to mother the partner and to be mothered in return. They can be moody at times.

♌

They need a partner who accepts teasing and playfulness as part of the sex game. They are sensuous and require lots of petting.

♍

These people need a partner who is highly skilled in the sex act. They do not like to display or discuss sexual emotions openly or in public.

♎

A romantic, flirtatious and aesthetic partner appeals to these people. They may have difficulty selecting the right partner, and even when they do, they may feel the wrong one has been chosen.

♏

These people need a partner who is passionate and who can create a constant challenge. They can be overly possessive and jealous.

♐

Someone who is willing to be more of a companion than a sex partner is the ideal choice for these people. They show excitement about sex but do not give their heart too easily.

♑

They require a partner who is demonstrative and who understands that under their seemingly cold exterior beats a warm heart.

♒

These people need a partner who is mentally stimulating. They are inconsistent in sex performance.

♓

These people are given to romantic daydreaming and need a partner who is romantic, intuitive and capable of alleviating fears.

12
Your Mental Expression— Mercury and the Sun

Mercury, which rules the mental functions and thought processes, can only be in the same sign as the Sun, in the sign that precedes the Sun or in the sign that follows the Sun. When reading the interpretations given below for Mercury and the Sun, keep in mind that Mercury positioned before the Sun shows that the mind is quicker and more alert than if Mercury is placed after the Sun.

Mercury and Sun in Same Sign, Mercury in Sign Before the Sun, Mercury in Sign Following the Sun

Sun in Aries — Mercury in Aries
This person must learn reasoning, detachment and logic. There is a tendency to jump to conclusions. A thorough education and knowledge of a situation is helpful since the person often reacts due to ignorance.

Sun in Aries — Mercury in Pisces
Here there is often a susceptibility to mental confusion. The intuition should not be trusted. This person easily falls for flattery.

Sun in Aries — Mercury in Taurus
This individual is practical, artistic and capable of achievement because he is determined. The mind is both thorough and active.

Sun in Taurus — Mercury in Taurus
This is a plodding mentality given to periodic mental laziness. Although this mind is stubborn, it is also artistic and tactful.

Sun in Taurus — Mercury in Aries
This combination denotes good executive abilities and mental agility. Although this mentality is visional, it is sometimes given to self-deception. It is not a courageous setup from a mental standpoint.

Sun in Taurus — Mercury in Gemini

Here there are versatile thinking patterns. This person is intuitive and can reach a conclusion quickly. The mind is perceptive, but it may leave a trail of unfinished tasks. This person could have literary success providing he learns self-discipline.

Sun in Gemini — Mercury in Gemini

This mind is in over-drive and can be profitably used to analyze business trends. In general, the thinking pattern tends to be more clever than profound. This person may also be deceptive.

Sun in Gemini — Mercury in Taurus

This is an excellent combination. The mind is stable and creative. This person can become successful in almost any area.

Sun in Gemini — Mercury in Cancer

This combination denotes a creative, articulate, sympathetic mind which may be too sensitive and touchy. It is greatly influenced by surrounding conditions and people.

Sun in Cancer — Mercury in Cancer

Here there is a tendency to collect both useful and useless information. The memory is retentive and the mind sensitive but subject to self-deception. This person can also be opinionated and pedantic.

Sun in Cancer — Mercury in Gemini

This combination is not particularly sensitive. With education, this person has the ability to succeed but also has a tendency to take things for granted. The mind is clever but somewhat superficial.

Sun in Cancer — Mercury in Leo

This mind is inflexible and has a tendency to stick with a situation or project even after it has proved worthless. The memory is fair but the person must learn tolerance.

Sun in Leo — Mercury in Leo

This person is difficult to please and often does not like to take the responsibility for mistakes. There is an egotistical, domineering streak. The mind can be stubborn and can repeat the same mistake over and over, not listening to reason. This individual must be boss — and usually is a good one, except that he is not always just. His redeeming qualities are that he can also be very generous and creative.

Sun in Leo — Mercury in Cancer

Sympathy and understanding are this mind's strong qualities. This person will always see the best in others. There is a tendency to self-deception, impressionability and sometimes laziness. However, there is a good business sense and often acting ability.

Sun in Leo — Mercury in Virgo

Here there is excellent executive ability, although the mind may be somewhat picky and fussy. This person functions in an orderly manner and pays attention to detail. Often there is medical and surgical skill and an interest in continued learning.

Sun in Virgo — Mercury in Virgo

This is a good setup for literary work. This person can be a persuasive writer and speaker and will flatter others if it serves his purpose. He has a good business sense and makes a good subordinate because of his developed sense of detail.

Sun in Virgo — Mercury in Leo

This person tends to be articulate in unimportant matters and inarticulate where deeper emotions and feelings are concerned. The mind is sensitive to impressions and sometimes touchy. Since he tends to self-delusion and daydreaming, he needs to learn practicality.

Sun in Virgo — Mercury in Libra

Although this person dislikes studying, he is capable of success if continuous effort is made. Because he has good physical coordination, he should undergo training in which both mental and physical agility are required.

Sun in Libra — Mercury in Libra

This mind is artistic, pleasant and refined. It is an excellent setup for an artist. However, this person tends to compromise too much for the sake of peace.

Sun in Libra — Mercury in Virgo

There is a tremendous need for affection and sympathy here. The mind is artistic, critical, logical, analytical and at times does not appear understanding or sympathetic.

Sun in Libra — Mercury in Scorpio

This person is highly analytical and extremely independent. The mind is active and has scientific leanings, but this person at times appears too reserved and detached. He does not anger easily but, once aroused, will not easily forgive. Although he tends to be stubborn, he can be moved by tact or flattery.

Sun in Scorpio — Mercury in Scorpio
This individual has a strong tendency to form personal conclusions quickly and to not change his mind once he does form an opinion. His speech and writing may be barbed and at times may be extremely cutting and malicious. He dislikes people who are idle and is himself tenacious, stubborn and immovable, never forgetting or forgiving an insult, real or imagined.

Sun in Scorpio — Mercury in Libra
Although these individuals are willing to see other people's viewpoints, this does not mean that they will necessarily change their own. They are artistic and appreciate beauty in all its forms. They may have good voices, capable of being trained, and executive ability, and are able to make money, which is helpful since they are also good spenders.

Sun in Scorpio — Mercury in Sagittarius
There is a quick but not terribly original thought pattern here. A good education is needed as the thinking pattern may be disorganized and disjointed, which is sometimes manifested in a tendency to talk first and think later. Too fast in everything, these people should learn to plan methodically. They should also take physical exercise.

Sun in Sagittarius — Mercury in Sagittarius
These people must learn to finish things as their tendency is to start work on a projected idea and then, halfway through, lose interest in it. They have a philosophical approach to life, but it may be only superficial and confused. However, they can be very successful if they are taught concentration in childhood.

Sun in Sagittarius — Mercury in Scorpio
This is a penetrating mind with a quick grasp of ideas. These people are logical, practical and honorable. They appreciate art from a collector's point of view. Often they have surgical aptitudes to a high degree. They are adventurous and appear tougher than they are.

Sun in Sagittarius — Mercury in Capricorn
This person is loyal and devoted to family and friends. The mind is stable and dependable; they have good mental balance. At times there is a strong pride and idealism, but sometimes attitudes are too rigid and conventional.

Sun in Capricorn — Mercury in Capricorn
Even in youth, these people see and accept conditions as they really are. They are total realists and because of this, depend only on themselves. They are proud, ambitious and ethical, espousing high moral standards. Because they are never confused, they can succeed in any type of activity.

Sun in Capricorn — Mercury in Sagittarius
This quick and alert mentality is at times prone to philosophize to an inordinate degree. The main problem is to maintain a fixed goal. These people must learn to be practical and realistic, for then their achievements can be great.

Sun in Capricorn — Mercury in Aquarius
Political and scientific leanings are usually present with this combination. Often there is a high degree of original thought, along with the ability to make the unusual acceptable. These people are community-oriented, humane and able to function on a broad scale, where they can analyze the whole.

Sun in Aquarius — Mercury in Aquarius
This is a highly idealistic person with noticeable impracticality. The native is aware of his impracticality but could not care less. He has a great need for freedom, loves to communicate and is kind and understanding, although his motives are often misunderstood by others. He has many dormant abilities, and once a choice is made and specific goals set, he can achieve much.

Sun in Aquarius — Mercury in Capricorn
This setup produces shrewd business heads. They think and operate on a large scale but always on a practical level. They may be interested in science and art and have mechanical aptitudes. Often they are more generous than their behavior indicates.

Sun in Aquarius — Mercury in Pisces
There is an impractical approach to life here, as well as a confused thinking pattern. At times, these people are kind and generous — at other times, they exhibit strange and unreasonable attitudes. They can also be imposed upon by strong-willed people, providing the latter use the

soft-sell approach. Often there are mystical interests.

Sun in Pisces — Mercury in Pisces
This kind of person is difficult to understand. His thinking is often confused and muddled, which causes him to be inarticulate on important matters and very articulate on unimportant things. However, he is highly imaginative and receptive to environmental influences. His undoing is a tendency to go to emotional extremes.

Sun in Pisces — Mercury in Aquarius
If properly trained, this individual may achieve great success in the arts or sciences. Although they have very understanding humanitarian attitudes, their motives are often misunderstood by others, which causes mental loneliness. They have a strong mystical leaning which should be developed to gain inner equilibrium and peace.

Sun in Pisces — Mercury in Aries
These people tend to be too direct and outspoken. Although they act touchy, they are not especially sensitive or easily hurt. Often they make enemies because they try to cover their mistakes with too much talk and not enough action. They should learn to analyze a situation thoroughly to overcome their predilection for blundering ahead thoughtlessly. They have mechanical aptitudes and an ability for detail work.

IV

Your Relationships with Others— Synastry

13

Using Your Chart to Find Relationships with Others

You can use your chart to delineate your relationships with your brothers and sisters, children, wife or husband (if there is more than one marriage, the chart will show your relationships with each marriage partner). Write down the names of all your brothers and sisters, even if some have died, starting with the oldest and continuing in chronological sequence to the youngest. Do not include yourself — you are ruled by the cusp of your first house.

Start with the cusp of your third house which rules your oldest brother or sister. Always include the house in question in your counting. Begin with the cusp of the first house (you) and count three cusps, which brings you to the cusp of the third house. This house now becomes the *first house* for your oldest brother or sister. The cusp of your fourth house becomes the second house for your oldest brother or sister and the cusp of your fifth house his or her third house, and so on. The cusp of your fifth house identifies your second oldest brother or sister. Since this house also represents your first child, you may find it in-

teresting to note that the relationships between you and your first child and between you and your second brother or sister are similar. Your fifth house now becomes the first house of your second oldest brother or sister. Your sixth house is his or her second, and your seventh house his or her third. The seventh house, logically enough, is the first house of your third oldest brother or sister. This — *your* seventh house — also identifies your first husband or wife. Continue in this manner around the zodiac to identify as many brothers and sisters as you have.

Now for the identification of your children: Your fifth house (five houses away from your first) shows your first child. Your second child — who would be the brother or sister of your first child — is shown by the cusp of your seventh house. So your seventh house becomes the first house of your second child. If you have a third child, he or she would be identified by the cusp of your ninth house (counting in threes again for all siblings).

Now if you have grasped the method of counting, you will know where to find your first child's own first child. Because *your* first child has been shown by your fifth house, *your child's* first child would be shown by your ninth house. Starting to count at your fifth cusp, turn the chart so that your fifth house is on the ascendant:

Your fifth is the first house for your first child.

Your sixth is the second house for your first child.

Your seventh is the third house for your first child.

Your eighth is the fourth house for your first child.

Your ninth is the fifth house for your first child.

Go over the previous identification setup several times until it becomes automatic.

Next, let's consider husbands and wives. The cusp of your seventh house rules your first husband or wife. *Then we skip one house* and go to your ninth house, which rules and identifies your second husband or wife. The cusp of the eleventh house (again we have skipped one house) would show your third husband or wife. And so on.

The reason your seventh house identifies your first marriage partner is because it is in opposition to your first house (you). Even though we utilize the ninth house, eleventh house, etc., for identification of further marriage partners, the seventh house must be considered in interpretations of all marriages. Let's say that the ruler of the cusp of your seventh house is afflicted.* This indicates problems that will have to be handled. On the other hand, if the ruler of the cusp of your

ninth house is better situated, this does not mean that all difficulties and restrictions indicated by the seventh house (the original marriage house) are lifted. It indicates only that you will face problems in your second marriage better than you did in your first.

The cusp of your eleventh house identifies the first husband or wife of your first child because the fifth (house of your first child) and the eleventh houses are in opposition. Notice that here again we have a first-to-seventh-house relationship (as in your own marriage). When possible, you should work with the natal chart of the person in question as the natal chart is the only real tool for a thorough interpretation. But if this is impossible, use the chart of one of that person's parents. (I have found the mother's chart better here than the father's.)

Do not try to read your own chart as one of your brother's, sister's, children's or husband's charts. The method given here is chiefly valuable because it shows the kind of relationship formed between the ruler of the specific house cusp for the person in question and your own ruler. (By ruler I mean the planet that rules *your* first house.) In other words, if you have Sagittarius rising, your own ruler would be Jupiter. If your child's house cusp is Aries, the ruler is Mars. Therefore to discover your relationship with your child, you would analyze the relationship between Jupiter and Mars.

* A planet is afflicted when it is in a stress aspect to another planet (semisquare, square, sesquare or opposition).

14

Planetary Comparison between Two People

Perhaps you have wondered why you have had an instant like or dislike for another person or why you can communicate with ease with one person and feel completely ill at ease with another. The aspect interpretation, which shows how each of your planets works in aspect with someone else's, will give you an understanding of your behavior patterns and reactions to others.

For a harmonious and lasting relationship between lovers, marriage partners, children, business partners and friends, the other person's planets in relationship to your own planetary setup must be evaluated. It is my hope that through this evaluation you will be in a better position to handle your relationships with others with understanding and compassion.

The Sun

☉ Vs. ☉

(Sun = Power — Ego — Ambition)

☉ ☌ ☉

This can create a mutual power drive toward similar objectives, or it can be a highly irritating aspect. Other planetary aspects will have to be evaluated.

☉ ✶ △ ☉

This gives similarity of aims and objectives.

☉ □ ☍ ☉

This gives frustrations and conflicts between two people.

☉ Vs. ☽

(Sun = Power — Ego — Ambition)
(Moon = Sensitivity — Mood Shifts — Domestic Urge)

☉ ☌ ✶ △ ☽

This gives harmony, compatibility and agreement on domestic issues and emotional affairs.

☉ □ ☍ ☽

This brings differences of temperament and problems between assertion (Sun) and oversensitivity (Moon).

☉ Vs. ☿

(Sun = Power — Ego — Ambition)
(Mercury = Mental Energy — Analysis — Communication)

☉ ☌ ✶ △ ☿

This brings mental agreement and mutual understanding.

☉ □ ☍ ☿

This brings differences of viewpoint.

☉ Vs. ♀

(Sun = Power — Ego — Ambition)
(Venus = Harmony — Affection — Social Urge)

☉ ☌ ✶ △ ♀

This brings cooperation, adoration, admiration and romantic interest.

☉ □ ☍ ♀

This brings emotional problems and disharmony due to differences in social or cultural backgrounds.

☉ Vs. ♂

(Sun = Power — Ego — Ambition)
(Mars = Physical Energy — Aggression — Rebellion)

☉ ☌ ♂

This brings aggression and impatience between two people. It can be a very stimulating type of aspect if other aspects are good. From a sexual standpoint, it gives compatibility, passion and excitement.

☉ ✶ △ ♂

This brings harmony, agreement and self-confidence. Both partners are able to develop their ambitions. It is also a favorable aspect for sexual excitement.

☉ □ ☍ ♂

This is an aspect of extreme mutual aggression. It fosters disharmony, quarrels and rebellion.

☉ Vs. ♃

(Sun = Power — Ego — Ambition)
(Jupiter = Benevolence — Protection — Tolerance)

☉ ☌ ✶ △ ♃

This is an aspect of tolerance, trust, sympathy and protection. Financial protection may be marked.

☉ □ ☍ ♃

This aspect brings conflict in ambitions. The Sun individual may expect too much from the Jupiter individual. Often selfish needs clash.

☉ Vs. ♄

(Sun = Power — Ego — Ambition)
(Saturn = Restriction — Discipline — Duty)

☉ ☌ ♄

This is an aspect of loyalty. The Sun individual can supply optimism to the Saturn individual, and in turn the Saturn person can teach the Sun person more responsibility. However, the Saturn person must guard against overplaying the role of disciplinarian.

☉ ✶ △ ♄

This gives mutual agreement about security and ambitions. It also indicates loyalty and is an excellent aspect for a lasting relationship.

☉ □ ☍ ♄

This aspect brings extreme frustration and mistrust. It is a condemning type of setup — it induces constant clashes, jealousy, disagreements and mutual disappointment.

☉ Vs. ♅

(Sun = Power — Ego — Ambition)
(Uranus = Excitement — Surprise — Change)

☉ ☌ ♅

This brings a very exciting but spasmodic type of relationship. If other aspects between the two charts are good, this could induce greater originality in both people, but if difficult aspects exist between two charts, this could cause explosive reactions to each other.

☉ ✶ △ ♅

Each partner will benefit tremendously from the other in the areas of intellect, creativity and romance. This aspect also indicates a strong romantic attraction.

☉ □ ☍ ♅

This aspect creates disharmony, separation, resentment and impatience.

☉ Vs. ♆
(Sun = Power — Ego — Ambition)
(Neptune = Spirituality — Compassion — Dissipation)

☉ ☌ ♆
This is considered a psychic and karmic tie. If other aspects are good between these people, it can bring sympathy and compassion, but if the aspects between the two charts are difficult, then this can bring escapism and deception. The Neptune person may be elusive, difficult to understand, untruthful and unfaithful.

☉ ⚹ △ ♆
This aspect shows a strong psychic tie. It inspires mutual confidence and a sharing of interests, as well as understanding and compassion.

☉ □ ☍ ♆
The Neptune person will prove to be very elusive. This is an aspect that breeds misunderstanding and mistrust through deception and manipulation.

☉ Vs. ♇
(Sun = Power — Ego — Ambition)
(Pluto = Destuction — Reformation — Hidden Ruthlessness)

☉ ☌ ♇
This aspect induces a struggle for power, dominance and self-assertion in both individuals. Each can be made over by the other.

☉ ⚹ □ ♇
This is a good aspect for business or political alliances since both people exhibit the same drive.

☉ □ ☍ ♇
This aspect creates serious frictions, vindictiveness and jealousies.

The Moon

☽ Vs. ☽
(Moon = Sensitivity — Mood Shifts — Domestic Urge)

☽ ☌ ⚹ △ ☽
These two people are very similar in moods and temperament. This is an aspect of harmony and cooperation.

☽ □ ☍ ☽
This brings occasional differences and lack of consideration about each other's feelings and therefore causes misunderstandings. If the other aspects between the two people are good, this is not too serious.

☽ Vs. ☿
(Moon = Sensitivity — Mood Shifts — Domestic Urge)
Mercury = Mental Energy — Analysis — Communication)

☽ ☌ ⚹ △ ☿
This is a good aspect for interchange of ideas between two people. It aids understanding. Telepathic interchanges may be experienced.

☽ □ ☍ ☿
This brings hypersensitivity, irritation and misunderstandings. The Mercury individual may occasionally be too critical and tactless, thus offending the Moon individual.

☽ Vs. ♀
(Moon = Sensitivity — Mood Shifts — Domestic Urge)
(Venus = Harmony — Affection — Social Urge)

☽ ☌ ⚹ △ ♀
This is a very harmonious combination, especially between marriage partners. It indicates sympathy and consideration for each other. These people have many similar social interests.

☽ □ ☍ ♀
Each individual should accept that many of the other's interests are dissimilar. The aspect is not too disturbing but could cause a few problems.

☽ Vs. ♂
(Moon = Sensitivity — Mood Shifts — Domestic Urge)

(Mars = Physical Energy — Aggression — Rebellion)

☽ ☌ ♂

For individuals of the opposite sex, this is a very stimulating aspect. However, the Mars individual must watch tactlessness, and the Moon individual must guard against emotional reactions.

☽ ✶ △ ♂

This aspect aids mutual cooperation and agreement. It is also a favorable aspect for sexual harmony.

☽ □ ☍ ♂

This aspect brings strong reactions and conflicts. The Mars individual will be too aggressive and the Moon individual too sensitive.

☽ Vs. ♃

(Moon = Sensitivity — Mood Shifts — Domestic Urge)

(Jupiter = Benevolence — Protection — Tolerance)

☽ ☌ ✶ □ ♃

This aspect is one of the most favorable. The Jupiter person gives protection and is always forgiving toward the Moon person. Each respects the other.

☽ □ ☍ ♃

The Jupiter individual may promise more than he can deliver, which can disturb the emotional equilibrium of the Moon individual.

☽ Vs. ♄

(Moon = Sensitivity — Mood Shifts — Domestic Urge)

(Saturn = Restriction — Discipline — Duty)

☽ ☌ ♄

With this aspect, other existing aspects between the two people, and aspects in each individual's chart, will have to be analyzed. The Saturn person may either have a stabilizing or a depressing and restrictive effect on the Moon person.

☽ ✶ △ ♄

This aspect brings mutual respect. The Saturn individual often becomes a teacher in some form, which can be of great benefit to the Moon person.

☽ □ ☍ ♄

The Saturn person is often cold and disagreeable toward the Moon person, which may cause serious depression in the latter. In a family setup, this aspect may cause financial difficulties.

☽ Vs. ♅

(Moon = Sensitivity — Mood Shifts — Domestic Urge)

(Uranus = Excitement — Surprise — Change)

☽ ☌ ✶ △ ♅

This is a magnetic aspect, and within any relationship, unexpected, unusual and sudden occurrences are the order. While this is a romantic setup, the relationship is often interrupted for long periods of time.

☽ □ ☍ ♅

Irritation and confusion are caused by this aspect. It also precipitates friction and separation.

☽ Vs. ♆

(Moon = Sensitivity — Mood Shifts — Domestic Urge)

(Neptune = Spirituality — Compassion — Dissipation)

☽ ☌ ✶ △ ♆

This is often called a karmic or psychic setup. Each person understands the other's moods and feelings.

☽ □ ☍ ♆

This aspect causes confusion and may trigger negative habit patterns in both people.

☽ Vs. ♇

(Moon = Sensitivity — Mood Shifts — Domestic Urge)

(Pluto = Destruction — Reformation — Hidden Ruthlessness)

☽ ☌ ♇

The Pluto individual may be too possessive, which would disturb the equilibrium of the Moon individual. From a sexual standpoint, this is an excellent combination.

☽ ✶ △ ♇

This aspect can cause a transformation of both people, which can be highly beneficial.

☽ □ ☍ ♇

Serious misunderstandings and mutual dislike are experienced with this aspect.

Mercury in Relation to Other Planets

☿ Vs. ☿
(Mercury = Mental Energy — Analysis — Communication)

☿ ☌ ⚹ △ ☿
This stimulates intellectual compatibility. Both people will find it easy to communicate with the other. The aspect brings acceptance and understanding of each other's plans and ideas.

☿ □ ☍ ☿
This aspect breeds misunderstandings and differences. The two people have different viewpoints. Confusion and misunderstandings lead to an argumentative situation.

☿ Vs. ♀
(Mercury = Mental Energy — Analysis — Communication)
(Venus = Harmony — Affection — Social Urge)

☿ ☌ ⚹ △ ♀
This is a very harmonious setup where the two people find many similar cultural interests. They also have sympathy and consideration for each other.

☿ □ ☍ ♀
This aspect causes minor conflicts and irritations. At times the Venus person may find the Mercury person too coarse, and the Mercury individual may in turn find the Venus individual too demanding.

☿ Vs. ♂
(Mercury = Mental Energy — Analysis — Communication)
(Mars = Physical Energy — Aggression — Rebellion)

☿ ☌ ⚹ △ ♂
This brings mental stimulation to the Mercury individual. The Mars individual can at times be too driving and forceful but will encourage the Mercury person to better utilize his or her potential. The Mercury person, in return, can reason things out for the Mars person.

☿ □ ☍ ♂
This brings serious conflicts that cause arguments and aggressive, combative reactions.

☿ Vs. ♃
(Mercury = Mental Energy — Analysis — Communication)
(Jupiter = Benevolence — Protection — Tolerance)

☿ ☌ ⚹ △ ♃
These two people will have tolerance and admiration for each other. In any form of partnership both can benefit mentally and materially.

☿ □ ☍ ♃
This may be an irritating aspect since the Mercury individual may expect more from the Jupiter individual than can be delivered.

☿ Vs. ♄
(Mercury = Mental Energy — Analysis — Communication)
(Saturn = Restriction — Discipline — Duty)

☿ ☌ ♄
If there are other negative aspects between the two charts, this could be an extremely difficult setup. The Saturn individual may make the Mercury individual feel inadequate. This is a restrictive aspect, and the Saturn person may often be jealous.

☿ ⚹ △ ♄
This is a stimulating aspect since the Saturn person can prove to be very wise, helpful and stable, which the Mercury individual appreciates.

☿ □ ☍ ♄
The Saturn person may belittle the efforts of the Mercury person and thus undermine his or her sef-confidence. Cooperation is difficult to achieve with this setup.

☿ Vs. ♅
(Mercury = Mental Energy — Analysis — Communication)
(Uranus = Excitement — Surprise — Change)

☿ ☌ ⚹ △ ♅
This is a beautiful aspect because it creates originality within the association. Many psychic experiences can occur between these two people.

☿ □ ☍ ♅
This aspect breeds misunderstandings and con-

fusion. It can also cause poor communication and many arguments.

☿ Vs. ♆

(Mercury = Mental Energy — Analysis — Communication)
(Neptune = Spirituality — Compassion — Dissipation)

☿ ☌ ⚹ △ ♆

This is called a psychic or karmic tie. These two people enjoy many of the same things. Confusion can occur if the aspects from these planets to other planets are detrimental. However, with other favorable aspects, this one can bring a deep empathy.

☿ □ ☍ ♆

This can bring serious misunderstandings between two people. One or the other may lie, which will have a destructive effect on the relationship.

☿ Vs. ♇

(Mercury = Mental Energy — Analysis — Communication)
(Pluto = Destruction — Reformation — Hidden Ruthlessness)

☿ ☌ ⚹ △ ♇

These people have common interests. Through their association, the world may benefit, especially if they are involved in research together.

☿ □ ☍ ♇

This brings aggression, critical attitudes and serious misunderstandings.

Venus

♀ Vs. ♀

(Venus = Harmony — Affection — Social Urge)

♀ ☌ ⚹ △ ♀

These two people like similar social activities. This aspect creates harmony and can override other difficult aspects. Love, tolerance and compassion are present here.

♀ □ ☍ ♀

These two may have different social backgrounds, which could create minor difficulties between them.

♀ Vs. ♂

(Venus = Harmony — Affection — Social Urge)
(Mars = Physical Energy — Aggression — Rebellion)

♀ ☌ ⚹ △ ♂

There is a strong sexual attraction here. The Venus individual is able to smooth the ruffled feathers of the Mars individual and thus maintain harmony.

♀ □ ☍ ♂

This also indicates a strong sex attraction but one that may be problematic. The Venus person will have to learn not to become disturbed by the aggression of the Mars person. Otherwise strife and irritations could arise.

♀ Vs. ♃

(Venus = Harmony — Affection — Social Urge)
(Jupiter = Benevolence — Protection — Tolerance)

♀ ☌ ⚹ △ ♃

These two people have similar social interests. They also have compassion and tolerance for each other.

♀ □ ☍ ♃

This may create wasteful tendencies and emotional excess in one or both, bringing about unhappiness and misunderstandings.

♀ Vs. ♄

(Venus = Harmony — Affection — Social Urge)
(Saturn = Restriction — Discipline — Duty)

♀ ☌ ♄

This is not a good setup for a marriage because the Saturn person will restrict the Venus person.

He or she may be too demanding and offend the sensitivities of the Venus person.

♀ ⚹ △ ♄

This is an aspect of loyalty and understanding, making any kind of partnership highly beneficial to both people.

♀ □ ☍ ♄

This works very much like the conjunction. The Saturn individual will resent the Venus individual, and the Venus individual will feel stifled and dominated.

♀ Vs. ♅

(Venus = Harmony — Affection — Social Urge)
(Uranus = Excitement — Surprise — Change)

♀ ☌ ⚹ △ ♅

This is excellent for a romantic setup, but unfortunately it is often not lasting. But while it does last, it is very magnetic and unusual.

♀ □ ☍ ♅

The romantic urge clashes with the desire for freedom and excitement, thus each will be disappointed and frustrated with the other. This is an aspect of divorce and separation.

♀ Vs. ♆

(Venus = Harmony — Affection — Social Urge)

(Neptune = Spirituality — Compassion — Dissipation)

♀ ☌ ⚹ △ ♆

Here there is enjoyment of the same cultural pastimes. If the individual charts show an affliction, this aspect could prove unsatisfactory for a lasting relationship because it may produce disillusionment.

♀ □ ☍ ♆

This brings about confusion, misunderstanding and deception by one or both of the people.

♀ Vs. ♇

(Venus = Harmony — Affection — Social Urge)
(Pluto = Destruction — Reformation — Hidden Ruthlessness)

♀ ☌ ♇

Here the Pluto individual may be too possessive and jealous.

♀ ⚹ △ ♇

This brings great understanding and achievement of constructive goals.

♀ □ ☍ ♇

This is often a very jealous, demanding and demeaning combination where the Pluto person imposes his will so much on the Venus person that the Venus person ultimately rejects him or her.

Mars

♂ Vs. ♂

(Mars = Physical Energy — Aggression — Rebellion)

♂ ☌ ♂

Either both individuals are subject to serious friction, or they channel their energies toward common constructive goals, depending on other aspects in their charts.

♂ ⚹ △ ♂

This brings cooperation and encouragement of each other's ambitions. Rarely, if ever, will these two people argue.

♂ □ ☍ ♂

This instills aggression and hostile behavior toward each other. Cooperation is almost impossible to attain.

♂ Vs. ♃

(Mars = Physical Energy — Aggression — Rebellion)
(Jupiter = Benevolence — Protection — Tolerance)

♂ ☌ ⚹ △ ♃

This is an excellent aspect for achievement as each will encourage the other.

♂ □ ☍ ♃
This aspect brings conflict, discontent and impatience. It also brings out the latent reckless traits in both people or encourages these traits if they are already manifest.

♂ Vs. ♄
(Mars = Physical Energy — Aggression — Rebellion)
(Saturn = Restriction — Discipline — Duty)

♂ ☌ ♄
This is an excellent aspect because the Saturn individual will check the recklessness of the Mars individual — if he is so inclined. But the Saturn person must guard against stifling the drive of the Mars person, or the latter's reactions could be detrimental to the relationship.

♂ ⚹ △ ♄
This aspect irons out many difficulties in a relationship as both people have a need for practical achievement.

♂ □ ☍ ♄
This is a highly frustrating setup and causes arguments, irritations and antagonisms between the two people.

♂ Vs. ♅
(Mars = Physical Energy — Aggression — Rebellion)
(Uranus = Excitement — Surprise — Change)

♂ ☌ ♅
Since both people are very independent and refuse to be dominated, this could prove to be a very unharmonious relationship. Although it is an excellent sex setup, each partner will have to understand that the other needs to function in a free and independent manner.

♂ ⚹ △ ♅
This is an excellent aspect because it creates originality and achievement that are beneficial to both parties.

♂ □ ☍ ♅
This is a serious conflicting aspect and causes arguments and aggressions of a serious nature.

♂ Vs. ♆
(Mars = Physical Energy — Agression — Rebellion)
(Neptune = Spirituality — Compassion — Dissipation)

♂ ☌ ⚹ △ ♆
Depending on other aspects, the conjunction could be a confusing and detrimental setup. Or, it could be an excellent aspect for similar interests of a spiritual nature. The effect that Neptune has on Mars may be very hypnotic. A karmic and psychic tie is indicated. The Mars individual may give the Neptune individual the necessary push to achieve.

♂ □ ☍ ♆
This aspect seems to bring out the worst in both people. It causes misunderstanding, disharmony and wasteful habits. The Mars individual has a tendency to shatter Neptune's dreams.

♂ Vs. ♇
(Mars = Physical Energy — Aggression — Rebellion)
(Pluto = Destruction — Reformation — Hidden Ruthlessness)

♂ ☌ ♇
These two people will resist each other. This aspect can seriously undermine any relationship.

♂ ⚹ △ ♇
Plans, organization and reorganization that will benefit both people can be achieved with this aspect.

♂ □ ☍ ♇
Rebellious attitudes and underhanded tactics, used by one or both individuals, can undermine the relationship.

Jupiter

♃ Vs. ♃
(Jupiter = Benevolence — Protection — Tolerance)

♃ ☌ ⚹ △ ♃
With this aspect two people can establish a relationship spiced with humor. They are helpful,

protective and understanding toward each other. This is a very beneficial aspect.

♃ □ ☍ ♃
These people may be of different social backgrounds. Their ideas on religion and morality may differ, causing mistrust and misunderstanding.

♃ Vs. ♄
(Jupiter = Benevolence — Protection — Tolerance)
(Saturn = Restriction — Discipline — Duty)

♃ ☌ ⚹ △ ♄
This creates a very stable association. With formulated goals, both people can achieve much.

♃ □ ☍ ♄
Saturn will hamper, hinder and dampen the enthusiasm and optimism of the Jupiter individual, which will ultimately create disagreements.

♃ Vs. ♅
(Jupiter = Benevolence — Protection — Tolerance)
(Uranus = Excitement — Surprise — Change)

♃ ☌ ⚹ △ ♅
This is an encouraging and optimistic setup. Each will accept and understand the other's needs. The conjunction may lead to overoptimism or recklessness in one or both of the people.

♃ □ ☍ ♅
This causes rebellion and serious reactions in both people. Depending on other aspects in the charts, this setup could cause serious rifts.

♃ Vs. ♆
(Jupiter = Benevolence — Protection — Tolerance)
(Neptune = Spirituality — Compassion — Dissipation)

♃ ☌ ⚹ △ ♆
This is called a karmic or psychic tie. Each will intuitively understand the other's needs and aspirations and will be helpful.

♃ □ ☍ ♆
This creates wasteful habits and may lead to confusion and dishonesty. This is not a good setup for any form of partnership unless many good aspects exist between the two charts.

♃ Vs. ♇
(Jupiter = Benevolence — Protection — Tolerance)
(Pluto = Destruction — Reformation — Hidden Ruthlessness)

♃ ☌ ⚹ △ ♇
Both people can be stimulated to greater social awareness. It is possible that both will become involved in humanitarian organizations that benefit mankind.
This creates misunderstandings and obstructions to both people's progress — even more so, perhaps, to the Jupiter person.

Saturn

♄ Vs. ♄
(Saturn = Restriction — Discipline — Duty)

♄ ☌ ⚹ △ ♄
Both will have similar drives and security needs. They can aid each other in working toward common goals. Under the conjunction, there may be a tendency to react negatively toward each other if natal aspects are of a detrimental nature.

♄ □ ☍ ♄
This creates mutual rivalry and mistrust. From a material standpoint, this aspect can create economic disaster.

♄ Vs. ♅
(Saturn = Restriction — Discipline — Duty)
(Uranus = Excitement — Surprise — Change)

♄ ☌ ⚹ △ ♅
This aspect can be highly beneficial to both people. Uranus, the progressive, and Saturn, the cautious, planet can join forces for constructive

and progressive activities. This is an aspect of cooperation and achievement.

♄ □ ☍ ♅
This creates unreliability and antagonism. Uranus may be too erratic for the slow, cautious Saturn, who may resent the freedom urge of Uranus.

♄ Vs. ♆
(Saturn = Restriction — Discipline — Duty)
(Neptune = Spirituality — Compassion — Dissipation)

♄ ☌ ⚹ △ ♆
Both can benefit by this aspect. The Saturn individual can gain greater spiritual insight, and the Neptune individual can gain greater crystallization of his or her concepts.

♄ □ ☍ ♆
This is a jealous, restrictive and misunderstanding type of aspect. It often creates intentional or unintentional fraud. Neptune seems somewhat confusing to Saturn.

♄ Vs. ♇
(Saturn = Restriction — Discipline — Duty)
(Pluto = Destruction — Reformation — Hidden Ruthlessness)

♄ ☌ ♇
This aspect can create serious dislike and spiteful behavior toward each other.

♄ ⚹ △ ♇
This brings striving for common goals and interests in a harmonious manner.

♄ □ ☍ ♇
This brings spitefulness and extreme mutual dislike.

Note: The semisquare (<) and sesquare (⚼) aspects between planets cause great irritation between people.

Uranus, Neptune, Pluto

These three outermost planets of the solar system are not important in interpersonal relationships because they influence society at large rather than individuals. Uranus, when the native is approximately fifteen, makes a sextile, which gives cooperation and interests in the areas of invention and science and makes it possible for the person to accept the conditions and plans of those in authority. When the native is about twenty-one, Uranus makes a square with the next generation, which shows dissimilar interests between children and parents and consequent rebellion at an early age on the part of the children. When the native is approximately thirty-five, Uranus makes a trine aspect, indicating understanding and cooperation between parents and offspring and acceptance by the parent of the goals of the younger generation. At approximately age forty-two, Uranus is in opposition, and since this brings transformation and change, it is often a turning point in the person's personal attitudes. Frustration is indicated between the younger and older generations. Uranus takes approximately eighty-four years to complete a transit of all the signs.

Neptune takes approximately 168 years to complete a transit of the zodiac, so the sextile, square and trine aspects are possible in the average lifetime, but the opposition aspect is rare. To find the time when these aspects occur, consult an ephemeris. The sextile occurs at approximately age thirty-five. The result is a spiritual groping toward an understanding of the self in relationship to the universe at large. At approximately age forty-five, the square occurs, which often brings a period of emotional and mental confusion about spiritual values. At approximately age seventy, the trine occurs, which induces a mellowing of attitudes and beliefs along with empathy with the younger generation.

Pluto takes approximately 248 years to complete

a transit of the zodiac. Pluto's movement is erratic in its path around the Sun, so it is difficult to establish even an approximate age at which sextiles and squares can be formed. Since the movement of Pluto is slow, trines and oppositions are impossible in a person's lifetime. Pluto deals with mass opinion, changes and transformation, and evokes reactions to a changed social order.

V
Important Planetary Parts

North and South
Nodes of
the Moon
in Signs
and Houses

Essentially, the position of the north node (also called *caput draconis*, or dragon's head) in the chart shows in what areas of life the native will receive extra benefits. Its nature is associated with Venus and Jupiter. The nature of the south node (*cauda draconis*, or dragon's tail) is more closely associated with Saturn, and it marks an area where the native must accomplish personal transformation through self-evaluation.

To find the position of the north and south nodes, look at Table 14 in Chapter 4. In the next to the last column you will see the Moon's node. In the example chart illustrated in Figure 38 in Appendix B, the north node is inserted in the eleventh house at 20° Capricorn 07'. The north node is recorded in an ephemeris every two days. Note in Table 14 how it retrogrades at the rate of 3 minutes a day, or 6 minutes every two days. It is unnecessary to do any math work to obtain the position of the north node; it can be done very quickly in your head. As you can see in Table 14, the north node on the 7th was 20° Capricorn 08'. In the example chart (Figure 38), after making the necessary planetary correction we were 10 hours and 24 minutes into the 7th. This is roughly less than half a day, so we deducted 1 minute from the position of the Moon's north node and inserted the result (20°07') on the chart.

The Moon's south node is always in *exact opposition* to the north node. In our example chart in Appendix B it would be 20° Cancer 07', and it would be found in the fifth house. It is not necessary to record the south node (it is not recorded in Figure 38), though you may if you like.

In order to interpret the north and south nodes, first read the interpretation of the north node by sign, then read the interpretation of the north node by house and, finally, blend the information. Do the same for the south node. This procedure gives you additional factors to blend for an accurate chart reading.

As an example, let's take someone who is born with the north node in Gemini in the eighth house, which would place the south node in opposition in Sagittarius in the second house. We know we have four factors to blend:

1. **North Node (☊) in Gemini**
   This indicates excellent mental agility, plenty of optimism and a general ability to adapt to circumstances.

2. **North Node (☊) in Eighth House**

The promise here is of a long life and possible gain through inheritance

3. **South Node (☋) in Sagittarius**

This indicates the native must learn tact. He or she may be subject to overoptimism and poor judgment. There is a possibility that real achievement may be withheld. In a previous life the native may have been superficial and reckless. Thus there is a subconscious tendency to inner discontent and restlessness which must be corrected.

4. **South Node (☋) in Second House**

The indications are a loss of prestige and financial difficulty resulting from a habit of taking rather than giving in previous incarnation.

From these factors we could synthesize the following interpretation:

Since this person has mental agility, he is able to adapt to circumstances quickly but he must learn tact. He must also learn to curb his excessive optimism because, unchecked, it may prevent him from reaching real achievement, especially in the financial area. His subconscious tendency to recklessness and discontent also needs to be corrected. It would be wise for this person to learn to sleep on a problem before taking any action.

Since the native is promised long life, he will have plenty of chances to work out his predisposition to superficiality. No matter how rough his life may become, his natural optimism and adaptability will make it possible for him to achieve a new or different approach to solving problems.

Try the interpretation of the north and south nodes by sign and house on your own chart and those of your friends and relatives for practice. First read through Table 25.

TABLE 25

INTERPRETATION of NORTH (☊) and SOUTH (☋) NODES of MOON by SIGNS and HOUSES

SIGN	HOUSE
☊ in Aries Creative and original, self-assertive.	**☊ in First** Strong powers of self-expression, independent, confident.
☋ in Aries Has business ability and is keenly analytical, but must correct subconscious, overaggressive tendencies from former lives.	**☋ in First** Encounters trials and tribulations until self-centered attitudes from past lives are overcome.
☊ in Taurus Optimistic, sensitive, materialistic, usually prosperous and protected.	**☊ in Second** Promised financial security, can teach others better utilization of resources.
☋ in Taurus Stubbornly adheres to ideas and conditions, must correct subconscious overpossessiveness of material goods and people.	**☋ in Second** Loses prestige and has financial difficulties because of habit of taking rather than giving in former lives.
☊ in Gemini Mentally agile, very optimistic, generally able to adapt to circumstances.	**☊ in Third** Interested in or successful through travel, writing, publishing or education.

☊ **in Gemini**

Could function excellently in the world of commerce. Because of instability and superficiality in former lives, may have concentration problems.

☋ **in Cancer**

Interested in and proud of home and family, strongly believes in family as an institution, sensitive to needs of others.

☊ **in Cancer**

Has selfish, self-centered, quarrelsome tendencies that alienate others. Hypersensitive leanings must be overcome in this life.

☋ **in Leo**

Able to lead, enjoys self-respect, can accomplish things on a large scale.

☊ **in Leo**

Can succeed in any enterprise but must conquer subconscious tendencies to over-emotionalism, overconfidence and delusions of grandeur from former life.

☋ **in Virgo**   '

Evidences critical but correct behavior patterns, analytical, sympathetic, stable.

☊ **in Virgo**

Tends to be hypercritical, sensitive, sarcastic. Subconscious tendency to hypochondria resulting from negativity in former lives must be controlled.

☋ **in Libra**

Cultured, social, kind, able to act as coordinator, sympathetic, sensitive and understanding.

☊ **in Libra**

Judgment may be impaired. Nonassertion in former life may result in subconscious tendency to overcriticize, which must be corrected.

☊ **in Third**

Encounters difficulty with and through blood relatives, neighbors and journeys. Should work at finding mental and emotional balance.

☋ **in Fourth**

Able to acquire property, lucky with the goods of this earth.

☊ **in Fourth**

Confused, has wasteful tendencies and difficult experiences within the family. Should learn to function more on a social and external level.

☋ **in Fifth**

Has promise of talented children, creative success, speculation and social intercourse.

☊ **in Fifth**

Has difficulty with children and speculation. Must learn to correct excessive tendency to self-indulgence.

☋ **in Sixth**

Enjoys excellent health pattern, is able to throw off diseases, makes an excellent employee or employer, is lucky with domesticated animals.

☊ **in Sixth**

Subject to strange diseases, has difficulties with employees and co-workers, should learn to give correct and proper service and develop positive behavior patterns.

☋ **in Seventh**

Benefits with and through any form of partnerships, has few or no enemies.

☊ **in Seventh**

Experiences difficulties with and through others, must learn cooperation, self-confidence and self-reliance.

☋ in Scorpio
Likes research, desires freedom of thought and action, courageous in a crisis.

☊ in Scorpio
Tends to dominate others, feels inadequate because greed and self-centeredness in former life give subconscious fear and resentment that should be overcome.

☋ in Sagittarius
Philosophical, educational and religious interests give direct approach to problems.

☊ in Sagittarius
Must learn tact, may be subject to overoptimism, poor judgment may prevent real achievement. Predisposition to superficiality and recklessness in former lives gives present inner discontent and restlessness that must be corrected.

☋ in Capricorn
Authoritative, responsible and ambitious. Development of self is geared to a specific objective that can be of benefit to mankind.

☊ in Capricorn
Has ruthless drive for achievement, is egocentric. Selfish habits in former lives give a subconscious tendency to assert power and control over others, which must be corrected.

☋ in Aquarius
Drive centers on social objectives. Ambition to reach top may be marked. Research, science and invention may hold special interest.

☊ in Aquarius
Aloofness and snobbishness may make smooth functioning with others difficult. Inclination to impulsive and egocentric behavior in former lives results in subconscious habits of control over others and self-glorification, which must be corrected.

☋ in Eighth
Promised a long life and, possibly, gain through inheritance.

☊ in Eighth
Difficulties over legal matters, inheritances and possessions of partner, and self-destructive subconscious pattern of negativity that should be brought to the surface and analyzed.

☋ in Ninth
Highly idealistic, visionary, religious, philosophical and intellectual.

☊ in Ninth
Must learn to attach proper value to education. Travel may be interrupted or prove unfortunate in some way. May have escapist tendencies, must learn to become realistic.

☋ in Tenth
Achievement, recognition and professional advancement are possible through native's personal initiative and industry.

☊ in Tenth
Difficulties with those in authority, business failures and fluctuations. Native must learn to concentrate on objective and not resent the achievements of others.

☋ in Eleventh
Friends will help in time of need. Group or universal service of some kind will give personal satisfaction.

☊ in Eleventh
Friends and associations may prove to be a source of difficulty. Loses opportunities because of great dependence on others.

☊ in Pisces
Renders selfless service to others, has compassionate nature, is kind and sympathetic.

☋ in Pisces
Should observe correct moral and ethical behavior, can be very undisciplined. Former inclination to self-indulgence and indifference toward reality may result in subconscious leanings toward intemperance and escapist habits, which should be corrected.

☊ in Twelfth
Interested in the occult and in institutional types of work.

☋ in Twelfth
May bottle feelings with detrimental results to physical and emotional well-being. May have difficulty facing life. Emotional problems or complexes should be analyzed.

16

The Arabian Parts: How to Figure Them and the Part of Fortune by Signs and Houses

The Arabian parts derive from an Arabian system of astrology that takes the degree cusp of the ascendant at birth, adds the degree of a specific planet, and then subtracts the degree of a specific planet. The final position indicates an imaginary point in a chart that is activated by a transiting or progressed planet. Any Arabian part may also be progressed by an age arc, which often times a future event.

The most commonly used Arabian part is the part of fortune, and it should be inserted into every chart. Refer to Figure 29 for an illustration of the math work involved in computing the part of fortune. Here the ascendant is 21° Pisces 38'. Pisces is the eleventh sign,* and this number is written down under "Signs." The position of the

Moon, which is 5° Sagittarius 57', is added to the figure for the ascendant. Sagittarius is the eighth sign, which number is written under "Signs." Added together, these figures give a total of 19 signs 26°105'. Next the position of the Sun, which is 15° Scorpio 37' (Scorpio is the seventh sign), was deducted, leaving a total of 12 signs 11°68'. For a final figure, the 68' were converted into 1°08', giving a total of 12 signs 12°08'. Since the 0 sign or the twelfth sign is Aries, the final figure is 12° Aries 08'.

Now, to ascertain the correct interpretation for the part of fortune, first read the interpretation of its element (fire, earth, air or water), and then read the interpretation of the house position.

Table 26 shows many more Arabian parts that can be utilized. None of them should be used when the moment of birth is unknown since the accuracy of most of them depends on knowing the correct ascendant. Some of them also depend on the sign and the degrees of other house cusps, such as the part of wedding or legalizing, where

*In the Arabian system the signs are numbered differently. Pisces is the twelfth sign of the zodiac counting from and including Aries, but in the Arabian system a sign is not counted until it is completed — 30° of Aries (which is Taurus) is one sign. Therefore Pisces is the eleventh sign in the Arabian system, and Aries is the twelfth.

Formula: Asc. + ☽ − ☉
Count Signs as Follows:

♈ - 0 s or 12 s	♋ - 3 s	♎ - 6 s	♑ - 9 s
♉ - 1 s	♌ - 4 s	♏ - 7 s	♒ - 10 s
♎ - 2 s	♍ - 5 s	♐ - 8 s	♓ - 11 s

	Signs	Degrees	Minutes
Asc. (21°♒38') _____ =	11	21°	48'
☽ (5°♐57') _____ =	+ 8	5°	57'
Total =	19	26°	105'
☉ (15°♏37') _____ =	− 7	15°	37'
	12	11°	68' = 12°♈08' for ⊕

FIGURE 29
How to figure the part of fortune.

the cusps of the ninth and third houses are utilized. The part of marriage utilizes the cusps of the first and seventh houses by signs and degrees. The part of bereavement adds the sign and the degrees of the cusp of the twelfth house to the ruler of that house and then subtracts the planet Neptune. If, for instance, the sign Capricorn is positioned on the cusp of the twelfth house, then Saturn's position (Saturn is the ruler of Capricorn) in the chart by sign and degree would be utilized.

TABLE 26 — THE ARABIAN PARTS

Assassination	Asc* + Ruler of 12th − ♅
Bereavement	Cusp of 12th + Ruler of 12th − ♅
Bankruptcy	♃ + ♃ − ♀
Weddings, legalizing	9th + 3rd − ♀
Water journeys	Asc. + ♋ 15° − ♄
Peril	Asc. + Ruler of 8th − ♄
Death, disaster	Asc. + Cusp of 8th − ☽
Marriage, partners	Asc. + Cusp of 7th − ♀
Suicide	Asc. + Cusp of 8th − ♆
Divorce	Asc. + ♀ − 7th
Catastrophy	Asc. + ♅ − ☉
Commerce, business	Asc. + ♂ − ☉
Daughters	Asc. + ♀ − ☽
Faith, belief, trust	Asc. + ☿ − ☽
Father	Asc. + ☉ − ♄
Fortune, substance ⊕	Asc. + ☽ − ☉
Increase, benefits	Asc. + ♃ − ☉
Inheritance, legacy	Asc. + ☽ − ♄

Intelligence, skill	Asc. + ♂ − ☿
Mother	Asc. + ♃ − ♀
Servants, service	Asc. + ☽ − ☿
Sickness, upsets	Asc. + ♂ − ♄
Sons	Asc. + ♃ − ☽
Surgery, cutting	Asc. + ♄ − ♂
Tragedy, fatality	Asc. + ♄ − ☉
Treachery, fraud, web	Asc. + ♆ − ☉
Waste, extravagance, discord	Asc. + ♃ − ♂
Love, appreciation	Asc. + ♀ − ☉
Spirit, soul	Asc. + ☉ − ☽

*Asc.-Ascendant.

Where a sign that is ruled by two planets — such as Pisces or Aquarius — appears on the cusp of the twelfth for the part of bereavement or on the cusp of the eighth for the part of peril, then *two* parts of fortune should be worked out, one for each ruler (Neptune and Jupiter for Pisces, and Saturn and Uranus for Aquarius).

To discover whether the Arabian parts register in your chart, find the preceding important years, years in which specific crucial events occurred. Check the transits and progressions existing at the time of these events. These specific Arabian parts should register, assuring you of a correct birthtime. It is not necessary to use all the Arabian parts listed, but it will be helpful to note the parts of fortune, peril, sickness and surgery. Most of you will probably also be interested in the part of marriage or legalizing.

Part of Fortune (Formula: Ascendant + ☽ − ☉)

The part of fortune represents worldly success, achieved mainly through the native's own efforts. It is as far distant from the ascendant as the Sun is from the Moon.

In the Signs

Fire Signs This imparts the energy to excel. Often there are interests in inventions, new projects and unusual methods for solving problems.

Earth Signs The part of fortune is evidenced in practical expressions. There is a need for security and a foundation.

Air Signs In air signs the part gives an interest in mental expressions and pursuits. Fulfillment may be achieved through literary, artistic or social work.

Water Signs Here the part of fortune emphasizes emotional, psychic and intuitive pursuits or interests.

In The Houses

First House Gain, development, happiness and progress are key words for this placement. But all of these will only come about through the native's own efforts.

Second House Gain through business or property is possible here. Friends and business associates may play a large part in helping the native reach financial security.

Third House This emphasizes a gain through intellectual pursuits and a tendency to examine the motives of one's self and others.

Fourth House Here there may be gain through the family, property and products of the earth. The native has a great need to establish harmony within his environment.

Fifth House A gain through artistic and pleasurable pursuits is emphasized here. The protection of and by children is also often indicated.

Sixth House Here there will be gain through employment and employees. The native is able to act in a responsible manner toward his inferiors.

Seventh House This position brings gain through any form of partnership, successful lawsuits and harmonious relationships.

Eighth House Here there is a tendency to gain through inheritance of goods of the dead. The native has the ability to utilize others' money.

Ninth House A gain through higher education, publishing, travel, religious and philosophical pursuits is indicated with this placement.

Tenth House Here a gain through unusual events helps the native to rise to a position of importance. This can be either in the family circle or in the professional world.

Eleventh House A gain through friends, organizations and affiliations is indicated here. The type of friends, whether original, conservative, intellectual or sensitive, will be indicated by the element that the part of fortune is found in.

Twelfth House Here there will be gain through meditation, introspection and self-examination. This position shows that confidence and self-worth must be assiduously cultivated.

If the part of fortune is heavily afflicted by the planets, the preceding interpretations will take on negative or opposite meanings. The native must then become aware that he has a greater than average responsibility to fulfill and satisfy his own needs.

17
The Solstice Points

The solstice points are also called the antiscions, though most writers and teachers of astrology refer to them as solstice points. These are the points in the ecliptic of the zodiac at which the Sun turns from 0° Cancer or 0° Capricorn back to the celestial equator.* At both 0° Cancer and 0° Capricorn, the Sun is at its greatest distance from the celestial equator. The summer solstice occurs about June 21, when the Sun is in 0° Cancer, and the winter solstice occurs about December 21, when the Sun is at 0° Capricorn. A planet's solstice point is figured from 0° Cancer or 0° Capricorn and carried in remaining degrees and minutes over to the other solstice axis.

When a progressed or transiting planet passes over the solstice point of a natal planet, the natal planet that this solstice point belongs to will be activated. The event will depend on the natal planet itself, the house position and the aspects that the natal planet makes in the native's chart. The reasons for many occurrences that are not apparent at first glance can thus be explained.

Solstice points are measured as illustrated in Figure 30. A planet in Cancer has its solstice point in Gemini; a planet in Virgo has its solstice point in Aries. The same holds true for the following combinations: Leo — Taurus, Virgo — Aries, Capricorn — Sagittarius, Aquarius — Scorpio and Pisces — Libra. Look, now, at Figure 31. If, for instance, you had a natal planet in 12° Aries, you would subtract 12° from 30° (the total number of degrees possible in a sign), and that planet's solstice point would be 18° Virgo. The opposition point of 18° Virgo is 18° Pisces, which would therefore also be affected. In this illustration you can see that the solstice very often works like a ricocheting bullet.

Let's do a few more examples so you can see what I mean. A planet in 20° Aries would have its solstice point in 10° Virgo. A planet in 25° Aries would have its solstice point in 5° Virgo. A planet in 5° Taurus would have it solstice point in 25° Leo. A planet in 10° Taurus would have its solstice

---

* The ecliptic of the zodiac is the *apparent* annual path of the Sun. (In astrology the motions of the planets are described as they appear to an observer on earth.) The celestial equator is the circle described in the heavens by the daily turning of the earth on its axis.

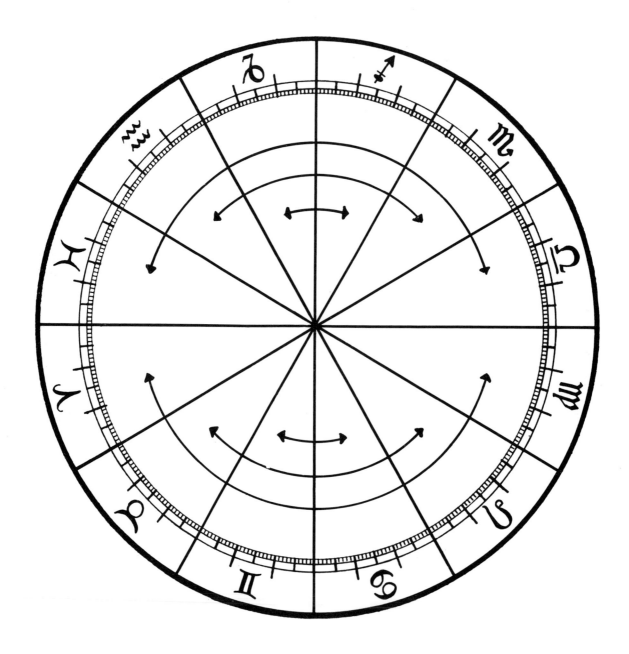

FIGURE 30

Solistice points: ♋—♊,♌—♉,♍—♈,♑—♎,♒—♏,♓—♌.

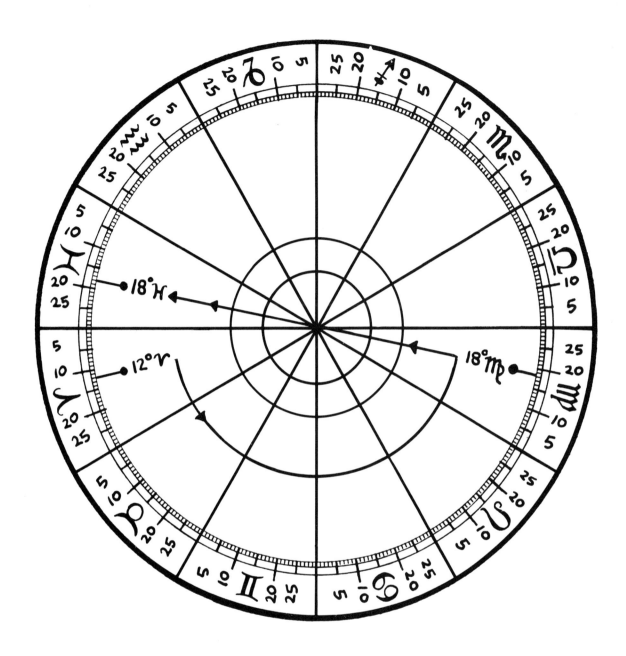

FIGURE 31
Natal planet in 12° Aries gives solstice point of 18° Virgo
and an opposite point of 18° Pisces.

point in 20° Leo. Can you see how in each of our examples the total number of degrees of a natal planet and its solstice position is always 30? In each case the opposition point is also affected. Therefore, if a natal planet — for instance, Jupiter (see Figure 40 in Appendix B) — is in 6° Capricorn 12', it would have its solstice point in 23° Sagittarius 48'. The opposite point would, of course, be 23° Gemini 48'. In other words, you can have a transiting planet or progressed planet at 23° Sagittarius 48', or 23° Gemini 48', and Jupiter would become activated.

All the solstice points for Figure 38 are listed in Table 34 in Appendix A. I suggest that you list your own natal planet's solstice points and note those days when the Moon transits these various points. (For transits, use a current ephemeris, the use of which is explained in Appendix A.)

VI
Timing Devices

18

Transits and Progressions of Planets through the Houses

The interpretations given in this chapter can be used for the progressions as well as for the transits. Transits are the positions of planets on any given day as they appear in a current ephemeris. They serve to trigger events promised by the natal and progressed planets. The progressed planets set up a situation, while the transits set it off.* Always look up the longitude of a planet in your emphemeris to see which house is being transited. Then read the interpretation as given in this chapter, which must be modified according to the aspect the transiting planet is making to a progressed or natal planet in your chart.

* For an explanation of progressions and transits, see Appendix C.

If you are serious about astrology, faithfully keep a two-year diary of mood changes and events concerning not only your family and friends, but also your neighborhood, business and the like. Alongside these events mark down the planetary positions for that day. This is one of the fastest ways to learn your actions and reactions in relation to a given planetary position. At the end of the two-year period you will realize that astrology is a law of recurring cycles.

The interpretation of planets through the houses is subject to modification depending on aspects. However, a knowledge of the houses being affected by either a transitory or progressed planet will give you an understanding of the specific areas of life that are brought into focus by these planetary movements.

Moon Moving through the Houses by Transit or Progression

First House
This marks a period of restlessness and dissatisfaction with existing circumstances. Often there is a desire to start something new.

Second House
Often a change in financial status is indicated. The native should guard against unnecessary expenditures and learn to budget.

Third House
This brings an interest in travel and study and often stimulates relationships with relatives and neighbors. The mind is often unstable and restless.

Fourth House
This can bring a desire for change of the home or for redecorating. Family interests become more important.

Fifth House
A desire for social activities, romance and creative expression is indicated. Children will become important in the chart of a parent.

Sixth House
Attention should be paid to health, hygiene and nutrition. A change in employment or in attitudes toward employees is also sometimes indicated.

Seventh House
Here there is a greater need for cooperation with others as well as for an active social life. All partnerships gain in importance.

Eighth House
This is a good time to evaluate financial setups and investigate insurance policies. Often there is an interest in occult subjects.

Ninth House
Religious and philosophical studies become more important. Travel may be indicated. This is a good time to expand horizons.

Tenth House
Here there is a strong desire for popularity. A change in career can also occur, but first the native should analyze whether change is advisable. This is a good time to consider reputation and finalize goals.

Eleventh House
This often brings changes in goals and life attitudes. The native becomes more community-oriented. New friendships may also begin around this time.

Twelfth House
This transit may give excessive dreams, moodiness and feelings of melancholy. It is important for the native to remain realistic while the Moon is going through this house. Fears and phobias should be analyzed.

Sun Moving through the Houses

First House
The native should practice self-confidence and work to improve his or her status. Success can be gained if effort is made.

Second House
This brings an opportunity for additional income. However, guard against extravagance — money is often spent on luxuries.

Third House
The native should now learn a new manual or mental skill. This is a good time to begin new studies and writing projects.

Fourth House
Attention is focused on the home. This is a good time for repair work or redecorating.

Fifth House
All social and artistic pursuits are favored. Children may become more important at this time. There may also be some activity in the native's love life.

Sixth House
The native should be sure to get enough rest and think about how he can improve his relationships with co-workers and employees.

Seventh House
This is excellent for making progress in all kinds of partnerships. If the Sun is well aspected, it is also a favorable time for winning lawsuits.

Eighth House
This may bring a monetary gift or inheritance. It is, in any case, a good time for building a nest egg. It is also a favorable time to pursue recent interests.

Ninth House
This is a good time for studies and travel. Religious and legal affairs may become prominent.

Tenth House
This is an excellent time for securing a position of authority. With work, the native can make gains in his or her vocation.

Eleventh House
Influential friends may be helpful for attainment of the native's goals and wishes. The pace of social life may also be stepped up.

Twelfth House
Quiet and rest are indicated. Success comes from working quietly behind the scenes. This is a good time to lay the groundwork for a creative project.

Mercury Moving through the Houses

First House
This brings a fluctuation of attitudes. The native should thoughtfully analyze his standing and position in life. He should also get enough rest because this placement may bring nervousness.

Second House
This is excellent for financial gain through any form of communication.

Third House
Literary interests become prominent. This is a good time to make careful travel plans, to write letters and to handle all information wisely.

Fourth House
Guard against restlessness due to fluctuating emotional moods. This often brings a desire to change residence.

Fifth House
An excellent time for all creative expressions, attending plays, sports activity, teaching or working with children.

Sixth House
Here the native should curb mental restlessness and try to decrease his anxieties through rest. There may be small annoyances from employees.

Seventh House
The native should get together with interesting and intellectual people. If Mercury is well aspected, this is an especially good time for signing contracts.

Eighth House
There may be a deepening interest in mystical subjects. The native should thoroughly analyze all documents and insurance policies before signing.

Ninth House
This is a favorable time to attend to details concerning trips and legal matters. The intellectual horizon is broadened. The mind may be extremely active under this transit.

Tenth House
Public and professional life are prominent. The

native should reconsider professional goals and avoid putting too many irons in the fire.

Eleventh House
Here the native's activity in groups and organizations increases. Intellectual relationships may be suddenly formed.

Twelfth House
This brings a desire for seclusion. It is an excellent time for inspired creative writing. There is an ability to concentrate on one objective.

Venus Moving through the Houses

First House
This is a time of optimism and popularity. The native experiences a need for admiration. A desire for luxuries may also be sparked.

Second House
Watch excessive spending. Although this position seems to bring money, the native has difficulty hanging onto it. Often, it is spent on luxuries and artwork.

Third House
Harmonious communication with neighbors, brothers and sisters is possible. This placing brings more optimistic attitudes. It may also be a time when the native hears from a loved one.

Fourth House
A desire to redecorate and be surrounded by color and luxury is often indicated by this position.

Fifth House
This is a good time for romance and artistic pursuits.

Sixth House
This aids cooperation with others as well as mutual sympathy. The native may experience weight gain.

Seventh House
This is a time of harmonious development within partnerships. There is also an increased love of peace and serenity.

Eighth House
The sex drive is suddenly accentuated. An inheritance or gift is also possible.

Ninth House
This is favorable for pleasant travel experiences. It is also a good time to pursue studies in music, art or drama.

Tenth House
Often honors and popularity are gained by this position. This is a favorable time to reap success.

Eleventh House
Friends, desires and gifts may suddenly spark the native's life. He may suddenly be overwhelmed with party invitations and social dinners.

Twelfth House
Artistic endeavors may flower in seclusion. A secret or unusual love affair may suddenly develop.

Mars Moving through the Houses

First House
This is a time of energy and impulsiveness. The native should guard against accidents due to hastiness and curb his or her temper.

Second House
If Mars is in good aspect, acquisition is possible. However, extravagance and waste will have to be watched, as this is a time of impulsive spending.

Third House

Mental energy is increased. The mind may be rash and restless. The native should try to be more diplomatic and think before speaking.

Fourth House

Here the native must try to avoid antagonisms within the home. This position can bring accidents and losses pertaining to the home.

Fifth House

This is a time of romantic excitement. However, the native should curb self-indulgence and try to be realistic. Children may become problematic.

Sixth House

The native should watch his or her health. This may be a time of increased work with employees, and a time of friction and disagreement.

Seventh House

The native must watch out for lawsuits. Partnerships may become strained and strife-ridden. An effort should be made to become more flexible to suit the needs of a partner or mate.

Eighth House

Here the native must watch reckless or impulsive spending. He should reassess long-range financial plans with others. With Mars in this position, it is a good time to check that insurance policies are up to date.

Ninth House

The native should guard against accidents during travel, look to self-improvement and try to avoid legal involvements. This is a good time to enthusiastically begin new studies.

Tenth House

This is a time to strive for independence and leadership but without damaging his reputation through too much outspokenness or indiscretion. Difficulties may arise with those in authority.

Eleventh House

Friends and acquaintances may prove troublesome. The native should be realistic in the execution of his goals.

Twelfth House

Hidden enemies may subject the native to false accusations. He should avoid gossip and watch his reputation. This position often brings inactivity and lethargy.

Jupiter Moving through the Houses

First House

A new personal cycle occurs with Jupiter in this house. There is increased optimism and often advancement and opportunity. This is a good position for health, although there may be a weight gain.

Second House

Financial prospects are increased. Unless Jupiter is in bad aspect, there is an opportunity to build up a bank account.

Third House

Mental optimism results from this influence. This is a most favorable time for journeys, correspondence and all mental activities.

Fourth House

Improving or redecorating the home or purchasing a new home should be favorable at this time. Benefits from land development may also be possible.

Fifth House

Interests turn to pleasure in all forms. There may be good fortune in both romance and speculation. This position often brings an inheritance.

Sixth House

This is an exceptionally good position for health and excellent for making progress in chosen work. The native will be successful with co-workers or employees, but he should watch excesses in eating and drinking.

Seventh House
Prosperity through the partner is favored. This is also a good position for lawsuits.

Eighth House
An inheritance or monetary sum may come. Religious and occult interests or experiences are possible.

Ninth House
This is excellent for pursuing an area of higher education. Favorable experiences will also come about through travel. There may also be a re-evaluation of faiths and beliefs.

Tenth House
This is favorable for popularity, for enhancing the reputation and for success.

Eleventh House
This is a time of wish attainment, goal realization and help through friends.

Twelfth House
This is good for studying the occult or mystical areas. Often the native desires to help the sick or underprivileged.

Saturn Moving through the Houses

First House
Dental and health checkups are often indicated. Patience has to be practiced because Saturn in this position demands mature behavior. Often there is a lack of vitality and a feeling of depression.

Second House
The native should learn to budget because heavy expenditures or loss of income may occur.

Third House
This gives great mental seriousness. Difficulties with brothers, sisters or neighbors may crop up.

Fourth House
Disappointments may arise in the home. Domestic difficulties should be handled calmly with patience.

Fifth House
This often brings the dissolvement of a romantic attachment and difficulty in creative expression. The native's children should be handled with understanding.

Sixth House
Health conditions should be carefully analyzed. Rest is needed. Routine chores are emphasized.

Seventh House
This often brings separations from a partner. However, it can also strengthen existing ties if both people are mature and if their charts indicate a lasting relationship.

Eighth House
Joint finances may become a source of trouble. This often indicates the death of older people.

Ninth House
In terms of legal involvements, this brings loss unless Saturn is well aspected. It is an excellent position for deepening religious beliefs. Often it brings a desire for additional learning.

Tenth House
The native must practice self-discipline. Advancement is slow and has to be earned. This position may bring major responsibilities that are burdensome yet significant learning experiences.

Eleventh House
Friends may be in need of help. Frustration may also be experienced in the pursuit of objectives.

Twelfth House
This will encourage reclusive habits and a need to withdraw. The native should be discreet as others may gossip or use information against him.

Uranus Moving through the Houses

First House
This position of Uranus brings tremendous restlessness and change. The native has a desire to begin something new and different from what he has formerly experienced. This can be a very progressive and freedom-enhancing period.

Second House
Enormous changes involving financial activities seem to occur here. It would be wise for the native to accumulate a nest egg for emergencies before Uranus transits this house. At this time, it is necessary to budget and handle finances with caution.

Third House
Sudden trips as well as sudden separations from relatives may occur. Unusual studies may be undertaken. If Uranus is afflicted, the native should exercise caution with all moving vehicles.

Fourth House
This position of Uranus often brings disruptions in the domestic sphere. Many times there is a move to a new residence, or the native may change the decor of his present home. In general, domestic harmony seems a little difficult to establish.

Fifth House
This may bring sudden romantic attachments, but they will probably not be lasting unless the two people's charts are harmonious. There may be difficulties through and with children, depending on the aspects of Uranus. There may also be interests in speculation, which may bring a windfall of some sort, but again, this depends on the aspects to Uranus.

Sixth House
Under this transit the native may suddenly change jobs. He may also experience sudden health changes. New co-workers or a change of employees may occur. More rest is generally indicated.

Seventh House
A hasty marriage may occur under this transit — or a sudden estrangement or separation from a business partner or mate. It is necessary to practice diplomacy when dealing with the public at this time.

Eighth House
This brings about the necessity to reorganize any joint holdings. It may also indicate a sudden inheritance or unexpected income, depending on other aspects.

Ninth House
Sudden travel is often indicated at this time. There may also be contact with brilliant, eccentric and important people. Changes in beliefs and attitudes often occur.

Tenth House
This brings a sudden change of status and often a complete change of profession. The native should be tactful when dealing with those in authority, since frictions may arise under this transit.

Eleventh House
This often brings unusual and impulsive attachments and friendships. The native's social life undergoes tremendous change because he meets many new and unusual people. He may also experience a radical change in his dreams and goals.

Twelfth House
This brings inner discontent. Mystical interests often come to the fore. Often there are behavioral changes that cause the native to be misunderstood by others.

Neptune Moving through the Houses

First House
The native should guard against self-deception. Life is often viewed through rose-colored glasses at this time.

Second House
Monetary affairs may become entangled causing chaotic financial conditions. The native should not become entangled in any schemes connected with money.

Third House
Imagination runs high, but the native should be careful not to sign papers without the advice of someone older and wiser. This is a good position for literary work.

Fourth House
Problems may arise concerning home or land holdings. All purchases of lasting value should be approached with caution.

Fifth House
Often this brings about a development of dormant artistic and creative abilities. The native should exercise care with regard to speculations. Love affairs will take on a romantic yet illusory quality.

Sixth House
Here the native must watch his appetite. There is a possibility of peculiar ailments. Employees or servants may become a source of difficulty.

Seventh House
The native should be careful of schemes proposed by others. Neptune in this position can bring very deceptive propositions and unions.

Eighth House
This may bring on chaotic financial conditions through the partner. All records of importance should be protected.

Ninth House
This often brings a desire to visit foreign countries. Mystical and religious interests are also indicated, although the perception of these things may be somewhat clouded.

Tenth House
The native must be careful not to become involved in scandals. This transit is most favorable for those who work in an artistic profession.

Eleventh House
Unusual friendships are formed. Often there is also involvement with groups that try to give life a deeper meaning. Friends might embroil the native in some form of notoriety.

Twelfth House
This may bring some mental disorganization. Vague fears, phobias and obsessions may be experienced.

Pluto Moving through the Houses

First House
This often brings personal upheaval, transformation, independence and a desire to establish oneself. This is a time of great change.

Second House
This position brings a desire to change financial conditions on a grand scale. It points to unforeseen dangerous financial fluctuations over which the native seems to have no control. Often all caution is thrown to the winds.

Third House
This is a very good position for studying and research. Unusual friends will be cultivated. The mind becomes penetrating and almost warlike.

Fourth House
The home may be thrown into a state of turmoil. It is not wise to deal in matters pertaining to property at this time.

Fifth House
If well aspected, Pluto in this house can bring about almost unbelievable success through speculation, the theater, sports activities, teaching and any form of creativity. Romantic affairs may be of an unusual nature. If this is an afflicted aspect, all of these activities should be approached with caution.

Sixth House
This may cause the native to change to a com-

pletely different occupation. The native must curb aggressive and dictatorial behavior toward co-workers and employees.

Seventh House
This brings about associations with many different people. The native can round out his knowledge through these associations. Marital or partnership status often undergoes some change.

Eighth House
With Pluto in this position, it is not advisable to take on greater financial obligations. Under this transit, there could be extreme losses.

Ninth House
The affairs of this house become charged with tremendous energy. Therefore this is an excellent time for travel, higher education, research and religious studies. However, overoptimism must be guarded against.

Tenth House
This gives a tremendous desire for wealth and power. Often it brings a complete reorganization of business ventures. The native may have the desire to go into business for himself.

Eleventh House
With Pluto in this position, the native is drawn to people of action and power. He may gain power in the organization or reorganization of group activities.

Twelfth House
Pluto in this position has a strangely beneficial effect on the native. Anything or anyone detrimental will in some manner be removed, discarded or rejected for the native in his own best interest. The native is subject to self-transformation and reevaluation of inner values.

19
Pregnancy Timing and the Determination of the Sex of Children

The ancients seem to have understood the Moon's influence on fertility, fluctuation and change. Since antiquity, the Moon's position has been utilized by farmers to determine the best time for planting and by the priesthood to determine religious holidays. Fertility rituals based on the position of the Moon are still practiced by various cultures.

We are indebted to the research of Dr. Eugen Jonas, a Czechoslovakian psychiatrist and gynecologist, who has studied the influence of the relationship between the Sun and the Moon on conception. Thanks to him, it is now possible for a woman to determine when she is fertile. (Many women are using astrological fertility charts as a method of birth control.)

If a woman wishes to determine her fertility period, she should figure the positions of the Sun and Moon (by degrees) and also her birth Moon's solstice at the moment when she was born. When the Moon reaches the same relationship with the Sun that was established at her birth, conception is possible. (To find this relationship, check a current ephemeris. A 5° orb is acceptable.)

The sign position of the Moon at the moment of conception (check the current ephemeris) determines the sex of the child. Fire and air signs indicate a male child; earth and water signs a female child.

A child conceived when the tide is incoming has a better chance of survival than a child conceived when the tide is outgoing. (Tidal data can be obtained from your local newspaper or Coast Guard.)

Let's assume a woman's birth Moon is in 14° Aries and her birth Sun in 10° Cancer. (See Figure 32.) This establishes an 86° relationship between the birth Sun and the birth Moon. Conception is possible when the Sun and Moon in the current ephemeris are 81° to 91° apart. (Remember, a 5° orb on either side of the exact aspect is permitted.) The Moon must be in an earlier sign

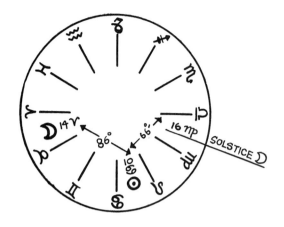

FIGURE 32
Conception chart for woman with birth Moon 14° Aries, birth Sun 10° Cancer and solstice point 16° Virgo.

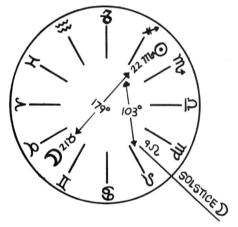

FIGURE 33
Conception chart for woman born during a full Moon.

than the Sun, the same as indicated in the horoscope. If you look at Table 14 in Chapter 4 (the reproduced page of the ephemeris), you will notice that the permitted setup for conception occurs on the 26th and the 27th. Late on the 26th the Moon is still in Leo, and therefore a male child would be conceived. On the 27th the Moon is in Virgo, and therefore a female child would be conceived.

The solstice point of the birth Moon, which in this case in 16° Virgo, must also be considered. The difference in degrees between the natal Sun and the solstice Moon is 66° in Figure 32. In this case the Sun is in an earlier sign than the Moon. Therefore when the Moon is from 61° to 71° and in a later sign than the Sun, conception is possible. Note in Table 14 that this condition exists on the eleventh, when the Moon is in Capricorn (an earth sign) and would thus produce a female child. These are the only possibilities for conception utilizing our particular example setup in the month of November 1972.

If a woman was born during a full Moon (see Figure 33), it is not advisable for her to become pregnant during a full Moon period because the Sun represents the positive factor and the Moon the negative factor, and when these two planets are in opposition at the time of conception, retardation of the offspring can occur if other planetary aspects are adverse. So for safety's sake, this woman should use the solstice position of the Moon in relation to her birth Sun to time her conceptions.

VII

Reading the Chart as a Whole

20
Synthesis of the Chart

This chapter describes the natal chart of a woman, whom we shall call Ann, born June 28, 1919, 11:32 P.M. Wartime, at 96°W24′ (west longitude) and 42°N30′ (north latitude).* Since she was born during Wartime, one hour has to be deducted from the birth hour (the same as would be done for Daylight Saving Time).† Ann's chart is given in Figure 34, her natal aspects in Table 27 and the position of the solstice points of her natal planets in Table 28.

If we categorize her chart by type, it is a combination of the bucket and the bundle types. We have a singleton planet (Uranus) on the east side of the chart, and at the same time an enormous concentration of planets between the range of the

*To find the longitude and the latitude of the native's birthplace, consult Dernay, *Longitudes and Latitudes in the United States* (see Bibliography), or a similar book.
†Doris Doane's *Time Changes in the U.S.A.* (see Bibliography) gives a complete listing of time changes in the United States.

fourth and seventh houses. This shows us that she has the capability to think and develop thoroughly within a given field of interest, but lacks the instinct for self-preservation. She is also subject to tremendous changes and upheavals since Uranus in Pisces is in the first house, which produces sudden changes.

Because Uranus is the co-ruler of her Aquarius ascendant — and the ascendant falls in the second decanate which is co-ruled by Libra, which, in turn, is ruled by Venus placed in the sixth house — Ann has the balance and determination she greatly needs to accept the many experiences and unusual occurrences she is subjected to.

Ann is also interested and well grounded in world affairs (Aquarius rising with ruler Uranus in first house) and likes to study history by her own admission. The ruler of the tenth house of employment is Jupiter, placed in her chart in the sixth house in Cancer, which shows that she is capable of functioning as an employee and giving loyal service. It also shows that she is cooperative and generous at times to a fault and is therefore often taken advantage of. That she has a very kind disposition is shown by Jupiter's conjunction with the Moon. This conjunction always endows the native with optimism — which, in Ann's case, is certainly needed.

Mars in her fourth house (home environment) shows problems within the home that continue throughout Ann's entire life. However, she has the ability to bear the domestic stresses and strains (Mars sextile Saturn) she encounters. (Human beings seem to come equipped with a planetary setup that enables them to cope with the stresses they are heir to. No greater lessons are imposed on us than we are able to handle.) Saturn in the seventh house gives loyalty to her mate.

Ann was born on the 28th day of the month, the day ruled by the Sun, which signifies inner strength. (The influence of the day of birth is explained in Chapter 21.) Ann's strength is evidenced by the way she handles the many difficulties in her life.

The Sun conjunct Pluto is another crisis-prone aspect. Since Uranus, the co-ruler of her first house, is in the intercepted sign of Pisces, and Saturn, the other ruler of her first house, is in opposition to her ascendant, and Venus, the co-significator of the ascendant, is also opposed to the ascendant, the indication is that Ann is not totally her own free agent and that in her life there will be many forces beyond her control.

The bundling of five planets in the sixth house shows that Ann functions best in a service type of profession. She worked as a clerk-typist and is now the office manager of an educational facility. She is adept at her job, which is shown by the Sun trine Uranus (bestowing organizing ability). The same is indicated by Pluto trine Uranus.

The solstice point of Mars is rather interesting because it falls directly conjunct her Sun and therefore can be read as an energy-giving conjunction. Pluto in the fifth house often indicates difficulty with or through children, especially since Pluto's solstice point is within a few minutes of being in conjunction to her natal Mars. The

Moon conjunct Mercury shows an above-average intelligence, so here we have an intelligent person very capable of handling difficulties.

In 1922 an aunt of Ann's shot herself accidentally. At the time of this accident, transiting Saturn (the Reaper) was squaring Pluto (co-ruler of Ann's ninth house, which rules aunts), transiting Mars (of firearms) was squaring Saturn, the progressed dragon's head was exactly conjunct the solstice point of the Moon (which rules males) and Mercury (which rules the cusp of the fourth house, representing an event within the family).

Mars in the fourth house is often an indication of early departure from home, and Ann moved out of her home and started working as a clerk-typist in 1938 at the age of nineteen. Uranus, co-ruler of her ascendant at that age, had just started by progression the trine to Jupiter (ruler of the tenth house — vocation). The Sun by progression was conjunct the Moon (ruler of the sixth house — giving service) and Mercury (ruler of papers).

At age twenty, Ann moved from her home state to California. The cusp of the ninth house by progression was exactly quincunx Pluto (change).

On June 18, 1940, ten days before her twenty-first birthday, Ann married her first husband who was a member of the Coast Guard. On Ann's chart the Sun, ruler of the seventh house (first marriage), is in Cancer (a water sign), and Mercury, the ruler of Ann's husband's tenth house (profession), which is her fourth house, is positioned also in a water sign and therefore signifies his profession. The transiting Moon on her day of marriage made a trine to Venus (ruler of her third house), indicating a signing of papers. Unfortunately, transiting Uranus, co-ruler of her ascendant, was exactly squaring her natal Saturn in the seventh house, which is an indication of marital disaster. Progressed Uranus was square to natal Mars in the fourth house, also showing disruption, and trining Jupiter and the Moon indicated a significant family event. Since her natal chart shows the part of marriage at 23° Aquarius 13' was conjunct her ascendant and in opposition to Saturn, there was an indication of marital disruption at birth. The part of wedding and legalizing at 9° Leo 05' is conjunct the planet Neptune, which also indicates confusing situations. By progression, both Neptune and the part of wedding and legalizing were in opposition to Ann's natal Uranus.

On February 4, 1941, Ann gave birth to a daughter whose Moon, Saturn and Jupiter unfortunately squares Ann's Neptune, which is indicative of a disharmonious relationship. That the daughter's Uranus squared the mother's natal Venus further indicated mutual disappointment. Even though Ann's water planets (five in Cancer and one in Pisces) gave her understanding and sensitivity, she was still unable to overcome the detrimental setup between her and her daughter.

Later in 1941 Ann went to work in an all-male section, again performing clerical work. The Moon, indicating service, at that time was by progression squaring the cusp of the third house — the result was the mental agony Ann had to endure under the needling and teasing of her male co-workers. Although she had been given sufficient strength to handle this, her overabundance of planets in water signs made her tremendously self-conscious.

In 1943 Ann had a miscarriage. The second child is ruled by the seventh house. Progressed Neptune, which is often an indicatior of miscarriage, was at that time in opposition to Ann's natal Uranus, co-ruler of her ascendant. The progressed Pluto and Sun were making a quincunx to the cusp of the eleventh house (hopes and wishes), showing a transformation through an unfavorable circumstance.

In 1944 Ann's only brother's first wife — the brother is shown by Ann's third house and his wife by her ninth house, which is ruled by Mars (firearms) — killed her girlfriend with a gun before killing herself. Deaths in the family are shown by the cusp of the eleventh house (the eleventh is eight houses after the family, which is the fourth house). Ann's chart shows 0° Capricorn — a critical degree — on the cusp of the eleventh house. At the time of the murder-suicide, the progressed cusp was in opposition to the Moon (rules females) and Mercury (rules the fourth house, the family).

Ann divorced her first husband at his request in 1945. At the time the Sun, ruler of her seventh house, and Pluto, the disruptive planet, formed a quincunx to Uranus, co-ruler of her natal ascendant. Ann's husband remarried five times.

On November 4, 1950, Ann remarried. Her second husband worked as a field engineer charting water maps. He was very intelligent and they had an excellent relationship, but — in her words — he suffered from "black moods." The second marriage is ruled by the ninth house, which in this case is Mars in Gemini (rules papers and interest in knowledge). Ann's husband's occupation is shown by Venus in Leo in the same sign as the water planet Neptune and Saturn (responsibility). His mental house is her eleventh house, with 0° Capricorn on the cusp and rulership by Saturn, planet of melancholy.

A second child was born to Ann on April 20, 1961 — a boy who, like his father, is subject to severe mood swings. This was her third pregnancy; the boy is also ruled by her ninth house.

On October 31, 1970, Ann's brother committed suicide. His mental house is the cusp of the fifth, with a critical position of 0° Cancer, and the cusp of family deaths was exactly conjunct Ann's ascendant by progression, which shows a personal family tragedy. Ann's eleventh house is also her brother's personal eighth house (regeneration and death). The progressed cusp of his eighth was also in opposition to Venus, ruler of his first house (which is Ann's third house). His birth was September 19, 1915.

In January, 1972, Ann's first husband died very suddenly of a heart attack. His birth was March 6, 1921. The following October 21st, her second husband also died very suddenly of a heart attack. His birth was March 8, 1916. Then on April 9, 1973, Ann's mother died of a heart attack. Her birth was June 1, 1884.

In all three cases the cusp of the eleventh house was by progression in close opposition to Saturn (rules elderly people), which rules Ann's twelfth house (sorrows). However, since Saturn is also co-ruler of the cusp of the first house, making a sextile aspect to Mars (the planet of energy), a tremendous longevity for Ann can reasonably be expected.

The reason I have included the birth data of the people involved in Ann's life is that you may wish to do some research. Her chart is excellent material for research.

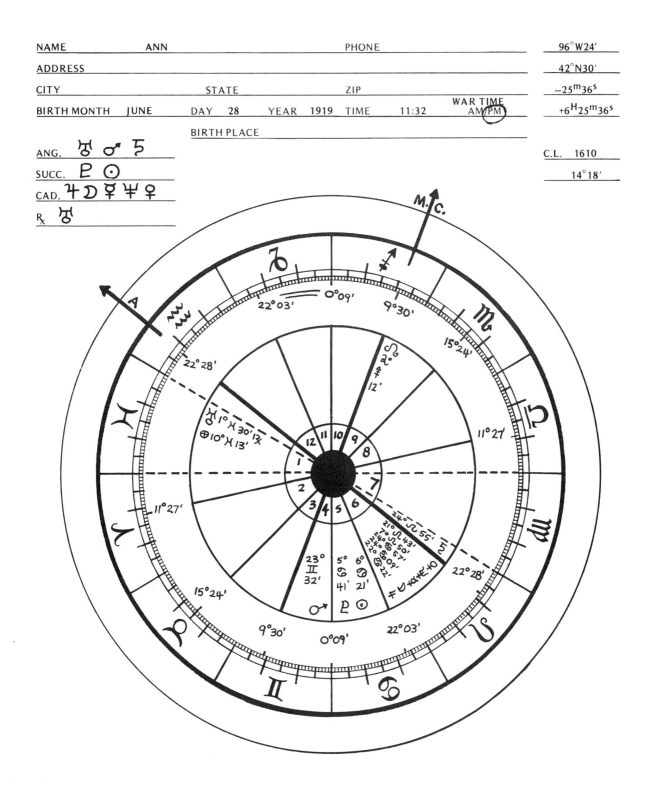

FIGURE 34
Natal chart (Ann).

TABLE 27

NATAL ASPECTS FOR FIG. 34 (ANN)

☌	⚺	∠	✱	Q	□	♆	△	⚼	±	⚻	☍
♇-☉	☽s♂	♂s♆				♀A.M.C.	♅A♇	☉-Asc.	☽A♅	♃-Asc.	♀ ☍ Asc.
	☿s♂	♀s♇				Asc.	♆-MC.	♇-Asc.	☿A♅	☽-Asc.	♄ ☍ Asc.
	☽A♄	♀s☉				M.C.	☉s♅			☿-Asc.	
	☿s♄						♂-Asc.			☉-MC.	
	☉A♆										
	♆s♇										
♃-☽											
♃-☿											
☽-☿											
♆-♀											
♀-♄											

☌ — Conjunction
⚺ — Semisextile
∠ — Semisquare
✱ — Sextile
Q — Quintile
□ — Square
♆ — Tredecile
△ — Trine
⚼ — Sesquare
± — Biquintile
⚻ — Quincunx
☍ — Opposition
S — Separating aspect
A — Applying aspect

TABLE 28

POSITION OF THE SOLSTICE POINTS FOR FIG. 34 (ANN)

Natal Position	Solstice Point	Opposition of Solstice Point
Asc. 22° ♒ 28′	7° ♏ 32′	7° ♉ 32′
♅ 1° ♃ 30′	28° ♎ 30′	28° ♈ 30′
♂ 23° ♊ 32′	6° ♋ 28′	6° ♑ 28′
♇ 5° ♋ 41′	24° ♊ 19′	24° ♐ 19′
☉ 6° ♋ 21′	23° ♊ 39′	23° ♐ 39′
♃ 22° ♋ 22′	7° ♊ 38′	7° ♐ 38′
☽ 24° ♋ 09′	5° ♊ 51′	5° ♐ 51′
☿ 24° ♋ 57′	5° ♊ 03′	5° ♐ 03′
♆ 7° ♌ 50′	22° ♉ 10′	22° ♏ 10′
♀ 21° ♌ 43′	8° ♉ 17′	8° ♏ 17′
♄ 24° ♌ 25′	5° ♉ 35′	5° ♏ 35′
MC 9° ♆ 30′	20° ♑ 30′	20° ♋ 30′

21
Influence of Your Day of Birth

What day of the month you were born on signifies what talents, abilities and tools you have brought with you into this life. Below, you will find the numerical significance of the various days:

First
"One" corresponds to the Sun in astrology. If you were born on the first day of any month, this shows that you are independent, original, creative and practical, but also idealistic. You handle all matters with more reason than feeling. You are a natural leader. At times you may be called selfish, obstinate, cold, undemonstrative and unsympathetic. You need praise and encouragement. You are fond of invention and eager to try your hand at many things. You possess a great deal of creativity.

The following are suggestions of occupations for which you may have an affinity: selling, inventing, teaching, writing.

Second
If you were born on the second day of any month, this number corresponds to the Moon in astrology and shows that you are sociable, warm-hearted and work better in a group than alone. You should try to overcome your periodic moods of depression. Do not become a doormat for others. You are fond of music and rhythm, and this can be an excellent emotional outlet for you as you may be somewhat high-strung or nervous.

The following are suggestions of occupations for which you may have an affinity: poetry, painting, dancing, physics, library work, civic work.

Third
If you were born on the third day of any month, this number corresponds to Venus in astrology and shows that you are a person of strong feelings — which, unfortunately, may change very suddenly and without warning. You have a great imagination and love communication. You are liked by both sexes and are a good storyteller. You must keep busy but be careful not to scatter your talents or abilities. You are able to make the best of any situation and are a good conversationalist.

The following are suggestions of occupations for which you may have an affinity: healing, hairdressing, cosmology, health food writing, music, art.

Fourth

"Four" corresponds to Mars. If you were born on the fourth day of any month, you are practical, methodical and love your home and country. Your somewhat materialistic inclinations serve you well in the business world. Since you are practical, you feel compelled to lay a good foundation for the future. At times you feel disappointed with yourself and others. You dislike showing affection and must overcome the habit of trying to force your opinions on others. Cultivate tact. You dislike change.

The following are suggestions of occupations for which you may have an affinity: banking, building, auditing, efficiency studies, architecture, accounting.

Fifth

If you were born on the fifth day of any month — this number corresponds to Mercury in astrology — this shows that you possess psychic abilities and should learn to follow your hunches. You are very sociable and have many acquaintances, both male and female. You may, however, have a lot of trouble with the opposite sex. You must learn self-discipline as you do not like to be tied down or disciplined by others. Do not burn your bridges behind you. You like to try your hand at many things and are somewhat restless. Therefore you must have an active occupation.

The following are suggestions of occupations for which you may have an affinity: stocks, bonds, buying, selling, athletics.

Sixth

The sixth day of the month corresponds to Venus, which gives those born on this day strong community loyalty. You appear mild but have a very strong character. You make a devoted parent to your own children or to others'. At times you keep your feelings too much to yourself. Though you contain your anger, once it flares up, it is difficult to suppress. You need love and approval. At times you are somewhat stubborn and argumentative.

The following are suggestions of occupations for which you may have an affinity: music, singing, acting, directing, institutional work, social work, restaurant or health food business, beauty schools, decorating.

Seventh

If you were born on the seventh day of any month, you are guided by Jupiter, which means you think everything through logically and are capable of deep mental analysis. You are psychic and sensitive; therefore you should learn to follow your hunches. Since you do not like to take orders, you work best alone. As you are not driven by feeling, you may be considered cold and unresponsive at times. You search after knowledge continuously. You are the perfectionist.

The following are suggestions of occupations for which you may have an affinity: science, teaching, occult, healing.

Eighth

If you were born on the eighth day of any month — this number corresponds to Saturn — you incline more to the material rather than to the spiritual level of existence. You have executive powers, are creative, progressive and a good judge of values. You are productive and generous, but at times you tend to dominate and force your will on others. It is important to you that you make a good impression. Deep within yourself you sometimes feel lonely, but you refuse to show it. You will treat the weak and the oppressed with charity.

The following are suggestions of occupations for which you may have an affinity: law, banking, industrial leadership, engineering, leadership in the music field, accounting, manufacturing.

Ninth

"Nine" corresponds to Uranus, which means those born on this day are humanitarians with both feeling and a strong will. You came into this world with the spirit of independence and try to dominate others. The losses and disappointments that touch you are usually superseded by something better. At times you behave impulsively and recklessly. You must serve others rather than lead a personal or selfish life.

The following are suggestions of occupations for which you may have an affinity: acting, writing, teaching, dramatics, interior decorating, lecturing, religious work.

Tenth

If you were born on the tenth day of any month, a number corresponding to the Sun in astrology, you have a strong will, are a delightful person to have around and very often enjoy excellent health. You seem to recover rather quickly from any illness. Many people born on the 10th possess creative abilities. You constantly try to improve your surroundings. You will be forced to stand on your own feet. You have an excellent mind.

The following are suggestions of occupations for which you may have an affinity: inventing, promoting, teaching, aviation, writing, selling.

Eleventh

You who were born on the eleventh day of any month are guided by Neptune, which means you are impulsive in thinking and behavior. You must avoid becoming a dreamer and strive to be a person of action. You are emotional and liable to worry too much over trivial matters. You must become aware of these defects and correct your tendency to vacillate in your desires so that you can become practical. You are psychic and should learn to pay attention to your hunches. You are extremely emotional and high-strung even when you appear calm on the outside.

The following are suggestions of occupations for which you may have an affinity: dancing, philosophy, art, movies, writing, accounting, promoting.

Twelfth

If you were born on the twelfth day of any month, a number corresponding to Venus, you are capable of reasoning things out quickly and of analyzing people and situations. You have artistic abilities, are able to communicate well, but must watch that you do not make enemies as you have a tendency to speak too bluntly. Do not scatter your energies. Cultivate the art of tact.

The following are suggestions of occupations for which you may have an affinity: law, writing, speaking, healing, restaurant work.

Thirteen

"Thirteen" corresponds to Mars, and those born on this day are practical. You appear mild but are secretly obstinate. Though you seem difficult to approach, you have a sympathetic nature. You are orderly and excellent at details. At times you are apt to be a little dictatorial — which makes those around you consider you obstinate and unreasonable — yet you dislike feuds and will try to achieve your own way through quiet stubbornness.

The following are suggestions of occupations for which you may have an affinity: accounting, designing, architecture, clerical work.

Fourteenth

If you were born on the fourteenth day of any month — this number corresponds to Mercury — you are positive in both speech and action. You like anything that is new and competitive. Gambling, alcohol and sex habits have to be watched. Even though you are conservative, you usually express some rather unique revolutionary ideas. You are psychic and often prophetic. Learn to follow your hunches.

The following are suggestions of occupations for which you may have an affinity: selling, buying, traveling, specialized medical fields.

Fifteenth

Those of you born on the fifteenth day of any month (Venus) appear gentle but carry some strong convictions. You are capable and responsible. Even though you appear cheerful and happy on the outside, you have a habit of constantly worrying about all sorts of things. You are sympathetic and affectionate, but carry a grudge for a long time. Learn not to sacrifice yourself for the sake of others. You are artistic and need to feel that you are serving.

The following are suggestions of occupations for which you may have an affinity: nursing, teaching, lecturing, medicine, designing, writing.

Sixteenth

If you were born on the sixteenth day of any month, the number that corresponds to Jupiter, you tend to be a perfectionist. On the outside you appear calm; however, your mind is in continuous turmoil, causing you to be somewhat short-tempered. You are slow in making decisions and at times somewhat moody. You dislike having your plans interfered with by others. You prefer a middle-of-the-road stand instead of taking the initiative. You are psychic, so learn to follow your hunches, even though this will be difficult since you cannot make quick decisions.

The following are suggestions of occupations for which you may have an affinity: education, teaching, writing, law, specialized fields of action.

Seventeenth

If you were born on the seventeenth day of any month — this number corresponds to Saturn in astrology — you are comparatively calm on the emotional level. This is a strong birthday. You are generous to a fault at times, while at other times you are very stingy. Essentially you are honest. You are very set in your ways and need people whom you can dominate. You search after knowledge. You are not spiritual and constantly require proof.

The following are suggestions of occupations for which you may have an affinity: writing, executive work, law, technical fields, historical fields, banking, dealing with earth products.

Eighteenth

Those of you born on the eighteenth day of any month are guided by Uranus. Therefore, you may have many disappointments and losses. You are somewhat emotional, have a knowledge of people and are clever at handling assets. You enjoy an argument just for the fun of it, and you love to exercise control over people and conditions. You have an enormous amount of independence. You give advice wisely.

The following are suggestions of occupations for which you may have an affinity: acting, music, art, surgery, medicine, care institutions, social work, politics, statistics.

Nineteenth

If you were born on the nineteenth day of any month, you are guided by the Sun, which means you are independent, original, but in some ways solitary. This day produces complicated characters. You are kind and patient and obstinate — all at the same time. You are subject to great changes in the area of finances. You always want to better a condition. You function best in a professional field rather than in the business world. Versatility seems to be the keynote for this birthday. You must learn through bitter experiences before you will make adjustments.

The following are suggestions of occupations for which you may have an affinity: politics, music, designing, art, theater, inventing, aviation.

Twentieth

If you were born on the twentieth day of any month — the number corresponding to the Moon in astrology — you have enormous affection for your fellowman and are therefore a natural peacemaker. You are respectful in your treatment of people. You notice even the most trivial things. You work best at your own business or in a small concern. Since you are not inclined to independence or foolhardiness, you work well

with others instead of being a leader. You love the nice and beautiful things in life and need a harmonious environment. See that people do not take advantage of your kindness. You express yourself better in writing than in speaking.

The following are suggestions of occupations for which you may have an affinity: writing, library work, collecting, music, analytical work.

Twenty-First

Those of you born on the twenty-first are influenced by Venus, and so are social, cheerful and pleasant. You make friends easily. You are endowed with enormous self-respect. At times you are highly suspicious. You are subject to moods and need to cultivate cheerfulness. You need change since you are somewhat restless and nervous.

The following are suggestions of occupations for which you may have an affinity: law, healing, publishing, music, art, speaking, writing.

Twenty-Second

If you were born on the twenty-second (Pluto), you function best in the material and business world. You tend to limit your associations to a few reliable friends. You need rest because you are somewhat high-strung and nervous. You are conservative and given to worry. You dislike arguments intensely. You have hunches, which you should follow. Affairs in your life seem to happen twice, for this is a double number. Make an effort to live constructively. Develop tact and your organizing ability.

The following are suggestions of occupations for which you may have an affinity: importing, exporting, buying, selling, teaching, poetry, corporational work.

Twenty-Third

If you were born on the twenty-third day of any month, the number that corresponds to Mercury in astrology, you are a person of action. You love freedom and dislike formalities. You live an active social life. You have a strong need for independence and may become easily enraptured with the opposite sex — in fact, you function better with the opposite sex. It is necessary for you to accomplish much from a psychological standpoint, so you need a good education. Otherwise, you will tend to bluff your way through life.

The following are suggestions of occupations

for which you may have an affinity: teaching, psychiatry, psychology, acting, entertaining, art, physical activities, diagnostic work.

Twenty-Fourth

The twenty-fourth day corresponds to Venus in astrology; if you were born on this day, you work and play equally hard. You are methodical but also an idealist and a dreamer. You are a natural parent and a natural teacher. Watch that you do not try to force your opinions on others. You are highly interested in your community. At times you are stubborn and argumentative and tend to publicize your sorrows and joys. Guard against jealousy, fault-finding and laziness, as these seem to occur at times.

The following are suggestions of occupations for which you may have an affinity: teaching, singing, restaurant work, social work, healing.

Twenty-Fifth

If you were born on the twenty-fifth day of any month, the number corresponding to Jupiter, you are intuitive but must learn to concentrate. You are extremely hasty at times; at other times you can be extremely hesitant. You should develop your creative talents. Occasionally you need to get away from the hustle and bustle of the city and out into the country to calm your nerves. Don't underestimate your own ability. Avoid erratic and critical behavior.

The following are suggestions of occupations for which you may have an affinity: science, politics, teaching, writing, detective work.

Twenty-Sixth

Those of you born on the twenty-sixth are guided by Saturn and thus must learn to finish what you start since you lack a certain amount of positiveness. This is an excellent financial day. You have too many worry habits. Cultivate optimism and do not live so much in the past. Since you are subject to extreme emotions, you must develop positive tendencies in order to stabilize your actions and behavior.

The following are suggestions of occupations for which you may have an affinity: art, publishing, music, traveling, diplomacy.

Twenty-Seventh

The twenty-seventh day corresponds to Uranus in astrology. Those born on this day can be described as very positive. You are self-assured and have nerve. You are independent, ambitious, capable, efficient and quietly determined. You are also highly emotional and dislike working under the dominion of others. You are extremely psychic and mediumistic. Perhaps because you are a natural leader, you dislike having to account for your behavior. You work best in an individual capacity. You are somewhat dogmatic. Your marriage may be disappointing. You are affectionate and emotional, but at times you may be somewhat high-strung and nervous.

The following are suggestions of occupations for which you may have an affinity: literary work, law, healing, poetry, art, teaching, health and religious work.

Twenty-Eighth

If you were born on the twenty-eighth day of any month you are guided by the Sun, which means you are positive and have a strong will. On the surface you appear calm — that is, you do not display your ingrained strength. You like freedom but often feel restrained. You begin many things but frequently fail to finish them. You must guard against daydreaming as this may lead to laziness. Learn not to magnify your problems. You will have to handle many difficulties, so learn to handle them wisely.

The following are suggestions of occupations for which you may have an affinity: inventions, law, decorating, executive positions, advertising.

Twenty-Ninth

The twenty-ninth corresponds to Neptune in astrology, and those born on this day are persons of action. At times you are impulsive because of your need for independence. You are an extremist — which can make you happy at times, and at other times moody. Try to find the middle of the road. You must learn not to suffer through others too intensely. Study religion. You need to develop calmness and you require a harmonious environment. There are many unhappy family experiences to be dealt with.

The following are suggestions of occupations for which you may have an affinity: law, selling, buying, speaking, art, acting.

Thirtieth

If you were born on the thirtieth day of any month — the number corresponding to Venus in astrology — you have a strong need for self-expression. You appear calm, gentle and sincere. In some ways you may be difficult to reach or understand because your behavior pattern is at times inconsistent. You are active and get restless; you are interested in many things. You appear weak but are not. You are set in your opinions and tend to think that you are always right. This tendency needs to be watched or it may turn into dominance. You are intuitive. You should guard against obsession and other fanatical tendencies.

The following are suggestions of occupations for which you may have an affinity: writing, art, advertising, speaking.

Thirty-First

If you were born on the thirty-first day of any month (Mars), you are practical and above all a realist. You personify logic and reason, but you experience difficulty in being on your own. You are a hard worker, honest and need responsibility early in life. You are much kinder to strangers than to your own relatives. You set very high standards for yourself and for your family and then become very disappointed when these standards are not lived up to.

The following are occupations for which you may have an affinity: medicine, health fields, statistics, manufacturing work, efficiency work.

Appendixes

A
How to Set Up a Chart

Since most people dislike math, I have compiled a list of reference works you can consult to make setting up a chart as easy as possible. These are in the Bibliography at the end of the book. If you decide to set up a chart, you will need certain tools:

1 A table of houses.

2 A book of longitude and latitude for the United States (if you are doing a chart for someone born in another country, you will, of course, need a world book).

3 A book showing time changes (or you could consult the post office for the state or town in question).

4 One ephemeris for the specific year that you are interested in (which shows longitude and latitude for planets in Greenwich Time for noon each day).

5 Table of proportional logarithms (Table 33, Appendix A).

6 A blank birth chart (Figure 47, Appendix C).

Now, let's get to work. Don't be terrified because it really isn't all that complicated. Just take your time.

Birth Data

On a piece of paper write down the person's birth name, month, day, year, time and place (state and town), just as it is indicated in Figure 35 (p. 143). (Figure 38 shows the completed chart.) Be certain that you circle A.M. or P.M. next to the birth time. This is *very* important.

In our first example (Table 29 p. 144), we are assuming that Person A, a female, is born

NAME   A, FEMALE   PHONE   118°W15'

ADDRESS   34°N03'

CITY   STATE   ZIP   +7ᵐ00ˢ

BIRTH MONTH   NOV.   DAY   7   YEAR   1972   TIME   2:24   ST.T.   +7ᴴ53ᵐ00ˢ
                                                           AM(PM)

                        BIRTH PLACE   LOS ANGELES, CA.

ANG.   C.L.

SUCC.   ☽

CAD.

Rₓ

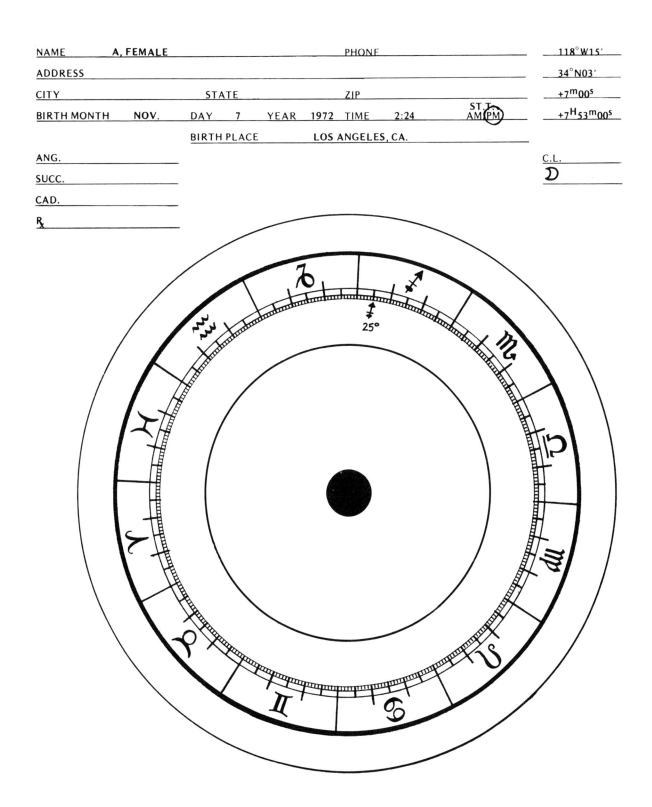

FIGURE 35

Sample birth chart with degree and sign marked for the tenth house.

November 7, 1972, at 2:24 P.M. in Los Angeles, California. This is the first information recorded. Note here whether the birth time was Standard or Daylight Saving.

Now open the longitude and latitude book for the United States and copy this information:

Los Angeles, California: Under the column "Longitude" we put 118°W15'. This is the distance in degrees and minutes Los Angeles is west of Greenwich Observatory.

Under the column "Latitude" we put 34°N03'.

This is the distance in degrees and minutes Los Angeles is north of the earth's equator.

The next column gives the L.M.T., which is the Local Mean Time variation from Standard Time. In this case, it is 7 minutes. (You see, our clocks are not quite correct unless we happen to live exactly on a meridian.) The last column in the longitude and latitude book shows how to obtain the G.M.T. (Greenwich Mean Time). In this case the exact distance that Los Angeles is from Greenwich is 7 hours, 53 minutes, 00 seconds.

TABLE 29

HOW TO FIGURE BIRTH DATA, HOUSE CUSPS AND DECLINATIONS FOR SAMPLE CHART

I. Birth Data

A. Female
November 7, 1972—2:24 P.M. ST.T. (Standard Time)—
Los Angeles, Ca.

Longitude	Latitude	L.M.T. Variation	E.G.M.T.
118°W15'	34°N03'	+7m00s	+7h53m00s

Steps:	Hours	Minutes	Seconds
1. Clock time at P.M. birth	02	24	00 ST.T.
2. *Local Mean Time* variation	+	7	00
	02	31	00
3. 10-Second Interval Correction	+		26
True Local Time =	02	31	26
	+15	07	08
4. Sidereal Time of the *7th* as birth occurred *after* 12 Noon	17	38	34
5. Longitudinal Correction (Formula: Multiply by 2, divide result by 3. Always *add* result when birthplace was *west of Greenwich;* deduct result when birthplace was *east of Greenwich*)	+	1	19
The Final Calculated Sidereal Time =	17	39	53

II. House Cusps

	Hours	Minutes	Seconds
6. *True* Local Time	02	31	26
7. *Equivalent Greenwich Mean Time*	+ 7	53	00
Greenwich Mean Time on 7th			
	9	84	26 or 10h24m26s

C.L. (Constant Log) for 10h24m = .3632 (for planetary correction between 7th and 8th)

☉ on 7th = 15° ♏ 11' = difference 60' = 1°
☉ on 8th = 16° ♏ 11'

(7th)   15° ♏ 11'
       +   49' ⟶ 49'
                        ⟶ +11'
    16° ♏ 00'
       +   11'   60' = 1° (Total movement in 24 hours)

(8th)   16° ♏ 11'   1.3802 (Log. for ☉)
                         + .3632 (C.L.)
                         1.7434 This total reconverted = 26'

☉ on 7th =   15° ♏ 11'
         +   26'
       15° ♏ 37' = ☉ Position for 10h24m

♆ on 7th = 4° ♎ 15' = difference 3'
♆ on 8th = 4° ♎ 18'

(7th) 4° ♎ 15'
      +   3'   = 3' (Total movement in 24 hours)
(8th) 4° ♎ 18'

            2.6812 (Log. for ♆)
         + .3632 (C.L.)
           3.0444 This total reconverted = 1'

♆ on 7th = 4° ♎ 15'
        +   1'
      4° ♎ 16' = ♆ Position for 10h24m

♅ on 7th = 20° ♎ 20' = difference 4'
♅ on 8th = 20° ♎ 24'

(7th) 20° ♎ 20'
      +   4'
(8th) 20° ♎ 24'   = 4' (Total movement in 24 hours)

$$2.5563 \text{ (Log. for } ♅)$$
$$+ \ .3632 \text{ (C.L.)}$$
$$2.9195 \text{ This total reconverted} = 2'$$

♅ on 7th =   20° ♎ 20'
$$\underline{+ \qquad\qquad 2'}$$
20° ♎ 22' = ♅ Position for 10h24m

♄ on 8th = 19° ♊ 24' ℞ = difference 4' ℞
♄ on 7th = 19° ♊ 28' ℞

(8th)   19° ♊ 24' ℞
$$\underline{+ \qquad\qquad 4'}$$ = 4' (Total movement in 24 hours
(7th)   19° ♊ 28' ℞

$$2.5563 \text{ (Log. for } ♄)$$
$$+ \ .3632 \text{ (C.L.)}$$
$$2.9195 \text{ This total reconverted} = 2'$$

♄ on 7th =   19° ♊ 28' ℞
$$\underline{- \qquad\qquad 2'}$$
19° ♊ 26' ℞ = ♄ Position for 10h24m

♃ on 7th = 6° ♑ 07' = difference 11'
♃ on 8th = 6° ♑ 18'

(7th)   6° ♑ 07'
$$\underline{+ \qquad\quad 11'}$$ = 11' (Total movement in 24 hours)
(8th)   6° ♑ 18'

$$2.1170 \text{ (Log. for } ♃)$$
$$+ \ .3632 \text{ (C.L.)}$$
$$2.4802 \text{ This total reconverted} = 5'$$

♃ on 7th =   6° ♑ 07'
$$\underline{+ \qquad\qquad 5'}$$
6° ♑ 12' = ♃ Position for 10h24m

♂ on 7th = 24° ♎ 26' = difference 40'
♂ on 8th = 25° ♎ 06'

146 Appendixes

(7th)   24° ♎ 26'

      +   34'——→34'

      25° ♎ 00'   + 6'

      +   6'   40'   = (Total movement in 24 hours)

(8th)   25° ♎ 06'

                     1.5563 (Log. for ♂)

                  + .3632 (C.L.)

                   1.9195 This total reconverted = 17'

♂ on 7th = 24° ♎ 26'

        +   17'

        24° ♎ 43 = ♂ Position for 10h24m

C.L. (Constant Log) .3632

♀ on 7th = 9° ♎ 10' = difference 1° 12'

♀ on 8th = 10° ♎ 22'

(7th)   9° ♎ 10'

      +   50'———→50'

      10° ♎ 00' +22'

      +   22'   72'   = 1° 12' (Total movement in 24 hours)

(8th)   10° ♎ 22'

                     1.3010 (Log. for ♀)

                  + .3632 (C.L.)

                   1.6642 This total reconverted = 32'

♀ on 7th = 9° ♎ 10'

        +   32'

       9° ♎ 42' = ♀ Position for 10h24m

C.L. (Constant Log) .3632

☿ on 7th = 8° ♎ 15' = difference 51'

☿ on 8th = 9' ♎ 06'

(7th)   8° ♎ 15'

      +   45'———→45'

      9° ♎ 00' + 6'

      +   6'   51'   = (Total movement in 24 hours)

(8th)   9° ♎ 06'

                    1.4508 (Log. for ☿)

                 + .3632 (C.L.)

               1.8140 This total reconverted = 22'

☿ on 7th = 8° ♎ 15'

        +   22'

      8° ♎ 37' = ☿ Position for 10h24m

☽ on 7th = 0° ♎ 50'
= difference 11°49'
☽ on 8th = 12° ♎ 39'

(7th)   0° ♎ 50'
        +   10' ——————→ 10'
         1° ♎ 00'   +11°00'
        +11° ♎ 00'   +   39'
         12° ♎ 00'   11°49'   = (Total movement in 24 hours)
        +   39'
(8th)   12° ♎ 39'   .3077 (Log. for ☽)
                          +.3632 (C.L.)
                           .6709 This total reconverted = 5°07'

☽ on 7th =   0° ♎ 50'

        +5°   07'
         5° ♎ 57' = ☽ Position for 10h24m

For the position of ♇ (Pluto), see text.

♇ 3° ♎ 26'

III. Declinations

♇ — 13°N18'   ♅ — 7°S23'
♆ — 19°S27'   ♄ — 21°N22'

♃ — 23°S24'

♂ on 7th = 8°S48'
= difference 30'
♂ on 9th = 9°S18'

30' divided by 2 days = 15' per day

1.9823 (Log. for 15')
+ .3632 (C.L.)
2.3455 This total reconverted = 7'

♂ on 7th =   8°S48'
        +   7'
         8°S55' = ♂ Declination position for 10h24m

♀ on 7th = 2°S04'   C.L. (Constant Log) .3632

                        = difference 55' (as this is an uneven figure, round it off to 56')

♀ on 9th = 2°S59'

                                                56' divided by 2 days = 28' per day

                                                1.7112 (Log. for 28')
                                              + .3632 (C.L.)
♀ on 7th =   2°S04'   2.0744 This total reconverted = 12'

            +   12'
            ───────
             2°S16' = ♀ Declination position for 10h24m

───

                                                                        C.L. (Constant Log) .3632

☿ on 7th = 24°S26'
                    = difference 12'
☿ on 9th = 24°S38'
                                                12' divided by 2 days = 6' per day

                                                2.3802 (Log. for 6')
                                              + .3632 (C.L.)
☿ on 7th =   24°S26'   2.7434 This total reconverted = 3'

            +   3'
            ───────
            24°S29' = ☿ Declination position for 10h24m

───

                                                                        C.L. (Constant Log) .3632

☉ on 7th = 16°S24'
                    = difference 17'
☉ on 8th = 16°S41'

(7th)   16°S24'
            +   17'   = 17' (Total movement in 24 hours)
(8th)   ───────
            16°S41'
                                                1.9279 (Log. for 17')
                                              + .3632 (C.L.)
                                                2.2911 This total reconverted = 7'

☉ on 7th =   16°S24'

            +   7'
            ───────
            16°S31' = ☉ Declination position for 10h24m

───

☽ on 7th = 24°S00'   C.L (Constant Log) .3632
                    = difference 1°16'
☽ on 8th = 25°S16'

(7th)   24°S00'
            + 1° 00' ────────→ 1° 00'
            ───────   +   16'
            25°S00'   ───────
            +   16'   1° 16'   = (Total movement in 24 hours)
(8th)   ───────
            25°S16'
                                                1.2775 (Log. for 1° 16')
                                              + .3632 (C.L.)
                                                1.6407 (This total reconverted = 33'
☽ on 7th =   24°S00'

            +   33'
            ───────
            24°S33' = ☽ Declination position for 10h24m

Note: I am giving the following information only for those of you who are interested in why this mathematical correction has to be made.

The earth is divided into twenty-four prime meridians, each one 15° distant from the next. Greenwich Observatory in England has been designated as 0°. (See Table 30.) In all places clocks are synchronized to the standard time in that prime meridian. This system has the obvious advantage of standardization, but it does not assure true time. Unless a person was born exactly on a prime meridian, the true time of his birth is not the same as the official time. Hence the official time has to be converted to True Local Time.

To return to our example: The clocks for Los Angeles are set for the 120th prime meridian, but since Los Angeles is only 118°N15' it is actually 1°45' east of its prime meridian or true time center. Now, the Sun travels 1° every 4 minutes, and 15° times 4 minutes equals 60 minutes, which equals 1 hour. (Can you see now why each of the prime meridians is 15° or 1 hour apart?) Since Los Angeles is short by 1°45' of the nearest prime meridian, and 1° is equivalent to 4 minutes of time and 45' is equivalent to 3 minutes of time, the difference between the True Local Time and the official time in Los Angeles is 7 minutes. The 7 minutes are *added* to the official time because Los Angeles is *east* of its true time center. (If the birthplace is *west* of a prime meridian, then the time difference is *subtracted*.)

Look again at Table 29. In Step 1 the clock time is noted as 2 hours, 24 minutes, 00 seconds. Since Daylight Saving Time was not in effect in November, 1972, it is marked ST.T., which stands for Standard Time. At this point let me note that we are working with a noontime ephemeris in which each day begins at Greenwich Noon Time and ends at noon the next day. From 12 Noon, November 7th, 1972, 2 hours, 24 minutes and 00 seconds have passed in our example case.

Step 2 concerns the Local Mean Time variation. In this case the adjustment is 7 minutes, 00 seconds, and it is added to the clock time.

Step 3 is a 10-second interval correction. Here we begin to adjust for Sidereal Time. Sidereal Time progresses by approximately 4 minutes per day.

The 4-minutes-per-day accumulation times 4 years equals slightly over 24 hours, or one

TABLE 30	
THE PRIME MERIDIANS	
Meridian	**Hours East of Greenwich**
180°	−12 (Date Line)
165°	−11
150°	−10
135°	− 9
120°	− 8
105°	− 7
90°	− 6
75°	− 5
60°	− 4
45°	− 3
30°	− 2
15°	− 1
0°	Greenwich Observatory, England
Meridian	**Hours West of Greenwich**
15°	+ 1
30°	+ 2
45°	+ 3
60°	+ 4
75°	+ 5
90°	+ 6
105°	+ 7
120°	+ 8
135°	+ 9
150°	+10
165°	+11
180°	+12 (Date Line)

extra day — which is inserted into our calendar as February 29 every four years. Sidereal Time is the most accurate method of time reckoning and is used in every astronomical observatory. A clock is set to register 0 hours, 0 minutes, 0 seconds the moment the earth crosses the intercepting point of the ecliptic and the earth's equator. On the zenith at that time is 0° Aries.

Since the ephemeris gives only one Sidereal Time per day — for noon in the noontime ephemeris we are using in this book — an adjustment has to be made if the birth time was not exactly noon. In our example case (Table 29) the correction is 26 seconds, which is obtained from Table 31. Two hours require a correction of 20 seconds, and 31 minutes require a correction of 6

TABLE 31

10-SECOND INTERVAL CORRECTIONS

	H	M	S
For 1 hour correct	00	00	10
For 2 hours correct	00	00	20
For 3 hours correct	00	00	30
For 4 hours correct	00	00	40
For 5 hours correct	00	00	50
For 6 hours correct	00	01	00
For 7 hours correct	00	01	10
For 8 hours correct	00	01	20
For 9 hours correct	00	01	30
For 10 hours correct	00	01	40
For 11 hours correct	00	01	50
For 12 hours correct	00	02	00
For 13 hours correct	00	02	10
For 14 hours correct	00	02	20
For 15 hours correct	00	02	30
For 16 hours correct	00	02	40
For 17 hours correct	00	02	50
For 18 hours correct	00	03	00
For 19 hours correct	00	03	10
For 20 hours correct	00	03	20
For 21 hours correct	00	03	30
For 22 hours correct	00	03	40
For 23 hours correct	00	03	50
For 24 hours correct	00	04	00
	H	M	S
For 1–6 minutes correct	00	00	01
For 7–12 minutes correct	00	00	02
For 13–18 minutes correct	00	00	03
For 19–24 minutes correct	00	00	04
For 25–30 minutes correct	00	00	05
For 31–36 minutes correct	00	00	06
For 37–42 minutes correct	00	00	07
For 43–48 minutes correct	00	00	08
For 49–54 minutes correct	00	00	09
For 55–60 minutes correct	00	00	10

Note: A 10-second correction can never be greater than 4 minutes in any given day.

seconds. The 10-second interval correction of 26 seconds is added to the L.M.T. of 2 hours, 31 minutes, 00 seconds for a total of 2 hours, 31 minutes, 26 seconds, which is the True Local Time (Step 1 plus 2, plus 3).

For Step 4 we have to consult Table 37 in Appendix B. This ephemeris page for November 7 shows the Sidereal Time as 15 hours, 07 minutes, 08 seconds. We add this Sidereal Time to the True Local Time, which gives a total of 17 hours, 38 minutes, 34 seconds.

Step 5 is the longitudinal correction. The rule for this is as follows: *Longitude times 2 divided by 3.* The longitude of Los Angeles is 118°W15'. Multiply 118 by 2, which gives 236. Divide this figure by 3 and the result is 78 with 2 remaining. Since the remainder is more than half the divisor, the total is rounded off to 79. This correction is *always* in seconds; 79 seconds would be 1 minute and 19 seconds. The longitudinal correction is added to the Sidereal Time: the result in Table 29 is 17 hours, 39 minutes, 53 seconds — the Final Calculated True Local Sidereal Time.

Notice that we dropped the 15' in the 118°W15' longitude figure. Whenever the minute figure is less than 30, it is dropped. If it is more than 30, the degree figure is increased by 1. Also note that the longitudinal correction is *added* if the birthplace was *west* of Greenwich but *deducted* if the birthplace was *east* of Greenwich. With the completion of Step 5, we are ready to set up the horoscope wheel.

The House Cusps

The Tenth House

Now open your table of houses or refer to Table 32. In the table the nearest Sidereal Time to our final figure is 17 hours, 38 minutes, 13 seconds (column 2), and next to it is indicated Sagittarius 25°. This figure *always* belongs on the cusp of the tenth house. (See Figure 35.) Starting with Sagit-

TABLE 32

TABLE OF HOUSES*

TABLE OF HOUSES FOR LATITUDES 22° TO 56°.

50 — UPPER MERIDIAN, CUSP OF 10th H.

SID. T. / ARC	SID. T. H. M. S. 17 33 51, ARC 263° 27'.8 ♐ 24°					H. M. S. 17 38 13, 264° 33'.1 ♐ 25°					H. M. S. 17 42 34, 265° 38'.5 ♐ 26°					H. M. S. 17 46 55, 266° 43'.8 ♐ 27°					H. M. S. 17 51 17, 267° 49'.2 ♐ 28°					H. M. S. 17 55 38, 268° 54'.6 ♐ 29°				
H.	11	12	1	2	3	11	12	1	2	3	11	12	1	2	3	11	12	1	2	3	11	12	1	2	3	11	12	1	2	3
Lat. °	♑ °	♒ °	♓ ° '	♈ °	♉ °	♑ °	♒ °	♓ ° '	♈ °	♉ °	♑ °	♒ °	♓ ° '	♉ °	♊ °	♑ °	♒ °	♓ ° '	♉ °	♊ °	♑ °	♒ °	♓ ° '	♉ °	♊ °	♑ °	♒ °	♓ ° '	♉ °	♊ °
22	18.8	16.6	21 23	28.5	28.5	19.8	17.8	22 49	29.8	29.6	20.8	19.0	24 15	1.0	0.7	21.9	20.2	25 41	2.3	1.7	22.9	21.5	27 7	3.6	2.8	24.0	22.7	28 33	4.8	3.9
23	6	3	21 17	7	6	6	5	22 44	9	7	7	18.8	24 11	2	8	7	0	25 38	5	9	8	2	27 5	8	3.0	23.8	5	28 33	5.0	4.0
24	4	1	21 11	9	8	5	3	22 39	♉ 0.1	9	5	5	24 7	4	1.0	6	19.8	25 35	7	2.0	6	0	27 3	4.0	1	7	2	28 32	2	2
25	3	15.8	21 5	29.1	9	3	0	22 34	3	♊	4	3	24 3	6	1	4	5	25 32	9	2	5	20.7	27 1	2	3	5	0	28 31	5	3
26	1	5	20 59	3	29.1	2	16.8	22 29	5	0.2	2	0	23 59	8	3	3	3	25 29	3.1	3	22.3	5	26 59	4	4	4	21.8	28 29	7	5
27	17.9	3	20 53	5	3	0	5	22 24	7	3	0	17.8	23 55	2.1	4	1	0	25 26	4	5	2	2	26 57	6	3.6	2	5	28 28	9	7
28	8	0	20 46	7	4	18.8	2	22 18	1.0	5	19.9	5	23 50	3	1.6	20.9	18.7	25 22	6	7	0	0	26 55	9	7	0	3	28 27	6.2	8
29	6	14.7	20 39	9	6	7	15.9	22 12	2	7	7	2	23 45	5	7	8	5	25 19	8	8	21.8	19.7	26 52	5.1	9	22.9	0	28 26	4	5.0
30	4	4	20 31	♉ 0.1	7	5	6	22 6	4	8	5	16.9	23 40	7	9	6	2	25 15	4.1	3.0	6	4	26 50	4	4.1	7	20.7	28 25	7	1
31	2	1	20 24	3	9	3	3	21 59	6	1.0	3	6	23 35	3.0	2.1	4	17.9	25 11	3	2	5	2	26 47	6	3	5	5	28 23	9	3
32	1	13.8	20 16	5	♊ 0.1	1	0	21 52	9	2	2	3	23 29	2	3	2	6	25 7	5	3	3	18.9	26 44	9	4	4	2	28 22	7.2	5
33	16.9	4	20 7	8	3	17.9	14.7	21 45	2.1	4	0	0	23 23	5	4	0	3	25 2	8	5	1	6	26 41	6.1	6	2	19.9	28 21	5	7
34	7	1	19 58	1.0	5	7	4	21 38	4	5	18.8	15.6	23 17	7	6	19.8	16.9	24 58	5.1	7	20.9	2	26 38	4	8	0	6	28 19	8	9
35	5	12.7	19 48	3	7	5	0	21 30	7	7	6	3	23 11	4.0	8	6	6	24 53	4	9	7	17.9	26 35	7	5.0	21.8	2	28 18	8.1	6.1
36	3	3	19 38	6	9	3	13.6	21 21	3.0	9	4	14.9	23 4	3	3.0	4	2	24 48	7	4.1	5	5	26 32	7.1	2	6	18.9	28 16	4	3
37	0	11.9	19 27	9	1.1	1	2	21 12	3	2.1	1	5	22 57	7	2	2	15.9	24 43	6.0	3	3	2	26 28	4	4	3	5	28 14	8	5
38	15.8	5	19 16	2.2	3	16.9	12.8	21 2	6	4	17.9	1	22 49	5.0	5	0	5	24 37	4	5	1	16.8	26 24	8	6	1	1	28 12	9.1	7
39	6	1	19 4	5	5	6	4	20 52	9	6	7	13.7	22 41	4	7	18.8	1	24 31	7	8	19.8	4	26 20	8.1	9	20.9	17.7	28 10	5	9
40	3	10.7	18 51	8	7	4	0	20 41	4.3	8	4	3	22 33	7	9	5	14.6	24 24	7.1	5.0	6	0	26 16	5	6.1	6	3	28 8	9	7.2
41	1	2	18 37	3.2	2.0	1	11.5	20 30	7	3.1	2	12.8	22 23	6.1	4.2	3	2	24 17	5	2	3	15.5	26 11	9	3	4	16.9	28 6	10.3	4
42	14.8	9.7	18 22	6	2	15.9	0	20 17	5.1	3	16.9	4	22 13	5	4	0	13.7	24 10	8.0	5	1	1	26 6	9.4	6	2	4	28 3	8	7
43	6	2	18 6	4.0	5	6	10.5	20 4	5	6	7	11.9	22 2	7.0	7	17.7	2	24 1	4	8	18.8	14.6	26 1	8	9	19.9	0	28 0	11.2	8.0
44	3	8.6	17 49	5	7	3	9.9	19 49	6.0	8	4	3	21 51	4	9	5	12.7	23 52	9	6.0	5	1	25 55	10.3	7.1	6	15.5	27 57	7	2
45	0	0	17 30	9	3.0	0	4	19 33	4	4.1	1	10.8	21 38	9	5.2	2	1	23 43	9.4	3	2	13.5	25 48	8	4	3	14.9	27 54	12.2	5
46	13.7	7.4	17 9	5.3	3	14.7	8.8	19 16	8	4	15.8	2	21 24	8.3	5	16.9	11.6	23 32	9	6	17.9	12.9	25 41	11.3	7	0	4	27 51	7	8
47	3	6.8	16 47	7	6	4	2	18 57	7.3	7	5	9.6	21 9	8	8	5	0	23 21	10.4	9	6	3	25 34	8	8.0	18.7	13.9	27 47	13.2	9.1
48	0	1	16 22	6.2	9	1	7.5	18 37	8	5.0	1	8.9	20 52	9.3	6.1	2	10.4	23 8	9	7.2	3	11.7	25 25	12.4	3	3	3	27 42	8	4
49	12.7	5.4	15 55	7	4.3	13.7	6.8	18 13	8.3	3	14.8	2	20 33	9	4	15.8	9.7	22 54	11.5	5	16.9	1	25 16	13.0	6	0	12.6	27 38	14.4	7
50	3	4.7	15 24	7.3	6	3	1	17 48	9	7	4	7.5	20 12	10.5	8	5	0	22 38	12.1	9	6	10.4	25 5	6	9.0	17.6	11.9	27 33	15.1	10.1
51	11.9	3.9	14 50	9	5.0	0	5.3	17 19	9.5	6.1	0	6.7	19 49	11.2	7.2	1	8.2	22 21	8	8.3	2	9.6	24 53	14.3	4	2	2	27 27	8	5
52	5	0	14 12	8.6	4	12.6	4.4	16 46	10.2	5	13.6	5.9	19 23	9	6	14.7	7.4	22 1	13.5	7	15.8	8.8	24 40	15.1	8	16.8	10.4	27 20	16.6	9
53	1	2.1	13 28	9.4	8	1	3.5	16 9	11.0	9	2	0	18 52	12.7	8.0	2	6.5	21 38	14.3	9.1	3	7.9	24 25	9	10.2	4	9.5	27 12	17.5	11.3
54	10.6	1.1	12 37	10.2	6.2	11.6	2.5	15 26	9	7.4	12.7	4.0	18 18	13.6	5	13.7	5.5	21 12	15.2	6	14.8	6.9	24 7	16.8	7	15.9	8.5	27 3	18.4	8
55	0	0.0	11 38	11.1	7	1	1.4	14 36	12.8	9	2	2.9	17 37	14.5	9.0	2	4.4	20 41	16.1	10.1	3	5.9	23 46	17.8	11.2	4	7.4	26 53	19.4	12.3
56	9.5	♑ 28.8	10 30	12.1	7.2	10.5	0.2	13 38	13.8	8.5	11.6	1.7	16 49	15.5	6	12.7	3.2	20 4	17.1	7	13.7	4.7	23 21	18.9	8	14.8	6.2	26 40	20.5	9

*Dalton's Table of Houses: Spherical Basis of Astrology, Macoy Publishing & Masonic Supply Company. Reproduced with permission of the publishers.

tarius on the cusp of the tenth house, we will fill in the cusp signs and their degrees in consecutive order around the wheel. To find these, consult Table 32.

The Eleventh House
Under "Lat." (Latitude = left side of page) you will find 34°N is the latitude of Los Angeles. Read across this line, beginning with the column for the cusp of the eleventh house ("H"), which is .7. As you glance up the column, you will notice right above that the governing degree figure — 17.9. Thus for 34°N we have 17.7'. The figure after the decimal point is multiplied by 6 to obtain the minutes. Here the result is 17°42'. (This is a simplified way of figuring seven-tenths of 1° or 60'.) In Table 32, the sign Capricorn appears under the eleventh house. (See Figure 36, where 17°42' is inserted under Capricorn.)

The Twelfth House
Looking up the cusp of the twelfth house in Table 30, we find 14.4°. Four is again multiplied by 6, giving us Aquarius 14° 24'. (See Figure 36.) Aquarius is found under the cusp of the twelfth house at the top of the column in the table.

The First House
The first house in *never* corrected. It is *copied exactly* as it appears. In this case, we find Pisces 21° 38' in Table 32. (See Figure 36.)

The Second House
The cusp of the second house is given in Table 32 as 2.4°. The 4 is again multiplied by 6, for a result of Taurus 2° 24'. If you cast your eye up the column for the second house in Table 30, you will notice there has been a sign change — from Aries to Taurus. This occurs in other columns, so always check. (See Figure 36.)

The Third House
The cusp of the third house is given as 1.5°. The 5 multiplied by 6 gives Gemini 1°30'. Notice, again, the sign change that occurs in the column. (See Figure 36.)

The remaining six house cusps are shown in Figure 37. Note that the six degree figures that are used are the same as those that appear in Figure 36 — but they are placed under opposing signs. For instance, for the cusp of the fourth house we used the same degree figure that appears for the cusp of the tenth house, and the sign it appears under is Gemini — the sign in opposition to Sagittarius.

How to Draw the Houses on the Chart
This same procedure is used for the remaining houses, and in Figure 37 the houses are marked and lines are drawn between them. The tenth–fourth house line is extra heavy and is extended beyond the wheel at the top and marked "M.C." (medium coeli or midheaven). The line for the first–seventh houses is also extra heavy and extends beyond the wheel at the left of the figure. It is marked "ASC." (ascendant). These heavy rules make it easier to identify the angular houses.

Notice that the cusps of the ninth and tenth houses are both ruled by the sign Sagittarius. A line is drawn between these cusps. A line is also drawn between the cusps of the third and fourth houses, which are both ruled by Gemini. The reason for this is so that you will not count the same sign twice when working with aspects.

In Figure 37 you can see that between the first house cusp of Pisces, 21°38', and the second house cusp of Taurus, 2°24', the entire 30° of the sign Aries is located, and it is in exact opposition to the entire 30° of the sign Libra. This situation is called an interception and occurs in certain latitudes at certain times of the day. Natal planets found in intercepted signs do not have full ability to express themselves until they move out by progression. In Figure 37 the sign of Aries is intercepted within the first house. Since the cusp of the first house is ruled by the sign Pisces, the planets that rule this sign — Neptune and Jupiter — have rulership over the entire house, which ends at the cusp of the second house of Taurus, 2°24'. So you can see how, depending on birth time and latitude, different signs may appear on the various house cusps.

Steps 1, 2, 3, 4 and 5 are *always* used to set up the wheel of a chart.

NAME   A, FEMALE   PHONE   118°W15'

ADDRESS   34°N03'

CITY   STATE   ZIP   +7^{m}00^s

BIRTH MONTH   NOV.   DAY   7   YEAR   1972   TIME   2:24   ST. T   +7^{H}53^{m}00^s
                                                               AM (PM)

                         BIRTH PLACE   LOS ANGELES, CA.

ANG. _____

SUCC. _____   C.L. _____

CAD. _____   ☽

R$_x$ _____

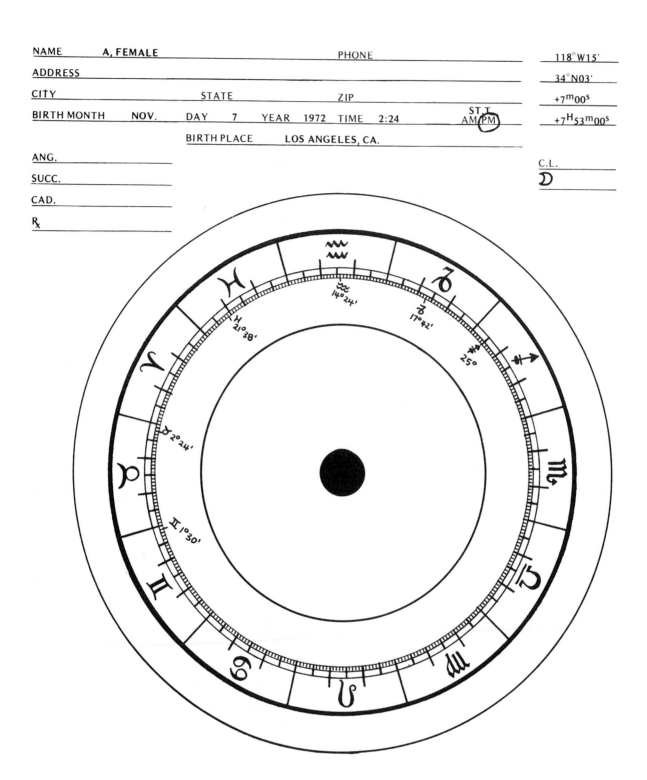

FIGURE 36

Sample birth chart with degrees and signs marked for the tenth, eleventh, twelfth, first, second and third houses.

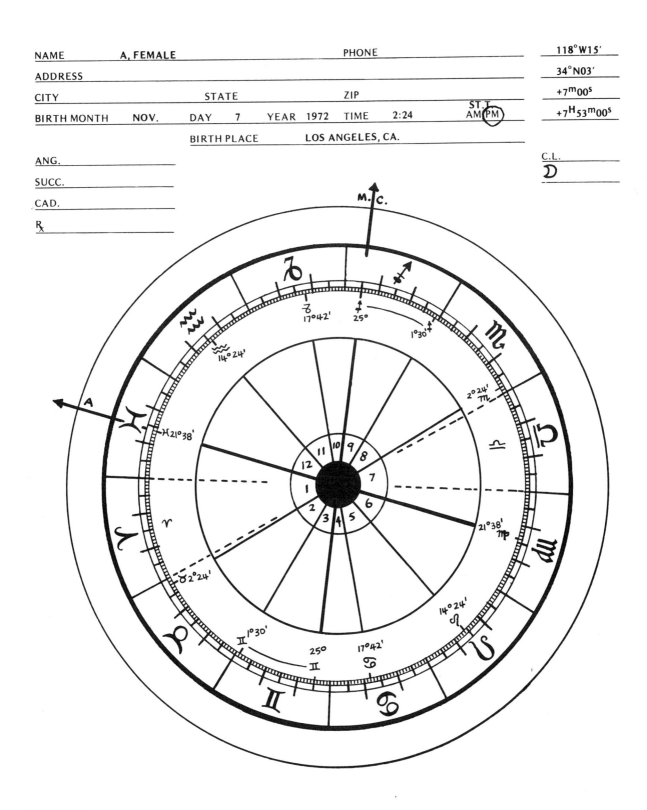

NAME   A, FEMALE   PHONE   118°W15'

ADDRESS   34°N03'

CITY   STATE   ZIP   +7^{m}00^s

BIRTH MONTH   NOV.   DAY   7   YEAR   1972   TIME   2:24   ST.T   AM (PM)   +7^{H}53^{m}00^s

BIRTH PLACE   LOS ANGELES, CA.

ANG.   C.L.

SUCC.   ☽

CAD.

R$_x$

FIGURE 37
Sample birth chart with degrees and signs marked for
all houses.

TABLE 33

PROPORTIONAL LOGARITHMS

Minutes	0	1	2	3	4	5	6	7	8	9	10	11	Minutes
	Hours and Degrees												
0	3.1584	1.3802	1.0792	9031	7781	6812	6021	5351	4771	4260	3802	3388	0
1	3.1584	1.3730	1.0756	9007	7763	6798	6009	5341	4762	4252	3795	3382	1
2	2.8573	1.3660	1.0720	8983	7745	6784	5997	5330	4753	4244	3788	3375	2
3	2.6812	1.3590	1.0685	8959	7728	6769	5985	5320	4744	4236	3780	3368	3
4	2.5563	1.3522	1.0649	8935	7710	6755	5973	5310	4735	4228	3773	3362	4
5	2.4594	1.3454	1.0614	8912	7692	6741	5961	5300	4726	4220	3766	3355	5
6	2.3802	1.3388	1.0580	8888	7674	6726	5949	5289	4717	4212	3759	3349	6
7	2.3133	1.3323	1.0546	8865	7657	6712	5937	5279	4708	4204	3752	3342	7
8	2.2553	1.3258	1.0511	8842	7639	6698	5925	5269	4699	4196	3745	3336	8
9	2.2041	1.3195	1.0478	8819	7622	6684	5913	5259	4690	4188	3738	3329	9
10	2.1584	1.3133	1.0444	8796	7604	6670	5902	5249	4682	4180	3730	3323	10
11	2.1170	1.3071	1.0411	8773	7587	6656	5890	5239	4673	4172	3723	3316	11
12	2.0792	1.3010	1.0378	8751	7570	6642	5878	5229	4664	4164	3716	3310	12
13	2.0444	1.2950	1.0345	8728	7552	6628	5866	5219	4655	4156	3709	3303	13
14	2.0122	1.2891	1.0313	8706	7535	6614	5855	5209	4646	4149	3702	3297	14
15	1.9823	1.2833	1.0280	8683	7518	6600	5843	5199	4638	4141	3695	3291	15
16	1.9542	1.2775	1.0248	8661	7501	6587	5832	5189	4629	4133	3688	3284	16
17	1.9279	1.2719	1.0216	8639	7484	6573	5820	5179	4620	4125	3681	3278	17
18	1.9031	1.2663	1.0185	8617	7467	6559	5809	5169	4611	4117	3674	3271	18
19	1.8796	1.2607	1.0153	8595	7451	6546	5797	5159	4603	4109	3667	3265	19
20	1.8573	1.2553	1.0122	8573	7434	6532	5786	5149	4594	4102	3660	3258	20
21	1.8361	1.2499	1.0091	8552	7417	6519	5774	5139	4585	4094	3653	3252	21
22	1.8159	1.2445	1.0061	8530	7401	6505	5763	5129	4577	4086	3646	3246	22
23	1.7966	1.2393	1.0030	8509	7384	6492	5752	5120	4568	4079	3639	3239	23
24	1.7781	1.2341	1.0000	8487	7368	6478	5740	5110	4559	4071	3632	3233	24
25	1.7604	1.2289	0.9970	8466	7351	6465	5729	5100	4551	4063	3625	3227	25
26	1.7434	1.2239	0.9940	8445	7335	6451	5718	5090	4542	4055	3618	3220	26
27	1.7270	1.2188	0.9910	8424	7318	6438	5706	5081	4534	4048	3611	3214	27
28	1.7112	1.2139	0.9881	8403	7302	6425	5692	5071	4525	4040	3604	3208	28
29	1.6969	1.2090	0.9852	8382	7286	6412	5684	5061	4516	4032	3597	3201	29
30	1.6812	1.2041	0.9823	8361	7270	6398	5673	5051	4508	4025	3590	3195	30
31	1.6670	1.1993	0.9794	8341	7254	6385	5662	5042	4499	4017	3583	3189	31
32	1.6532	1.1946	0.9765	8321	7238	6372	5651	5032	4491	4010	3577	3183	32
33	1.6398	1.1899	0.9737	8300	7222	6359	5640	5023	4482	4002	3570	3176	33
34	1.6269	1.1852	0.9708	8279	7206	6346	5629	5013	4474	3995	3563	3170	34
35	1.6143	1.1806	0.9680	8259	7190	6333	5618	5003	4466	3987	3556	3164	35
36	1.6021	1.1761	0.9652	8239	7174	6320	5607	4994	4457	3979	3549	3157	36
37	1.5902	1.1716	0.9625	8219	7159	6307	5596	4984	4449	3972	3542	3151	37
38	1.5786	1.1671	0.9597	8199	7143	6294	5585	4975	4440	3964	3535	3145	38
39	1.5673	1.1627	0.9570	8179	7128	6282	5574	4965	4432	3957	3529	3139	39
40	1.5563	1.1584	0.9542	8159	7112	6269	5563	4956	4424	3949	3522	3133	40
41	1.5456	1.1540	0.9515	8140	7097	6256	5552	4947	4415	3942	3515	3126	41
42	1.5351	1.1498	0.9488	8120	7081	6243	5541	4937	4407	3934	3508	3120	42
43	1.5249	1.1455	0.9462	8101	7066	6231	5531	4928	4399	3927	3501	3114	43
44	1.5149	1.1413	0.9435	8081	7050	6218	5520	4918	4390	3919	3495	3108	44
45	1.5051	1.1372	0.9409	8062	7035	6205	5509	4909	4382	3912	3488	3102	45
46	1.4956	1.1331	0.9383	8043	7020	6193	5498	4900	4374	3905	3481	3096	46
47	1.4863	1.1290	0.9356	8023	7005	6180	5488	4890	4365	3897	3475	3089	47
48	1.4771	1.1249	0.9330	8004	6990	6168	5477	4881	4357	3890	3468	3083	48
49	1.4682	1.1209	0.9305	7985	6975	6155	5466	4872	4349	3882	3461	3077	49
50	1.4594	1.1170	0.9279	7966	6960	6143	5456	4863	4341	3875	3455	3071	50
51	1.4508	1.1130	0.9254	7947	6945	6131	5445	4853	4333	3868	3448	3065	51
52	1.4424	1.1091	0.9228	7929	6930	6118	5435	4844	4324	3860	3441	3059	52
53	1.4341	1.1053	0.9203	7910	6915	6106	5424	4835	4316	3853	3435	3053	53
54	1.4260	1.1015	0.9178	7891	6900	6094	5414	4826	4308	3846	3428	3047	54
55	1.4180	1.0977	0.9153	7873	6885	6081	5403	4817	4300	3838	3421	3041	55
56	1.4102	1.0939	0.9128	7854	6871	6069	5393	4808	4292	3831	3415	3035	56
57	1.4025	1.0902	0.9104	7836	6856	6057	5382	4799	4284	3824	3408	3028	57
58	1.3949	1.0865	0.9079	7818	6841	6045	5372	4789	4276	3817	3401	3022	58
59	1.3875	1.0828	0.9055	7800	6827	6033	5361	4780	4268	3809	3395	3016	59

Minutes					Hours and Degrees								Minutes
	12	13	14	15	16	17	18	19	20	21	22	23	
0	3010	2663	2341	2041	1761	1498	1249	1015	0792	0580	0378	0185	0
1	3004	2657	2336	2036	1756	1493	1245	1011	0788	0577	0375	0182	1
2	2998	2652	2330	2032	1752	1489	1241	1007	0785	0573	0337	0179	2
3	2992	2646	2325	2027	1747	1485	1237	1003	0781	0570	0368	0175	3
4	2986	2641	2320	2022	1743	1481	1234	0999	0777	0566	0364	0172	4
5	2980	2635	2315	2017	1738	1476	1229	0996	0774	0563	0361	0169	5
6	2974	2629	2310	2012	1734	1472	1225	0992	0770	0559	0358	0166	6
7	2968	2624	2305	2008	1729	1468	1221	0988	0766	0556	0355	0163	7
8	2962	2618	2300	2003	1725	1464	1217	0984	0763	0552	0352	0160	8
9	2956	2613	2295	1998	1720	1460	1213	0980	0759	0549	0348	0157	9
10	2950	2607	2289	1993	1716	1455	1209	0977	0756	0546	0345	0153	10
11	2945	2602	2284	1989	1711	1451	1205	0973	0752	0542	0342	0150	11
12	2938	2596	2279	1984	1707	1447	1201	0969	0749	0539	0339	0147	12
13	2933	2591	2274	1979	1702	1443	1197	0965	0745	0535	0335	0144	13
14	2927	2585	2269	1974	1698	1438	1193	0962	0742	0532	0332	0141	14
15	2921	2580	2264	1969	1694	1434	1189	0958	0738	0529	0329	0138	15
16	2915	2575	2259	1965	1689	1430	1185	0954	0734	0525	0326	0135	16
17	2909	2569	2254	1960	1685	1426	1182	0950	0731	0522	0322	0132	17
18	2903	2564	2249	1955	1680	1422	1178	0947	0727	0518	0319	0129	18
19	2897	2558	2244	1950	1676	1417	1174	0943	0724	0515	0316	0125	19
20	2891	2553	2239	1946	1671	1413	1170	0939	0720	0511	0313	0122	20
21	2885	2547	2234	1941	1667	1409	1166	0935	0717	0508	0309	0119	21
22	2880	2542	2229	1936	1663	1405	1162	0932	0713	0505	0306	0116	22
23	2874	2536	2223	1932	1658	1401	1158	0928	0709	0501	0303	0113	23
24	2868	2531	2218	1927	1654	1397	1154	0924	0706	0498	0300	0110	24
25	2862	2526	2213	1922	1649	1393	1150	0920	0702	0495	0296	0107	25
26	2856	2520	2208	1917	1645	1388	1146	0917	0699	0491	0292	0104	26
27	2850	2515	2203	1913	1640	1384	1142	0913	0695	0488	0290	0101	27
28	2845	2509	2198	1908	1636	1380	1138	0909	0692	0485	0287	0098	28
29	2839	2504	2193	1903	1632	1376	1134	0905	0688	0481	0283	0094	29
30	2833	2499	2188	1899	1627	1372	1130	0902	0685	0478	0280	0091	30
31	2827	2493	2183	1894	1623	1368	1126	0898	0681	0474	0277	0088	31
32	2821	2488	2178	1890	1619	1363	1123	0894	0678	0471	0274	0085	32
33	2816	2483	2173	1885	1614	1359	1118	0891	0674	0468	0271	0082	33
34	2810	2477	2168	1880	1610	1355	1115	0887	0670	0464	0267	0079	34
35	2804	2472	2164	1875	1605	1351	1111	0883	0667	0461	0264	0076	35
36	2798	2467	2159	1871	1601	1347	1107	0880	0664	0458	0261	0073	36
37	2793	2461	2154	1866	1597	1343	1103	0876	0660	0454	0258	0070	37
38	2787	2456	2149	1862	1592	1339	1099	0872	0656	0451	0255	0067	38
39	2781	2451	2144	1857	1588	1335	1095	0868	0653	0448	0251	0064	39
40	2775	2445	2139	1852	1584	1331	1092	0865	0649	0444	0248	0061	40
41	2770	2440	2134	1848	1579	1327	1088	0861	0646	0441	0245	0058	41
42	2764	2435	2129	1843	1575	1322	1084	0857	0642	0437	0242	0055	42
43	2758	2430	2124	1838	1571	1318	1080	0854	0639	0434	0239	0052	43
44	2753	2424	2119	1834	1566	1314	1076	0850	0635	0431	0235	0048	44
45	2747	2419	2114	1829	1562	1310	1072	0846	0632	0428	0232	0045	45
46	2741	2414	2109	1825	1558	1306	1068	0843	0629	0424	0229	0042	46
47	2736	2409	2104	1820	1553	1302	1064	0839	0625	0421	0226	0039	47
48	2730	2403	2099	1816	1549	1298	1061	0835	0621	0418	0223	0036	48
49	2724	2398	2095	1811	1545	1294	1057	0832	0618	0414	0220	0033	49
50	2719	2393	2090	1806	1540	1290	1053	0828	0614	0411	0216	0030	50
51	2713	2388	2085	1802	1536	1286	1049	0824	0611	0408	0213	0027	51
52	2707	2382	2080	1797	1532	1282	1045	0821	0608	0404	0210	0024	52
53	2702	2377	2075	1793	1528	1278	1041	0817	0604	0401	0207	0021	53
54	2696	2372	2070	1788	1523	1274	1037	0814	0601	0398	0204	0018	54
55	2691	2367	2065	1784	1519	1270	1034	0810	0597	0394	0201	0015	55
56	2685	2362	2061	1779	1515	1266	1030	0806	0594	0391	0197	0012	56
57	2679	2356	2056	1774	1510	1261	1026	0803	0590	0388	0194	0009	57
58	2674	2351	2051	1770	1506	1257	1022	0799	0587	0384	0191	0006	58
59	2668	2346	2046	1765	1502	1253	1018	0795	0583	0381	0188	0003	59

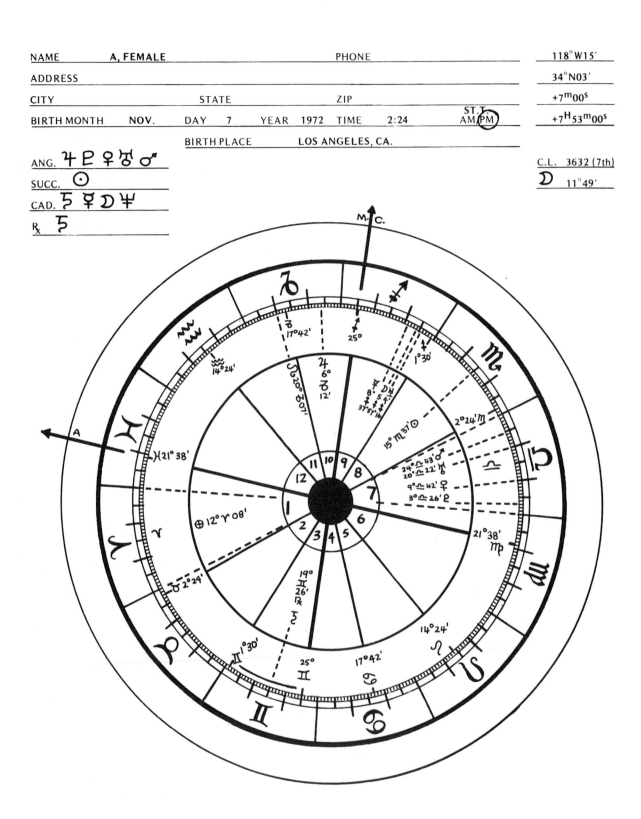

FIGURE 38
Completed sample birth chart.

The Position of the Planets

The next step involves filling in the *exact* position of the planets for the birth time and place. Refer back to Table 29. Notice that in Step 6 once again the True Local Time is recorded — 2 hours, 31 minutes, 26 seconds. To this is added the E.G.M.T. (Equivalent Greenwich Mean Time) of 7 hours, 53 minutes, 00 seconds, which is found in a longitude and latitude book. This gives a total of 9 hours, 84 minutes, 26 seconds — or 10 hours, 24 minutes, 26 seconds. This final result is marked G.M.T. (Greenwich Mean Time) (Step 7).

Note: 1 day cannot have more than 24 hours.
   1 hour cannot have more than 60 minutes.
   1 minute cannot have more than 60 seconds.
   1 astrological sign cannot have more than 30°.
   1° cannot have more than 60'.

Next look at Table 33, Proportional Logarithms. At the top, horizontally, are the numbers 0 through 23, which are used for *both* hours and degree interpretation. The extreme vertical columns on either side contain the numbers used for minute interpretation. Our example reads 10 hours, 24 minutes, 26 seconds. Drop the seconds since there are less than 30. (If there were more than 30 seconds, you would round off the figure to the next minute.) For 10 hours and 24 minutes the log number reads .3632. This number is inserted on Table 29 as the C.L. (Constant Log) figure. This is the figure used to correct the position of every planet in the chart.

The Sun

Under "C.L. (Constant Log)" in Table 29 the longitude for the Sun on November 7, 1972, is given as 15° Scorpio 11'. (The actual longitude is 15° Scorpio 10' 52" — obtained from Table 37 — but the figure was rounded off.) For the next day, November 8, the longitude of the Sun is shown as 16° Scorpio 11'. (Again, the actual figure — obtained from Table 37 — is 16° 11' 08' — was rounded off.) This shows that the Sun's

movement in a 24-hour period was exactly 60', or 1°. In this example case the difference is very easy to see. However, you must become used to figuring *forward* from a lesser degree and minute to a greater degree and minute so that you do not make mistakes. Look at Table 29. By adding 49' to the 15° Scorpio 11', we get a total of an even 16°. Since our next highest figure for the Sun reads 16° 11', the 11' were added to the 49' for a total movement of 60' or 1° for a 24-hour period.

The longarithm figure for the Sun's total movement in 24 hours is found in Table 33 under 1° — 1.3802. To this figure is added the C.L. (Constant Logarithm) for the Sun's movement in 10 hours and 24 minutes — .3632. This gives a total of 1.7434, which must be reconverted. In the vertical 0° column in Table 33 you will find this figure next to 26'. These 26' are added to the Sun's position on the 7th. The result shows us that the Sun was in 15° Scorpio 37' at the time of the native's birth, and this is inserted into the birth chart (Figure 38).

Neptune

We will leave the Moon's correction until last and continue instead with the longitude of Neptune. (All longitudes are found in Table 37 in Appendix B.) Neptune on the 7th is 4° Sagittarius 15', and on the 8th, 4° Sagittarius 18'. This gives a difference of 3' in a 24-hour period, and, in Table 33, a logarithm of 2.6812. When added to C.L., .3632, the total is 3.0444. In Table 33 the *nearest* figure to this total is 3.1584, which appears next to 1'. This 1' added to the position of Neptune on the 7th gives a total of 4° Sagittarius 16', which is inserted as Neptune's position on Figure 38.

Uranus

The longitude of Uranus on the 7th is 20° Libra 20', and on the 8th, 20° Libra 24', which gives a difference of 4' in a 24-hour period. The logarithm for 4' is 2.5563 (Table 33), and to this is added the C.L. of .3632, which gives a total of 2.9195. The *nearest* figure to this total in Table 33 is 2.8573, which appears next to 2'. These 2' added to the position of Uranus on the 7th gives a total of 20° Libra 22' which is inserted as Uranus's position on Figure 38.

Saturn

The longitude of Saturn on the 7th was 19° Gemini 28′ *retrograde*. If you cast your eye up the column for Saturn in Table 37, you will see the retrograde symbol (℞).

The term *retrograde* denotes a planet's apparent backward motion in the zodiac and its decrease in longitude as viewed from the earth. Retrograde motion has no correspondence to the actual speed of the planet, but rather to the change in its relationship to the earth. When a planet is retrograde, the dates as they appear in the ephemeris are always *reversed* to obtain the difference between the two days in question. Thus Saturn, which on the 7th was 19° Gemini 28′, and on the 8th, 19° Gemini 24′, shows a difference of 4′ retrogression. Again, convert the 4′ (Table 33), add the C.L. and reconvert the total figure into minutes. In this case the figure is 2′. Since Saturn is retrograde, these 2′ have to be *deducted* from Saturn on the 7th, which leaves a total of 19° Gemini 26′ retrograde for the position of Saturn. This is inserted as Saturn's position on Figure 38.

Any planet that is retrograde in a birth chart shows introversion or introspection. It gives the native more depth than is apparent on the surface. The house that a retrograde planet is in and the house that this planet rules become important because they show that the native has the power to reconcile and reconstruct matters and people ruled by the houses in question.

Jupiter

The longitude of Jupiter on the 7th is 6° Capricorn 07′, and on the 8th, 6° Capricorn 18′, which gives a difference of 11′ between the two days. Note the math in Table 29. The final position of Jupiter is 6° Capricorn 12′, which is inserted on Figure 38.

Mars

The longitude of Mars on the 7th is 24° Libra 26′ and on the 8th 25° Libra 06′ which gives a difference of 40 minutes. Again look at the math work.

The final position for Mars is 24° Libra 43′, which is inserted on Figure 38.

Venus

The longitude of Venus on the 7th is 9° Libra 10′ and on the 8th 10° Libra 22′ which gives a difference of 1°12′. Again look at the math work. The final position for Venus is 9° Libra 42′, which is inserted on Figure 38.

Mercury

The longitude of Mercury on the 7th is 8° Sagittarius 15′ and on the 8th 9° Sagittarius 06′ which gives a difference of 51′. Again look at the math work. The final position for Mercury is 8° Sagittarius 37′ which is inserted on Figure 38.

The Moon

Now let's go back to the Moon. The longitude of the Moon on the 7th is 0° Sagittarius 50′, and on the 8th, 12° Sagittarius 39′, which gives a total difference between the two days of 11°49′. Look at the math work in Table 29. Remember, you must always add so that you do not make a mistake. If 10′ are added to the 0° Sagittarius 50′, the result is an even 1° Sagittarius. If another 11° are added, the result is an even 12° Sagittarius. Add another 39′ and the result is 12° Sagittarius 39′ — which is the position of the Moon on the 8th. This math shows that the total movement in 24 hours was 11°49′. Using Table 33 to convert the figure — the conversion figure, .3077 — is found where the 11 hour or degree column intersects with the 49′ column. As usual, add the C.L. of .3632; the total is .6709. The closest figure in Table 33 is .6712. Thus the reconverted figure is equivalent to 5°07′ — the total movement of the Moon for 10 hours, 34 minutes. The 5°07′ are added to the position of the Moon on the 7th, giving a total of 5° Sagittarius 57′ as the Moon's position, which is inserted on Figure 38.

Pluto

Pluto's longitude for the entire year is always given on a separate page in an ephemeris and is listed approximately two to three times per month because the planet moves very slowly. In Table 38 in Appendix B the longitude of Pluto on November 6 is 3° Libra 25', and ten days later, on November 16, Pluto's position is 3° Libra 42' — which means a ten-day difference of 17'. This shows that Pluto moves approximately 1' to 2' per day. We are looking for the position of Pluto on the 7th, so we mentally add 1' to its position on the 6th, which gives 3° Libra 26'. This is inserted on Figure 38.

Declination

Pluto
To obtain the declination of the planets, we will start with Pluto. Since Pluto moves so slowly, we have inserted the declination position on November 6 (found in Table 38) — 13°N18' — in Table 29.

Neptune, Uranus, Saturn and Jupiter
Neptune, Uranus, Saturn and Jupiter are also very slow-moving planets. In Table 37 Neptune is given on the 7th as 19°S27', Uranus as 7°S23', Saturn as 21°N22' and Jupiter as 23°S24'. (Notice that the declinations are always given at two-day intervals.) The figures for these four planets are inserted in Table 29. They are the closest to the birth date in question.

Mars
For Mars, a correction is necessary. The math work is very similar to that done for the planets. Remember, the C.L. is .3632. Look at Figure 46 in Appendix B. Mars on the 7th is 8°S48', and on the 9th, two days later, is 9°S18', which gives a difference of 30' for two days. As we need to know the movement for one day, we have to divide the 30' in half; the result is 15' for one day. This is converted into the log. figure of 1.9823, to which the C.L. is added. The total is reconverted, and the closest figure, 7', is added to the position of Mars on the 7th. The position for Mars now is 8°S55' and is inserted on Figure 38.

Follow the same procedure for Venus and Mercury, the Sun and the Moon.

Finishing the Chart

Note that the north node of the Moon appears in the eleventh house and the part of fortune in the first house in Figure 38. How to arrive at the positions for these is discussed in Chapters 15 and 16.

The only thing that remains to be finished is the recording of the angular, succedent, cadent and retrograde planets. The tenth house, an angular house, shows Jupiter. The seventh house, another angular house, shows Pluto, Venus, Uranus and Mars. In succedent houses there is only one planet — the Sun. The cadent houses show Saturn in the third house, and Mercury, the Moon and Neptune in the ninth house. Saturn is the only retrograde planet. These are recorded in the lower left-hand corner of Figure 38.

On the lower right-hand side of Figure 38 the planets are recorded as they appear in cardinal, fixed, and mutable *qualities*, in the correct fire, earth, air or water *element*.

The position of the solstice points for Figure 38 is given in Table 34.

TABLE 34

POSITION OF THE SOLSTICE POINTS FOR FIG. 38

Natal Position			Solstice Point			Opposition of Solstice Point		
Asc.	21° ♊	38'		8° ♎	22'		8° ♈	22'
♄	19° ♊	26'		10° ♋	34'		10° ♑	34'
♇	3° ♎	26'		26° ♊	34'		26° ♏	34'
♀	9° ♎	42'		20° ♊	18'		20° ♏	18'
♅	20° ♎	22'		9° ♊	38'		9° ♏	38'
♂	24° ♎	43'		5° ♊	17'		5° ♏	17'
☉	15° ♏	37'		14° ♒	23'		15° ♌	23'
♆	4° ♐	16'		25° ♑	44'		25° ♋	44'
☽	5° ♐	57'		24° ♑	03'		24° ♋	03'
☿	8° ♐	37'		21° ♑	23'		21° ♋	23'
MC	25° ♐	00'		5° ♑	00'		5° ♋	00'
♃	6° ♑	12'		23° ♐	48'		23° ♊	48'

Practice Math

In Table 35 I have given two math examples which I strongly advise you to do for practice.

Mercury on the 28th is in 0° Sagittarius 57' retrograde. The C.L. is 116. The position of Mercury has to be reversed because the planet is retrograde, and the reconverted final figure has to be deducted from the position of Mercury on the 28th. When you look at the math work, you will realize that it is impossible to deduct the reconverted figure of 59' from the position of Mercury in 0° Sagittarius 57'. The solution is to borrow all 30° of the sign previous to Sagittarius, which is Scorpio. To this is added 0° Sagittarius 57', giving a total of 30°57'. When 1°09' is deducted from this figure, the result shows the position of Mercury for 23 hours, 22 minutes as 29° Scorpio 48'.

The longitude of the Moon on the 22nd uses a C.L. of .1532. The Moon on the 22nd appears in 22° Gemini 10', and on the 23rd in 7° Cancer 05', which gives a difference of 14°55'. Look at the math work in Table 35. On the 22nd the Moon appears in 22° Gemini 10'. By adding 50', the figure of the Moon is rounded off to 23°00'. The addition of another 7° completed the sign of Gemini and brings us to 0° Cancer 00'. This, added to the remaining 7° Cancer 05', gives a total movement in 24 hours of 14°55'. Table 33 is used to convert this figure. The C.L. — .1532 — is added to the log. Then the total is reconverted and added to the position on the 22nd. When this figure is added, the result is 32°39', and as a sign can only contain 30° it shows that the sign Gemini is finished and we are 2°39' into the sign of Cancer for the position of the Moon for 16 hours, 52 minutes.

I suggest that you review setting up of the chart several times — perhaps once a day for two weeks. Then work with different charts, always utilizing a P.M. birth. *Do not* go on Appendix B until you have mastered the P.M. birth charts.

TABLE 35

PRACTICE MATH INVOLVING MERCURY AND THE MOON

23h22m = C.L. (Constant Log) 116

☿ on 28th = 0° ♎ 57′ ℞

= difference 61′ = 1° 01′

☿ on 29th = 29° ♏ 46′ ℞

(29th)   29° ♏ 46′

    +   14′ ⟶ 14′

    00° ♎ 00′ ⟶ +57′

    +   57′ ⟶ 71′ = 1° 11′ (Total movement in 24 hours)

(28)   00° ♎ 57′

1.3071 (Log. for 1° 11′)

+   116 (C.L.)

1.3187 This total reconverted = 1°09′

☿ on 28th 0° ♎ 57′

    −1°   09′ = 30° ♏ 00′

    + 0° ♎ 57′

    30°   57′

    − 1°   9′

    29° ♏ 48′ = ☿ Position for 23h22m

16h52m = C.L. (Constant Log) .1532

☽ on 22nd = 22° ♊ 10′

= difference 14° 55′

☽ on 23rd = 7° ♋ 05′

(22nd)   22° ♊ 10′

    +   50′ ⟶ 50′

    23° ♊ 00′ ⟶ + 7°

    + 7°   00′ ⟶ + 7° 05′

    00° ♋ 00′ ⟶ 14° 55′ = (Total movement in 24 hours)

    + 7° ♋ 05′

(23rd)   7° ♋ 05′

.2065 (Log. for 14° 55′)

+.1532 (C.L.)

.3597 This total reconverted = 10° 29′

☽ on 22nd = 22° ♊ 10′

    +10°   29′

    32°   39′ = 2° ♋ 39′ ☽ Position for 16h52m

B

Special Charts

How to Set Up a Birth Chart with a Noon Ephemeris if Birth Occurred before Noon with Planetary Correction between Seventh and Eighth Day

Let's assume that a male is born on November 7, 1972, at 8:45 A.M., in Los Angeles, California. Look at Table 36 for the math work. It is the same as the math work for the sample chart in Appendix A, except: there is an additional step —1A — where 12 hours are added because all figuring in a noon ephemeris (Tables 37 and 38) must start at 12 noon and in this case the birth took place before noon on the 7th. The procedure is to count forward from November 6, noontime to midnight, which gives 12 hours plus the birth time of 8 hours, 45 minutes. Together these figures give a total of 20 hours, 45 minutes, 00 seconds.

The Sidereal Time (Step 4) also had to be taken from the 6th because the birth occurred before noon on the 7th. The total after Step 4 reads 35 hours, 58 minutes, 40 seconds. However, since the earth rotates on its axis once in approximately 24 hours, there has to be an extra step here — Step 4A — the circle of 24 hours, which is *deducted*. The total reads 11 hours, 58 minutes, 40 seconds.

The total result after Step 5 (Final Calculated Sidereal Time), is 11 hours, 59 minutes, 59 seconds. See how the chart is set up in Figure 39.

On the cusp of the tenth house is 0° Libra. Look down the latitude column in your Table of Houses, and where the tenth house of 0° Libra and 34° latitude intersect, you will find that the eleventh house cusp has 29°30' Libra; the cusp of the twelfth house has 23°16' Scorpio; the cusp of the first house has 14°59' Sagittarius; the cusp of the second house has 17°59' Capricorn; and the cusp of the third house has 24°42' Aquarius. (See

TABLE 36

MATH WORK FOR FIGURES 39 AND 40

I. Birth Data

B. Male

November 7, 1972 — 8:42 A.M. ST.T. (Standard Time) — Los Angeles, Ca.

	Longitude	Latitude	L.M.T.	E.G.M.T.
	118°W15′	34°N03′	+7m00s	+7h53m00s

Steps:

		Hours	Minutes	Seconds
1.	Clock Time at A.M. Birth	08	45	00 ST.T.
1A.	+12 Hours, as all timing starts at 12 noon the previous day	+12	00	00
		20	45	00
		+	7	00
2.	Local *Mean* Time Variation	20	52	00
3.	10-Second Interval Correction	+	3	29
	True Local Time =	20	55	29
4.	Sidereal Time of the 6th, as birth occurred *before* 12 noon	+15	03	12
		35	58	41
4A.	Minus the Circle of 24 hours	−24	00	00
		11	58	41
5.	Longitudinal Correction (Formula: Multiply by 2, divide result by 3. Always *add* result when birthplace was *west of Greenwhich; deduct* result when birthplace was *east of Greenwich.*	+	1	19
	The Final Calculated Sidereal Time =	11	59	00

II. House Cusps

		Hours	Minutes	Seconds
Step: 6.	*True* Local Time	20	52	00
Step: 7.	Equivalent *Greenwich* Mean Time	+ 7	53	00
		27	105	00 =
		28	45	00
		−24	00	00
	Greenwich *Mean* Time on 7th =	4	45	00

= C.L. .7035

C.L. (Constant Log.) for 4h45m = .7035 (for planetary correction between 7th and 8th)

TABLE 37

RAPHAEL'S EPHEMERIS, November, 1972*

New Moon—November 6d. 1h. 22m. a.m.

22   **NOVEMBER, 1972**   [*RAPHAEL'S*

D M	Neptune Lat.	Neptune Dec.	Herschel Lat.	Herschel Dec.	Saturn Lat.	Saturn Dec.	Jupiter Lat.	Jupiter Dec.	Mars Lat.	Mars Dec.	Mars Dec.
1	1 N 35	19 S 24	0 N 36	7 S 15	1 S 40	21 N 23	0 S 5	23 S 26	0 N 46	7 S 18	7 S 33
3	1 35	19 25	0 36	7 18	1 40	21 23	0 5	23 25	0 45	7 48	8 3
5	1 35	19 26	0 36	7 21	1 40	21 22	0 5	23 24	0 44	8 18	8 33
7	1 35	19 27	0 36	7 23	1 40	21 22	0 6	23 24	0 44	8 48	9 3
9	1 35	19 28	0 36	7 26	1 40	21 21	0 6	23 23	0 43	9 18	9 32
11	1 35	19 29	0 36	7 29	1 40	21 20	0 6	23 22	0 42	9 47	10 1
13	1 35	19 29	0 36	7 31	1 40	21 20	0 6	23 21	0 41	10 16	10 30
15	1 35	19 30	0 36	7 34	1 40	21 19	0 6	23 20	0 40	10 45	10 59
17	1 34	19 31	0 36	7 36	1 40	21 18	0 6	23 18	0 39	11 13	11 28
19	1 34	19 32	0 36	7 39	1 40	21 18	0 7	23 17	0 39	11 42	11 56
21	1 34	19 33	0 36	7 41	1 40	21 17	0 7	23 16	0 38	12 10	12 23
23	1 34	19 34	0 36	7 43	1 40	21 16	0 7	23 14	0 37	12 37	12 51
25	1 34	19 34	0 36	7 46	1 40	21 15	0 7	23 13	0 36	13 4	13 18
27	1 34	19 35	0 36	7 48	1 40	21 15	0 7	23 11	0 35	13 31	13 S 45
29	1 34	19 36	0 36	7 50	1 40	21 14	0 7	23 9	0 34	13 58	—
30	1 N 34	19 S 36	0 N 36	7 S 51	1 S 40	21 N 13	0 S 8	23 S 8	0 N 33	14 S 11	

D M	D W	Sidereal Time H. M. S.	☉ Long.	☉ Dec.	☽ Long.	☽ Lat.	☽ Dec.	MIDNIGHT ☽ Long.	☽ Dec.
1	W	14 43 29	9 ♏ 9 51	14 S 33	18 ♍ 24 46	4 S 18	0 N 37	24 ♍ 37 21	2 S 3
2	Th	14 47 26	10 9 57	14 52	0 ♎ 47 20	4 46	4 S 41	6 ♎ 54 59	7 15
3	F	14 51 22	11 10 4	15 11	13 0 31	5 0	9 44	19 4 11	12 7
4	S	14 55 19	12 10 13	15 30	25 6 7	5 0	14 22	1 ♏ 6 31	16 28
5	☉	14 59 15	13 10 24	15 48	7 ♏ 5 31	4 47	18 24	13 3 17	20 9
6	M	15 3 12	14 10 37	16 6	18 59 57	4 22	21 40	24 55 42	22 58
7	Tu	15 7 8	15 10 52	16 24	0 ♐ 50 44	3 45	24 0	6 ♐ 45 15	24 47
8	W	15 11 5	16 11 8	16 41	12 39 30	2 59	25 16	18 33 48	25 29
9	Th	15 15 1	17 11 27	16 58	24 28 29	2 4	25 24	0 ♑ 23 56	25 1
10	F	15 18 58	18 11 46	17 15	6 ♑ 20 34	1 4	24 22	12 18 52	23 25
11	S	15 22 55	19 12 8	17 32	18 19 22	0 S 1	22 12	24 22 35	20 43
12	☉	15 26 51	20 12 30	17 48	0 ♒ 29 9	1 N 4	19 0	6 ♒ 39 38	17 3
13	M	15 30 48	21 12 54	18 4	12 54 41	2 7	14 54	19 14 55	12 33
14	Tu	15 34 44	22 13 20	18 20	25 40 55	3 6	10 2	2 ♓ 13 13	7 22
15	W	15 38 41	23 13 46	18 35	8 ♓ 52 20	3 57	4 S 35	15 38 38	1 S 41
16	Th	15 42 37	24 14 14	18 50	22 32 21	4 36	1 N 16	29 33 37	4 N 16
17	F	15 46 34	25 14 44	19 5	6 ♈ 42 19	5 1	7 16	13 ♈ 58 9	10 12
18	S	15 50 30	26 15 14	19 19	21 20 36	5 6	13 3	28 48 52	15 45
19	☉	15 54 27	27 15 46	19 33	6 ♉ 22 1	4 51	18 13	13 ♉ 58 50	20 26
20	M	15 58 24	28 16 20	19 47	21 38 1	4 16	22 17	29 18 9	23 45
21	Tu	16 2 20	29 ♏ 16 55	20 0	6 ♊ 57 48	3 21	24 47	14 ♊ 35 34	25 21
22	W	16 6 17	0 ♐ 17 31	20 13	22 10 9	2 13	25 26	29 40 26	25 2
23	Th	16 10 13	1 18 10	20 25	7 ♋ 5 26	0 N 57	24 12	14 ♋ 24 27	22 47
24	F	16 14 10	2 18 49	20 38	21 36 56	0 S 21	21 21	28 42 35	19 27
25	S	16 18 6	3 19 30	20 49	5 ♌ 41 16	1 36	17 18	12 ♌ 33 3	14 57
26	☉	16 22 3	4 20 13	21 1	19 18 6	2 43	12 27	25 56 43	9 51
27	M	16 26 0	5 20 57	21 12	2 ♍ 29 17	3 39	7 11	8 ♍ 56 15	4 N 28
28	Tu	16 29 56	6 21 43	21 22	15 18 6	4 22	1 N 45	21 35 20	0 S 56
29	W	16 33 53	7 22 31	21 33	27 48 27	4 52	3 S 36	3 ♎ 57 58	6 11
30	Th	16 37 49	8 ♐ 23 20	21 S 42	10 ♎ 4 20	5 S 7	8 S 42	16 ♎ 8 1	11 S 7

First Quarter—November 14d. 5h. 1m. a.m.

*© W. Foulsham & Co. Ltd., England. Reproduced with permission of the publishers.
† Uranus.

Full Moon—November 20*d.* 11*h.* 7*m.* *p.m.*

D M	Venus Lat. ° ′	Venus Dec. ° ′	Venus Dec. ° ′	Mercury Lat. ° ′	Mercury Dec. ° ′	Mercury Dec. ° ′	☽ Node ° ′
1	1N 33	0N 39	0N 12	2 S 41	23 S 12	23 S 28	20♑27
3	1 36	0 S 15	0 S 42	2 46	23 43	23 56	20 21
5	1 39	1 9	1 37	2 47	24 8	24 18	20 14
7	1 42	2 4	2 31	2 47	24 26	24 33	20 8
9	1 44	2 59	3 26	2 44	24 38	24 41	20 2
11	1 46	3 54	4 21	2 36	24 42	24 41	19 55
13	1 48	4 48	5 16	2 24	24 38	24 32	19 49
15	1 49	5 43	6 10	2 7	24 24	24 13	19 43
17	1 50	6 37	7 4	1 45	24 0	23 43	19 36
19	1 51	7 31	7 58	1 16	23 24	23 1	19 30
21	1 51	8 24	8 51	0 41	22 36	22 7	19 24
23	1 51	9 17	9 43	0 S 2	21 36	21 3	19 17
25	1 50	10 9	10 35	0N 39	20 29	19 54	19 11
27	1 50	11 1	11 S 26	1 18	19 20	18 S 48	19 4
29	1 48	11 51		1 51	18 18		18 58
30	1N 48	12 S 16	—	2N 5	17 S 51	—	18♑55

Mutual Aspects

1. ☉⊥♇. ♂P♅.
2. ☿✱♀, P♃, ✱♇. ♂☌♇.
3. ☿☌♆. ♀✱♆.
4. ☿⚺♃, ∠♅. ♀□♃.
5. ☉±♄. 6. ♂Q♃.
7. ☉⊥♀. 10. ☉∠♇.
11. ☉∇♄. 12. ☉⚺♅.
13. ♂⊥♆. 14. ☉∠♃.
15. ☿ Stat. ♀△♄.
16. ♀∠♆. 17. ♀☌♅.
19. ☉⊥♅, P♆. ☿P♃. ♀P♅.
20. ☿∠♀.
21. ☿⊥♂. ♂⚼♄, ⚺♇.
22. ☿⚺♃. ♀Q♃.
23. ♀⊥♆. ♂⚺♆.
24. ☿⊥♀, ⚺♂, P♄, ∠♅.
25. ☉P☿, ⊥♃. ☿☌♆.
26. ☉☌☿, ✱♇. ☿⚺♀, ⊥♃, [✱♇. ♂P♇.
27. ☉P♄, ☌♆. ☿P♆. ♀⚼ [♄, ⚺♇.
28. ☉∠♅. ♀⚺♆.

D M	♆ Long. ° ′	♅ Long. ° ′	♄ Long. ° ′	♃ Long. ° ′	♂ Long. ° ′	♀ Long. ° ′	☿ Long. ° ′	☉	♇	♆	♅	♄	♃	♂	♀	☿
1	4♐ 3	19♎59	19♊48	5♑ 3	20♎30	1♎55	2♐ 1				⚺	□		⚺		
2	4 5	20 3	19 ℞45	5 13	21 9	3 7	3 9	∠	☌	✱			□		☌	✱
3	4 7	20 6	19 42	5 24	21 49	4 20	4 16	⚺								
4	4 9	20 10	19 38	5 34	22 28	5 32	5 20			∠	☌	△		☌		∠
5	4 11	20 13	19 35	5 45	23 8	6 44	6 22		⚺	⚺		⚼	✱		⚺	⚺
6	4 13	20 17	19 31	5 56	23 47	7 57	7 20	☌	∠		⚺		∠	⚺	∠	
7	4 15	20 20	19 28	6 7	24 26	9 10	8 15		✱	☌	∠		⚺			
8	4 18	20 24	19 24	6 18	25 6	10 22	9 6	⚺						∠	✱	☌
9	4 20	20 28	19 20	6 30	25 45	11 35	9 52				✱	☍		✱		
10	4 22	20 31	19 17	6 41	26 25	12 48	10 34	∠	□	⚺			☌			⚺
11	4 24	20 34	19 13	6 52	27 4	14 1	11 10	✱		∠	□				□	
12	4 26	20 38	19 9	7 4	27 44	15 14	11 40		△	✱		⚼		□		∠
13	4 28	20 41	19 5	7 15	28 24	16 27	12 3		⚼			△	⚺		△	✱
14	4 31	20 45	19 1	7 27	29 3	17 40	12 19	□			△		∠	△		
15	4 33	20 48	18 56	7 39	29♎43	18 54	12 27			□	⚼		✱	⚼	⚼	□
16	4 35	20 51	18 52	7 51	0♏23	20 7	12 ℞25	△				□				
17	4 37	20 55	18 48	8 3	1 2	21 20	12 14	⚼	☍	△			□			△
18	4 40	20 58	18 44	8 15	1 42	22 34	11 53			⚼	☍	✱			☍	⚼
19	4 42	21 1	18 39	8 27	2 22	23 47	11 22					∠	△	☍		
20	4 44	21 4	18 35	8 39	3 2	25 1	10 39	☍	⚼			⚺	⚼			
21	4 46	21 8	18 30	8 51	3 41	26 14	9 47		△	☍	⚼				⚼	☍
22	4 49	21 11	18 26	9 3	4 21	27 28	8 45				△	☌		⚼	△	
23	4 51	21 14	18 21	9 15	5 1	28 42	7 35		□				☍	△		
24	4 53	21 17	18 17	9 28	5 41	29♎56	6 18	⚼		⚼	□	⚺				⚼
25	4 55	21 20	18 12	9 40	6 21	0♏10	4 58	△	✱	△		∠		□	□	△
26	4 58	21 23	18 7	9 53	7 1	2 23	3 35		∠		✱	✱	⚼			
27	5 0	21 26	18 3	10 6	7 41	3 37	2 14	□	⚺	□	∠			✱	✱	□
28	5 2	21 29	17 58	10 18	8 21	4 51	0♐57				⚺	□	△		∠	
29	5 4	21 32	17 53	10 31	9 1	6 5	29♏46							∠		✱
30	5♐ 7	21♎35	17♊48	10♑44	9♏41	7♏20	28♏44	✱	☌	✱			□	⚺	⚺	∠

Last Quarter—November 27*d.* 5*h.* 45*m.* *p.m.*

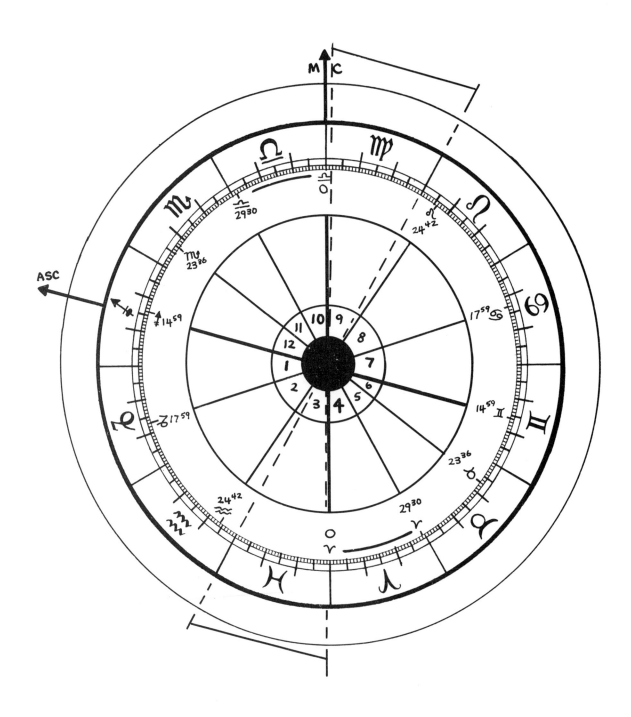

FIGURE 39
Sample birth chart (B, male) with degrees and signs
marked.

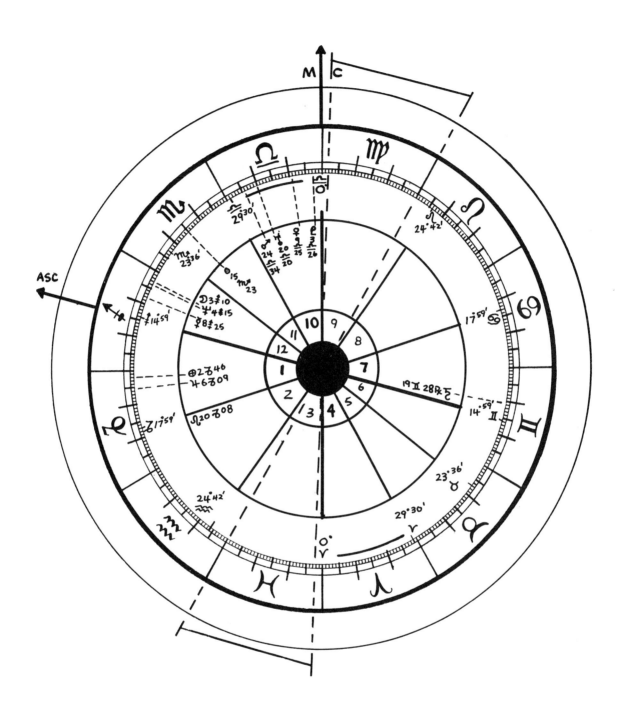

FIGURE 40
Completed sample birth chart (B, male).

NAME   C, FEMALE   PHONE   118°W15'

ADDRESS   34°N03'

CITY   STATE   ZIP   +7ᵐ00ˢ

BIRTH MONTH   NOV.   DAY   7   YEAR 1972   TIME   1:42   ST.T.   +7ᴴ53ᵐ00ˢ
                                                              AM/PM

                       BIRTH PLACE   LOS ANGELES, CA.

ANG.   C.L. 431 (6th)

SUCC.   ☽

CAD.

Rₓ

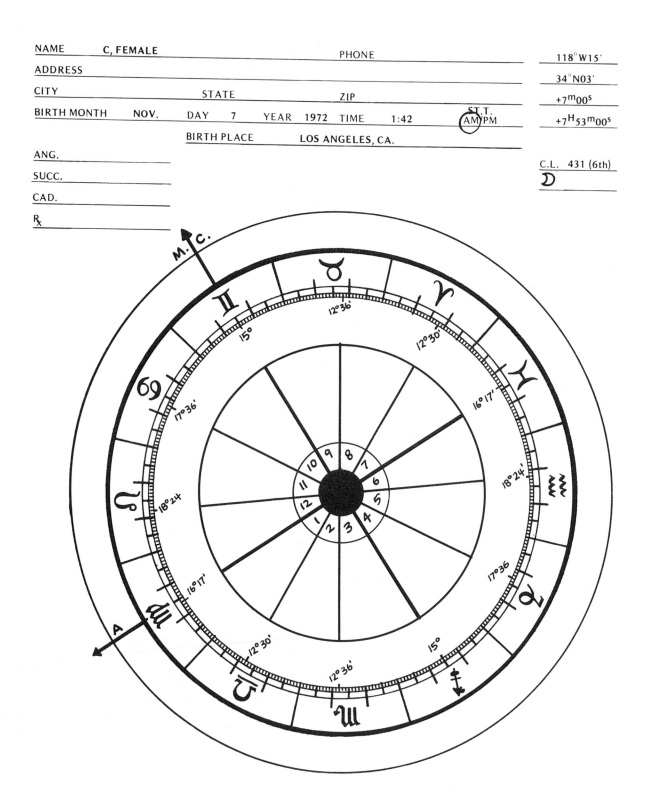

FIGURE 41
Sample birth chart (C, female) with degrees and signs
marked.

Figure 39.)

To insert the correct planetary position, look at Table 36, Step 6. The True Local Time is again recorded; it is 20 hours, 52 minutes, 00 seconds. To this is added the E.G.M.T. for a total of 27 hours, 105 minutes, 00 seconds — or 28 hours, 45 minutes, 00 seconds. This total shows that we have finished with the sixth day and are 4 hours, 45 minutes, 00 seconds into the seventh.

The C.L. for 4 hours, 45 minutes is .7035. The planets are inserted into the chart, using the same math work described in Appendix A — except that the C.L. is different. Figure 40 is the completed chart.

TABLE 38

THE POSITION OF PLUTO ♇ IN 1972

Date	Long.	Lat.	Dec.	Date	Long.	Lat.	Dec.	Date	Long.	Lat.	Dec.
	° ′	° ′	° ′		° ′	° ′	° ′		° ′	° ′	° ′
Jan. 1	2≏ 3	16N 16	14N 5	May 10	29♍33	16N 37	15N 23	Sept. 17	1≏37	15N 50	13N 52
11	2 ℞ 2	16 21	14 10	20	29 25	16 33	15 22	27	2 0	15 51	13 43
21	1 58	16 27	14 17	30	29 20	16 28	15 20	Oct. 7	2 23	15 52	13 35
31	1 51	16 32	14 24	June 9	29D 19	16 23	15 17	17	2 45	15 54	13 28
Feb. 10	1 41	16 36	14 32	19	29 20	16 18	15 12	27	3 6	15 56	13 22
20	1 28	16 40	14 40	29	29 25	16 14	15 5	Nov. 6	3 25	15 59	13 18
Mar. 1	1 14	16 43	14 49	July 9	29 33	16 9	14 58	16	3 42	16 3	13 15
11	0 58	16 45	14 57	19	29 45	16 5	14 49	26	3 57	16 8	13 13
21	0 42	16 46	15 4	29	29♍58	16 1	14 40	Dec. 6	4 9	16 13	13 13
31	0 26	16 46	15 10	Aug. 8	0≏15	15 57	14 31	16	4 18	16 19	13 14
Apr. 10	0≏10	16 45	15 16	18	0 33	15 55	14 21	26	4 24	16 24	13 18
20	29♍56	16 43	15 20	28	0 53	15 52	14 11	Jan. 1	4≏25	16N 28	13N 20
30	29♍43	16N 40	15N 22	Sept. 7	1≏15	15N 51	14N 1				

How to Set Up a Birth Chart with a Noon Ephemeris if Birth Occurred before Noon with Planetary Correction between Sixth and Seventh Day

Here we will assume that C., a female, is also born in Los Angeles on November 7, 1972, but at 1:44 A.M. (Figures 41, 42). I believe the math work (Table 39) is at this point self-explanatory, but note that since no 24-hour deduction was necessary, all planetary correction lies between November 6 and November 7. In other words, all planets are corrected from the 6th forward because 12 noon on November 7 had not been reached at the moment of birth. The C.L. is 431.

Figure 45 will help you verify your math work.

The Sun will always appear in or near the house indicated for the time of birth, regardless of the place of birth. In other words, if a person is born around 5:00 A.M. anywhere in the world, the Sun *must* be on the east side of his chart, in or near the first house. If the Sun shows up on the west side in any such chart you are drawing, it is on the P.M. half of the chart, and you have made a math error of 12 hours. In any chart you set up always check what position the Sun is occupying to see if it corresponds to the proper birth time.

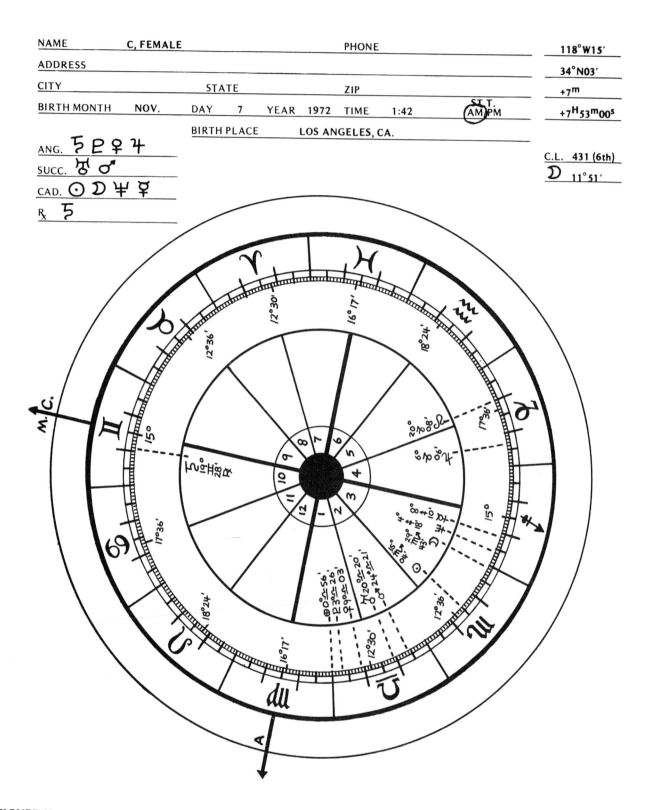

FIGURE 42
Completed sample birth chart (C, female).

TABLE 39
MATH WORK FOR FIGS. 41 AND 42

I. Birth Data

C. Female
November 7, 1972 — 1:42 A.M ST.T. (Standard Time) — Los Angeles, Ca.

	Longitude	Latitude	L.M.T.	E.G.M.T.		
	118°W15'	34°N03'	+7m00s	+7h53m00s		
				Hours	Minutes	Seconds
1.	Clock Time at A.M. Birth			01	44	00 ST.T.
1A.	+12 Hours, as all timing starts at 12 noon the previous day			+12	00	00
				13	44	00
2.	Local *Mean Time* Variation			+	7	00
3.	10-Second Interval Correction					
	True Local Time =			13	51	00
				+	2	18
				13	53	18
4.	Sidereal Time of the 6th, as birth occurred *before* 12 noon			+15	03	12
				28	56	30
4A.	Minus the Circle of 24 hours			−24	00	00
5.	Longitudinal Correction (Formula: Multiply by 2, divide result by 3. Always *add* result when birthplace was *west of Greenwich; deduct* result when birthplace was *east of Greenwich*)			4	56	30
				+	1	19
	The Final Calculated Sidereal Time =			4	57	49

II. House Cusps

		Hours	Minutes	Seconds
Step 6.	*True* Local Time =	13	51	00
Step 7.	Equivalent *Greenwich Mean Time*	+ 7	53	00
		20	104	00
	Greenwich Mean Time on 6th	21	44	00 = C.L. 431

C.L. (Constant Log.) for 21h44m = 431 (for planetary correction between 6th and 7th)

If Birth Occurred East of Greenwich P.M., but with Planetary Correction between the Sixth and Seventh Days

Let's assume that D., a male, was born November 7, 1972, at 12:05 P.M., in Berlin, Germany. In Figure 43 I have recorded the needed information from *Longitudes and Latitudes Throughout the World* (listed in the Bibliography).

In Table 40 notice Step 1 — only 05' appears

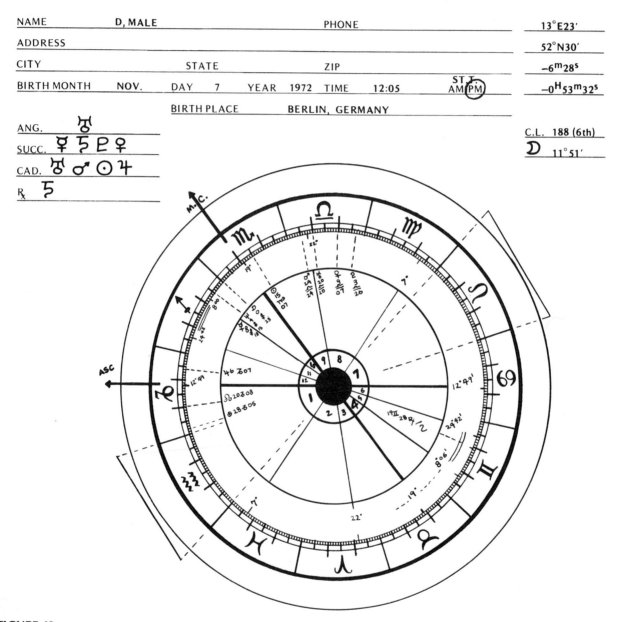

NAME	D, MALE			PHONE				13°E23'
ADDRESS								52°N30'
CITY		STATE			ZIP			−6ᵐ28ˢ
BIRTH MONTH NOV.	DAY 7	YEAR 1972	TIME 12:05	ST.T. AM(PM)				−0ᴴ53ᵐ32ˢ
		BIRTH PLACE	BERLIN, GERMANY					

C.L. 188 (6th)

☾ 11°51'

FIGURE 43
Completed sample birth chart (D, male).

TABLE 40

MATH WORK FOR FIG. 43

I. Birth Data

D. Male

November 7, 1972 — 12:05 P.M. ST.T. (Standard Time) — Berlin, Germany

Longitude	Latitude	L.M.T.	E.G.M.T.
13°E23′	52°N30′	−6m28s	−0h53m32s

Steps:	Hours	Minutes	Seconds
1. Clock Time at P.M. Birth	00	05	00 ST.T.
1A. From previous day	+24	00	00
1B. Convert 1 Hour into Minutes and 1 Minute	24	05	00
into Seconds	23	64	60
2. *Local Mean Time Variation*	−00	06	28
	23	58	32
	+	3	59
3. 10-Second Interval Correction			
True Local Time =	24	02	31
4. Sidereal Time of the 6th, as birth occurred *before* 12 noon	+15	03	12
	39	05	43
4A. Minus the Circle of 24 hours	−24	00	00
5. Longitudinal Correction (Formula: Multiply by 2, divide result by 3. Always *add* result when birthplace was *west of Greenwich;* *deduct* result when birthplace was *east of Greenwich*)	15	05	43
	−		08
The Final Calculated Sidereal Time =	15	05	35

II. House Cusps

6. *True* Local Time	23	58	32
7. *Equivalent Greenwich Mean Time*	−00	53	32
Greenwich Mean Time on the 6th	23	05	00 = GMT

C.L. (Constant Log.) for 23h05m = 169 (for planetary correction between 6th and 7th)

because the day starts at 12 noon. In other words, there are no hours to record. We need to borrow time from the previous day (Step 1A) since it is obviously impossible to deduct 6 minutes, 28 seconds (Step 2) from 05 minutes, 00 seconds. It is also necessary to add Step 1B — which is converting 1 hour into 60 minutes and 1 minute into 60 seconds. Afterward, we can proceed to Step 2 and deduct the 6 minutes, 28 seconds for a result of 23 hours, 58 minutes, 32 seconds.

The 10-Second Interval Correction (Step 3) is 3 minutes, 59 seconds, which gives 24 hours, 02 minutes, 31 seconds. But the birth actually occurred before noon, so the Sidereal Time has to be borrowed from the previous day, the 6th. This is Step 4, which gives a total of 39 hours, 05 minutes, 43 seconds. When the circle of 24 hours is deducted from this, the result is 15 hours, 05 minutes, 43 seconds.

Step 5, the longitude, is east of Greenwich, so it is multiplied by 2 and divided by 3, which gives a total of 8 seconds. In this case, since the birth occurred east of Greenwich, the total has to be *deducted*. This gives a final Calculated Sidereal Time of 15 hours, 05 minutes, 35 seconds. Now we can set up the house cusps on the chart (Figure 43).

The house cusps in this case are set up where the Midheaven of 19° Scorpio and the latitude of 52°N intersect. In the column of the twelfth house and in the column of the first house, notice how the sign changes.

Step 6 gave us 23 hours, 58 minutes, 32 seconds for the True Local Time. Subtract Step 7, the E.G.M.T. of 00 hours, 53 minutes, 32 seconds. The result is a G.M.T. of 23 hours, 05 minutes, 00 seconds. The C.L. is 169. All planetary corrections are made from the 6th to the 7th.

How to Set Up a Birth Chart if Birth Occurred in P.M. in Southern Latitude West of Greenwich

In this example we are assuming that E., a female, was born on November 7, 1972, at 9:51 P.M. in Rio de Janeiro, Brazil. Look at Table 41 for the math work. Figure 44 is the completed chart.

For a southern latitude chart there is only one change, and that is Step 5A. Always add 12 hours to the final figure — which in this case gives 13 hours, 07 minutes, 13 seconds — and reverse the wheel.

The final figure shows 18° Libra for the cusp of the tenth house, but since we are setting up a southern latitude chart, we must reverse this so that 18° Libra is recorded in the fourth house. The

cusp of the eleventh house for the 23rd latitude is 16°36′ Scorpio and is recorded as the fifth house cusp. The cusp of the twelfth house shows 11°30′ Sagittarius and is recorded as the sixth house. The figures for the cusp of the first house are recorded on the seventh house cusp. The figures for the cusp of the second house are recorded on the eighth house cusp, and the figures for the cusp of the third house are recorded on the ninth house cusp. Then the opposite side of the wheel is filled in. (See Figure 44.) To fill in the planets, look at Table 41; the planets are recorded for the correct position between November 7 and 8.

NAME   C, FEMALE   PHONE   43°W15'

ADDRESS   22°S54'

CITY   STATE   ZIP   +7ᵐ00ˢ

BIRTH MONTH♂ NOV.   DAY 7   YEAR 1972   TIME   9:51   ST.Ⓣ   +2ᴴ53ᵐ00ˢ
                                                      AM⟨PM⟩

            BIRTH PLACE   RIO DE JANEIRO, BRAZIL

ANG. ♅   ☉♃   C.L. 2702 (7th)
SUCC. ♆ ☽ ☿   ☽ 11°49'
CAD. ♄ ♇ ♀

℞ ♄

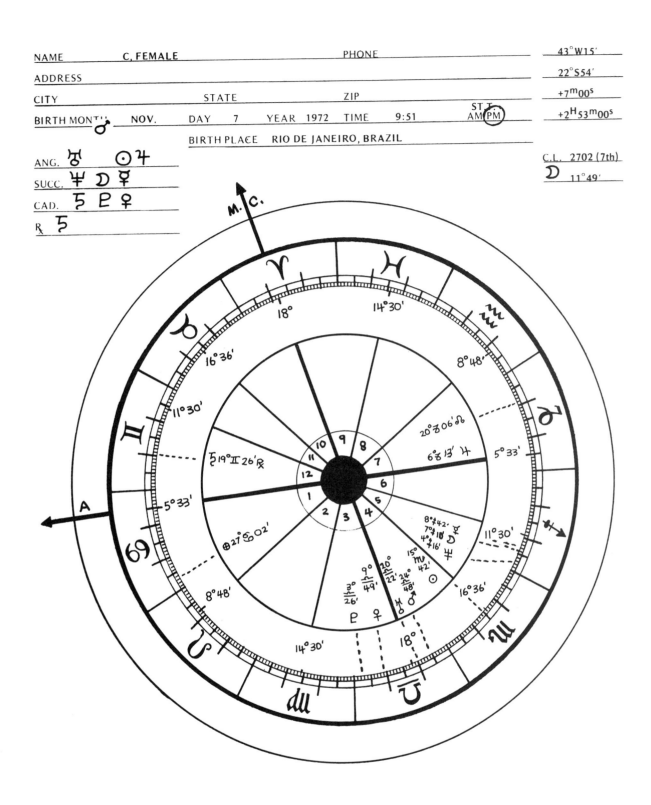

FIGURE 44
Completed sample birth chart (E, female).

TABLE 41

MATH WORK FOR FIG. 44

I. Birth Data

E. Female

November 7, 1972 — 9:51 P.M. ST.T. (Standard Time) — Rio de Janeiro, Brazil

Longitude	Latitude	L.M.T.	E.G.M.T.
43°W15'	22°S54'	+7m00s	+2h53m00s

		Hours	Minutes	Seconds
1.	Clock Time at P.M. Birth	09	51	00 ST.T.
2.	*Local Mean Time Variation*	+	7	00
		09	58	00
3.	10-Second Interval Correction	+	1	39
	True Local Time =	09	59	39
4.	Sidereal Time of the 7th as birth occurred *after* 12 noon	+15	07	08
		25	06	47
4A.	Circle of 24 hours	−24	00	00
5.	Longitudinal Correction (Formula: Multiply by 2, divide result by 3. Always *add* result when birthplace was *west of Greenwich; deduct* result when birthplace was *east of Greenwich*)	1	06	47
		+		26
		1	07	13
5A.	Add 12 Hours to Wheel	+12	00	00
	The Final Calculated Sidereal Time =	13	07	13

II. House Cusps

		Hours	Minutes	Seconds
Step 6.	*True* Local Time	09	58	00
Step 7.	Equivalent Greenwich Mean Time	+02	53	00
	Greenwich Mean Time	13	51	00

C.L. (Constant Log.) for 12h53m = .2702 (for planetary correction between 7th and 8th)

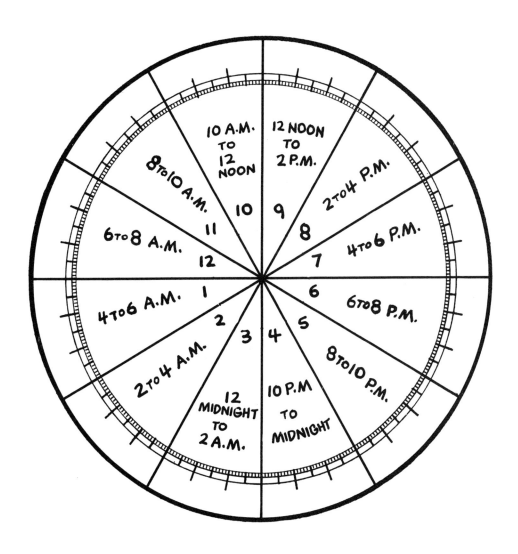

FIGURE 45
Birth time will determine house position of ☉.

C

The Calculations of Progressions

The progressions are used for calculating the timing of future events. One popular type of progression is called the major arc, which points to a year in question; another is the minor arc, which points to the month of an event. A birth chart is much like a clock face with its numbers permanently imprinted: the major progression corresponds to the hour hand; the minor progression corresponds to the minute hand; and the transiting planets, as they are moving through the heavens, are analogous to the sweeping second hand.

Major Arc

We will do a major progression for the tenth year of life using the chart in Figure 46. The rule for progressions is that each day in the ephemeris (Table 37) corresponds to one year of life. Therefore, assuming the birth date is November 7, 1972, and the sun on day of birth (as listed on 7th in ephemering) is at 15° Scorpio 10', and counting ten days forward (representing ten years), we reach the seventeenth day, with the Sun in 25° Scorpio 14'. The difference in degrees between those two dates is 9°04', and this is called the major arc. Keep in mind that the Sun moves at approximately 1° per year, and for every additional month between years, 5' are added. The major arc stands for the tenth year of life. Refer to Table 42. After adding this arc to the natal ascendant of 21° Pisces 38' the ascendant for the tenth year of life would be in 1° Aries 42'. Saturn's natal position is 19° Gemini 26'. After adding the arc of 10°04', Saturn's position for the tenth year of life would be 29° Gemini 30'. All planets are progressed in the same manner. Any Arabian parts, and the dragon's head, can also be progressed the same way. All major progressions are indicated on Figure 46.

Always read a progressed planet's position

against that of the natal planets. In other words, progressed planets in relationship to natal planets point to future events. For interpretation, use the same type of aspects that were explained in Chapters 4, 5 and 6. The progressed and transiting posi-

tion of planets through the different houses of the chart is discussed in Chapter 18. In Chapter 20, where the complete reading of a chart is given, progressions are interpreted to show the timing of actual events.

Minor Arc

For a minor arc, utilize the new position of the Moon. In our example case, on the 7th, the Moon was at 0° Sagittarius 50′, and ten days later, on the 17th, it was at 6° Aries 42′. The difference is 4 signs 05°52′. The figure of the minor arc stands for November 7, 1982, which is ten years later. In order to find the position for the Moon for ten years *and one month*, you would have to find the difference in the Moon's motion between the seventeenth day and the eighteenth day; this difference is 14°38′. (See Table 43.) Since 1° equals 60′, 14° must equal 840′ — plus 38′, for a total of 878′. Divided by twelve months, this gives 73′ or 1°13′ per month for the Moon. So, if you want to know where the Moon is for *one year and one month*, 1°13′ has to be added to the arc of the Moon for the tenth year — showing that the Moon's arc would be 4 signs 07°05′. In other

words, for any additional month, another 1°13′ would have to be added. From one day to the next the Moon will move anywhere between 11°48′ to 15°19′. Minor progressions are applied to natal planets and natal house cusps.

Major progressed planetary positions with accompanying aspects only set the stage or point a finger toward a coming event during a given year. The minor progressed position of a planet will narrow the timing, but remember that *without* the transits, none of these aspects can be activated. Transits are the current planetary positions given in an ephemeris; these act as the triggers that activate an event.

Of the ten planets, the Moon is the fastest. It transits the entire twelve signs once in a little less than a month. Therefore this planet is the most important significator.

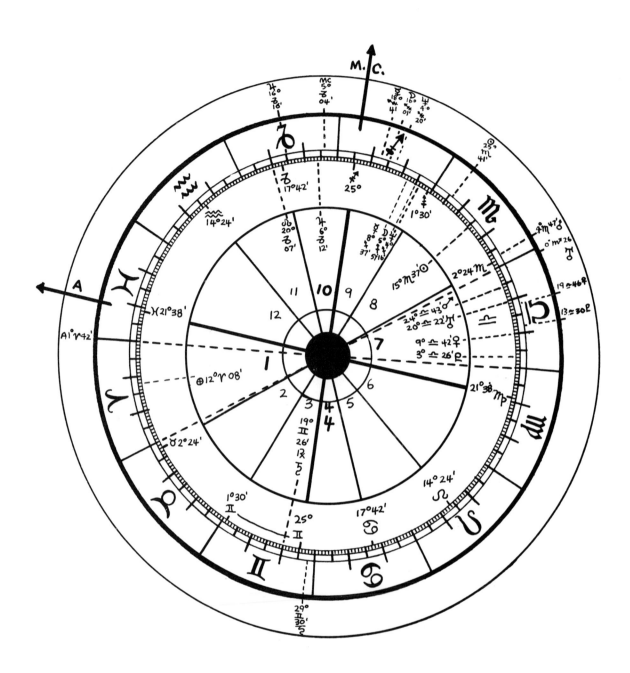

FIGURE 46
Major arc progression in outer rim.

TABLE 42
MAJOR PROGRESSION FOR TENTH YEAR

☉ on 7th (Day of Birth) —— 15° ♏ 10'   = difference of 10°04'

☉ on 17th (Representing 10th Year) – 24° ♏ 14'

Major Arc (☉) is 9°04'. All planets, and especially the cusps of the ascendant and midheaven, are moved forward by this amount.

Example:

    21° ♅ 38' (Natal Asc.)
    +10°   04' (Major Arc)
     1° ♈ 42' = Position of Major Progressed

Ascendant for Tenth Year — November 7, 1982.

Example:

    19° ♊ 26' (Natal Saturn)
    +10°   04' (Major Arc)
    29° ♊ 30' = Position of Major Progressed

Saturn for Tenth Year — November 7, 1982

TABLE 43
MINOR PROGRESSION FOR TENTH YEAR

☽ on 7th (Day of Birth) —— 0° ♎ 50'   = difference 4ˢ* 05°52' (Minor Arc)

☽ on 17th (Representing 10th Year) – 6° ♈ 42'

Minor Arc (☽) is 4ˢ 05°52'. All planets, and especially the ascendant and midheaven house cusps, are moved forward by this amount.

Example:

Plus 4 signs = 21° ♋ 38'
             + 5°   52'
              27° ♋ 30' = Position of Progressed

Ascendant for Tenth Year — November 7, 1982.

Total motion of ☽ between:

    17th day = 6° ♈ 42'   = difference 14°38'
    18th day = 21° ♈ 20'

    14 times 60' =   840'
                 +   38
                   878' divided by 12 months
                 = 73' = 1°13' per month

For 10th Year — November 7, 1982 ——— 4ˢ 05°52'
             +1 month ——— +   1°13'
Minor Arc for 10 years and 1 month ——— = 4ˢ 07°05'

NAME _____ PHONE _____ W _____

ADDRESS _____ N _____

CITY _____ STATE _____ ZIP _____

BIRTH MONTH _____ DAY _____ YEAR _____ TIME _____ AM/PM _____

BIRTH PLACE _____

ANG. _____ C.L. _____

SUCC. _____ ☽ _____

CAD. _____

R︎ _____

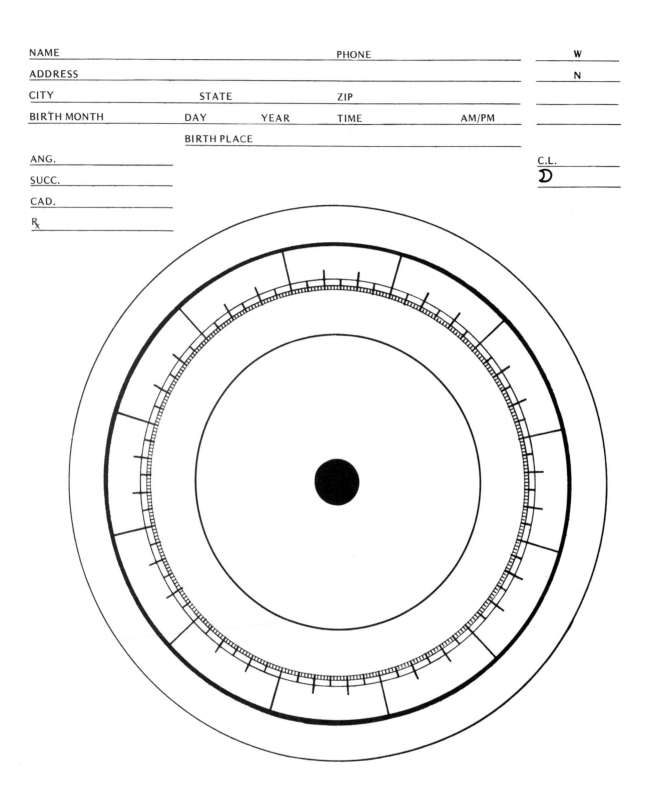

FIGURE 47
Blank birth chart.

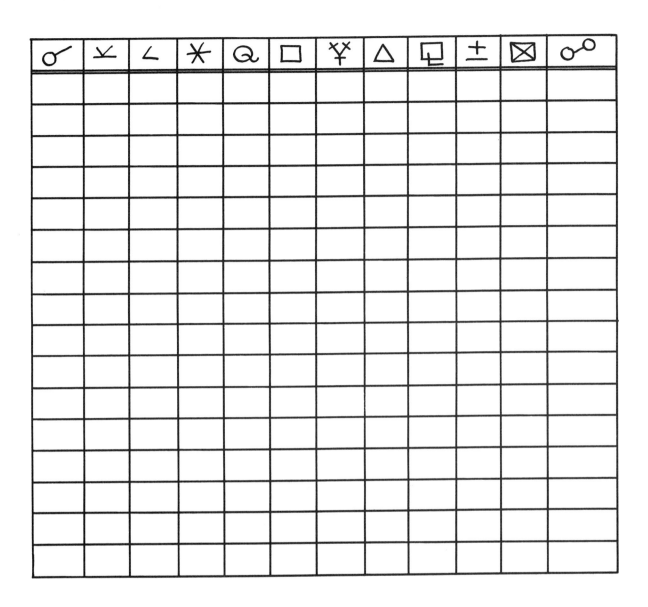

♂	⊻	∠	✳	Q	☐	♉	△	⊡	±	⊠	☊

♂ — Conjunction   △ — Trine
⊻ — Semisextile   ⊡ — Sesquare
∠ — Semisquare   ± — Biquintile
✳ — Sextile   ⊠ — Quincunx
Q — Quintile   ☊ — Opposition
☐ — Square   S — Separating aspect
♉ — Tredecile   A — Applying aspect

FIGURE 48
Natal Aspect form.

Bibliography

Dalton, Joseph G. *Dalton's Tables of Houses: Spherical Basis of Astrology*. Richmond, Virginia: Macoy Publishing and Masonic Supply Company, 1975.

Dernay, Eugene. *Longitudes and Latitudes in the United States*. Washington, D.C.: National Astrological Library, 1945.

———. *Longitudes and Latitudes Throughout the World*. Washington, D.C.: National Astrological Library, 1948.

Doane, Doris Chase. *Time Changes in the U.S.A.* Los Angeles: The Church of Light, 1966.

———. *Time Changes in the World (Except Canada, Mexico, U.S.A.)*. Hollywood, Cal.: Professional Astrologers Incorporated, 1971.

———. *Time Changes in Canada and Mexico*. Los Angeles: The Church of Light, 1968.

Raphael. *Raphael's Astronomical Ephemeris of the Planets' Places*. London: W. Foulsham and Company, Ltd.; New York, Toronto, Cape Town, Sydney. Published annually.

De Vore, Nicholas. *Encyclopedia of Astrology*. New York: Philosophical Library, Incorporated, 1947.

Jones, Marc Edmund. *The Guide to Horoscope Interpretation*. New York: Sabian Publishing Society, 1961.

Index

Boldface page numbers indicate material in tables or illustrations.

Afflicted planets, definition of, 91n
Air signs, 15
  when rising, 41
Angular houses, 66–67
Antiscions (solstice points), 113–16, 134, 162
Aquarius
  decanates of, 78
  house ruled by, 18
  key words for, 17
  nature of, 15, 25
  rulers of, 17
  sun-mercury relationship in, 87–88
  symbol for, 17

Arabian parts, 109–12
Aries
  decanates of, 77
  house ruled by, 18
  key words for, 16
  nature of, 14, 21
  ruler of, 17
  sun-mercury relationship in, 85
  symbol for, 16
Ascendants (rising signs)
  key words for, 20
  planets in, **42**
  by sign, **41–42**

Aspects
    applying and separating, 62–64
    in comparisons between two people, 92–101
    definitions of, 43–51
    example of, 134
    interpretations of, 52–53
    major vs. minor, 62
    with planets, **53–61**
    symbols for, 43–44, 63–64

Biquintile, 64
Birth data, 142–44
Body parts
    planets associated with, 16
    signs associated with, 16–17, 18
Bowl type, 71
Brothers, relationships with, 90
Bucket type, 71, 130
Bundle type, 72, 130

Cadent houses, 66–67
Calculations for charts. *See* Setting up charts
Cancer
    decanates of, 77
    house ruled by, 18
    key words for, 16
    nature of, 15, 22
    ruler of, 17
    sun-mercury relationship in, 86
    symbol for, 16
Capricorn
    decanates of, 77
    house ruled by, 18
    key words for, 17
    nature of, 15, 24
    ruler of, 17
    sun-mercury relationship in, 87
    symbol for, 17
Caput draconis, 104
Cardinal signs, 14, 67–68
Cauda draconis, 104
Charts, setting up, 142–63
    completed examples of, 158, 168–70, 172, 174, 177
    special calculations in, 164–79
Children
    determination of sex of, 127
    relationships with, 90–91
Common cross, 67–68
Comparisons between two people, 92–102
Conception timing, 127–28
Conjunction, 43–44

Constant Log (C.L.), 159–63, 165, 171, 172, 173, 175, 176
Cusps
    calculations for finding, 144–48, 151–55
    definition of, 18.
    See also Houses
Cycles, 11

Day of birth, meaning of, 135–40
Daylight Saving Time, 130, 144, 150
Decanates, 76–78
Declinations. *See* Parallels
Diurnal hemisphere, 69

Earth, the, motions of, 14
Earth signs, 15
    when rising, 41
Eastern hemisphere, 68–69
Ecliptic of the zodiac, 113n
Elements, 14–15
Ephemeris, 142
    Raphael's, 47, 166–67, 186
Equivalent Greenwich Mean Time (E.G.M.T.), 144, 159, 165, 171, 173, 175, 176, 178

Fifth house, sexual expression and, 80, 84
Fire signs, 14–15
    when rising, 41
Fixed signs, 15, 67–68
Flat chart (natural wheel), 14, 18–19
Fortune, part of, 109–12

Gemini
    decanates of, 77
    house ruled by, 18
    key words for, 16
    nature of, 15, 22
    ruler of, 17
    sun-mercury relationship in, 86
    symbol for, 16
Grand cross, 72
Grand trine, 73
Greenwich Mean Time (G.M.T.), 144, 150, 159, 176

Hemispheres, 68–69
Houses
    angular, 66–67
    cadent, 66–67
    calculations for setting up of, 144–48, 151–55
    definition of, 14
    fifth, sexual expression and, 80, 84

key words for, 20
nodes in, 104–108
part of fortune in, 111–12
planets in, **27–41**
planets moving through, 118, 26
relationships with relatives delineated by
    counting, 90–91
rulers of, 14, 18
succedent, 66–67
Husbands, relationships with, 91

Inconjunct (quincunx), 44, 50, 51, 64

Jonas, Eugen, 127
Jupiter
    aspects with, **54–59**
    charting position of, 160, 161
    in comparisons between two people, 93, 95–100
    in the houses, **34–35**
    key words for, 16
    moving through the houses, 122–23
    north node and, 104
    in the signs, **34–35**
    signs ruled by, 17
    symbol for, 16

Key words
    for houses, 20
    for planets, 16
    for signs, 16–17

Latitude and longitude, 142, 144, 150–51, 186
Leo
    decanates of, 77
    house ruled by, 18
    key words for, 16
    nature of, 14–15, 22–23
    ruler of, 17
    sun-mercury relationship in, 86
    symbol for, 16
Libra
    decanates of, 77
    house ruled by, 18
    key words for, 17
    nature of, 15, 23
    ruler of, 17
    sun-mercury relationship in, 86–87
    symbol for, 17
Local Mean Time (L.M.T.), 144, 165, 173, 175, 178
Locomotive type, 70
Logarithms, proportional, **156–58**

Longitude. See Latitude and Longitude

Major arc. 180–81, 183
Marriages, seventh house in interpretation of, 91
Mars
    aspects with, **54–58**
    charting position of, 160, 161
    in comparisons between two people, 93–99
    in the houses, **33–34**
    key words for, 16
    moving through the houses, 121–22
    sexual expression indicated by, 81–82
    in the signs, **33–34**
    signs ruled by, 17
    symbol for, 16
Mental expression, 85–88
Mercury
    aspects with, **53, 54, 56**
    charting position of, 160, 163
    in comparisons between two people, 93, 94,
      96–97
    in the houses, **30–31**
    key words for, 16
    moving through the houses, 120–21
    in the signs, **30–31**
    signs ruled by, 17
    sun and, as sign of mental expression, 85–88
    symbol for, 16
Minor arc, 181, 183
Moon
    aspects with, **54–55**
    charting position of, 160, 163
    in comparisons between two people, 92–93,
      94–95
    in conception timing, 127–28
    in the houses, **28–29**
    key words for, 16
    moving through the houses, 119
    nodes of, 104–108
    progressions of, 181, 183
    in the signs, **28–29**
    sign ruled by, 17
    symbol for, 16
Moveable signs (cardinal signs), 14, 67–68
Mutable signs, 15, 67–68

Natal chart, definition of, 49n
Native, definition of, 49n
Nativity, definition of, 49n
Natural wheel. See Flat chart
Neptune

aspects with, **54–61**
charting position of, 159, 161
in comparisons between two people, 95, 97–101
discovery of, 17
in the houses, **38–39**
key words for, 16
moving through the houses, 124–25
in the signs, **38–39**
sign ruled by, 17
symbol for, 16
Nocturnal hemisphere, 69
Nodes, 104–108
North hemisphere, 69

Occidental hemisphere, 68–69
Opposition, 44, 50, 51, 64
Oriental hemisphere, 68–69

Parallels (declinations), 44, 46–49, 62
calculations for, 148–49, 161
Part of fortune, 109–12
Physique, rising planets and, **42**
Pisces
decanates of, 78
as first sign in Arabian system, 109n
house ruled by, 18
key words for, 17
nature of, 15, 25
rulers of, 17
sun-mercury relationship in, 88
symbol for, 17
Planets
afflicted, definition of, 91n
calculating declination of, 161
charting position of, 159–61
classification of distributions of, 70–72
in comparisons between two people, 92–102
configurations of, 72–73
conjunct, 44
key words for, 16
negative and positive positions of, 74–75
number of, 14
progressions of. *See* Progressions
in rising sign, **42**
rulers of, 17
as rulers of houses, 14, 18
singleton, 71, 130
symbols for, 16
transits of. *See* Transits
See also specific planets
Pluto
aspects with, **54–61**

charting position of, 160–61
in comparisons between two people, 95, 97–102
discovery of, 17–18, 40
in the houses, **40–41**
key words for, 16
moving through the houses, 125–26
1972 position of, **171**
in the signs, **40**
sign ruled by, 17
symbol for, 16
Pregnancy timing, 127–28
Prime meridians, 150
Progressions, 118–26
calculations of, 180–85
example of, 131–32
rule for, 180
Proportional logarithms, **156–57**

Quadruplicities, 15, 67–68
Quincunx (inconjunct), 44, 50, 51, 64
Quintile, 44, 49–51, 63

Raphael's Ephemeris, 47, **166–67**, 186
Reading the chart as a whole, 130–34
Relatives, relationships with, delineated by
counting houses, 90–91
Rhythms, 11
Rising signs (ascendants)
key words for, 20
planets in, **42**
by sign, **41–42**
Rulers
of houses, 14, 18
of signs, 17

Sagittarius
decanates of, 77
house ruled by, 18
key words for, 17
nature of, 15, 24
ruler of, 17
sun-mercury relationship in, 87
symbol for, 17
Saturn
aspects with, **60**
charting position of, 160, 161
in comparisons between two people, 93, 95–101
in the houses, **35–37**
key words for, 16
moving through the houses, 123
in the signs, **35–37**
signs ruled by, 17

south node and, 104
symbol for, 16
Scorpio
decanates of, 77
house ruled by, 18
key words for, 17
nature of, 15, 23–24
rulers of, 17
sun-mercury relationships in, 87
symbol for, 17
Seesaw type, 71
Semiquintile, 63
Semisextile, 63
Semisquare, 44, 49, 50, 63
Sesquare, 44, 50, 51, 64
Setting up charts, 142–63
completed examples of, 158, 168–70, 172, 174, 177
special calculations in, 164–79
Seventh house, in interpretation of marriages, 91
Sex of children, determination of, 127
Sextile, 44, 49, 50, 63
Sexual expression, 80–84
Sidereal Time, 150–51, 165, 173, 175, 176, 178
Signs
ascendants by, **41–42**
body parts associated with, 18
decanates of, 76–78
definition of, 14
key words for, 16–17
nodes in, 104–108
part of fortune in, 111
planets in, **27–40**
rulers of, 17
symbols for, 17
Simple trine, 73
Singleton planet, 71
Sisters, relationships with, 90
Society, planets that influence, 101–102
Solstice points, 113–16, 134, 162
South hemisphere, 69
South node, 104–108
Splash type, 72
Splay type, 71
Square, 44, 50, 51, 63
Standard Time (ST.T), 144, 150, 165, 178
Stellium, definition of, 72
Succedent houses, 66–67
Sun
aspects with, **53–54**
charting position of, 159
in comparisons between two people, 92–94
in the houses, **27–28**

individuality as delineated by, 21–25
key words for, 16
mercury and, as sign of mental expression, 85–88
moving through the houses, 119–20
in the signs, **27–28**
sign ruled by, 17
symbol for, 16
Symbols
for aspects, 43–44, 63–64
for planets, 16
for signs, 16–17

T-square, 71, 72–73
Table of houses, 152
Taurus
decanates of, 77
house ruled by, 18
key words for, 16
nature of, 15, 22
ruler of, 17
sun-mercury relationship in, 85–86
symbol for, 16
Tide, conception and, 127
Time changes, 130, 142, 186
Time of birth, calculations for, 144, 150–51
Transits, 118–26
definition of, 118, 181
Tredecile, 63–64
Trine
definition of, 14, 44, 50, 51, 64
grand, 73
simple, 73
True Local Time, 150, 151, 165
Two people, comparisons between, 92–102
Tyl, Noel, 12

Uranus
aspects with, **54–60**
charting position of, 159–60
in comparisons between two people, 93, 95, 96–101
discovery of, 17
in the houses, **37–38**
key words for, 16
moving through the houses, 124
in the signs, **37–38**
sign ruled by, 17
symbol for, 16

Venus
aspects with, **53–57**

charting position of, 160, 161
in comparisons between two people, 93, 94,
   97–98
in the houses, **31–32**
key words for, 16
moving through the houses, 121
north node and, 104
sexual expression indicated by, 82–84
in the signs, **31–32**
signs ruled by, 17
symbol for, 16
Virgo
  decanates of, 77
  house ruled by, 18
  key words for, 16

nature of, 15, 23
ruler of, 17
sun-mercury relationship in, 86
symbol for, 16

Water signs, 15
  when rising, 41
Welsh, John H., 11
Western hemisphere, 68–69
Wives, relationships with, 91

Zodiac
  definition of, 14
  ecliptic of, 113n